# Pervasive Social Computing

Muhammad Ashad Kabir • Jun Han
Alan Colman

# Pervasive Social Computing

Socially-Aware Pervasive Systems
and Mobile Applications

 Springer

Muhammad Ashad Kabir
School of Computing and Mathematics
Charles Sturt University
Bathurst, NSW, Australia

Alan Colman
School of Software and Electrical
  Engineering
Swinburne University of Technology
Melbourne, VIC, Australia

Jun Han
School of Software and Electrical
  Engineering
Swinburne University of Technology
Melbourne, VIC, Australia

ISBN 978-3-319-29949-5          ISBN 978-3-319-29951-8   (eBook)
DOI 10.1007/978-3-319-29951-8

Library of Congress Control Number: 2016933335

Printed on acid-free paper

This springer imprint is published by Springer Nature
The registered company is Springer International Publishing AG Switzerland

# Preface

**Pervasive computing** envisions "smart" places where people are assisted in their daily life by various technologies that move to the background, being invisible yet significantly helpful. To provide such technologies a rapidly growing research area called *context-awareness* has emerged, to make pervasive applications more intelligent and accessible. Humans, the centre of pervasive computing, however, are social beings. Hence, the notion of *social context-awareness* can advance the field further in achieving the vision of pervasive computing. As such, recently a vibrant research direction is introduced, entitled *Pervasive Social Computing*, which is a novel collective paradigm derived from pervasive computing, social media, social networking, social signal processing and multi-modal human-computer interaction. It aims to take advantage of human *social context* to enable the fulfilment of user tasks on the move, ultimately promoting individual well being and social productivity. With the increasing prevalence and features of advanced mobile devices, interest has grown in *socially aware* mobile applications, where the applications will be aware of users' social context and be able to assist them in their daily activities.

Developing socially aware applications is challenging. **First**, the socially aware applications need different types of social context information such as *social roles*, *social relationships*, *social interactions* and *situations*. These different types of social context information need to be *modelled*, *represented* and *acquired* from various sources for use by the applications. **Second**, an application may need social context information that is not directly available from context sources but can be inferred from the acquired basic information. Thus, there is the need to define and obtain *inferred* social context information from the acquired basic information. **Third**, the users' social context information is inherently sensitive and can be used to infer further information. The users should be allowed to specify their *privacy preferences* regarding access to their information. **Fourth**, much of the users' social context information is *dynamic* and continuously changes. The socially aware applications need to support *adaptation* to cope with the changes in social context information.

This book introduces a novel *framework* to address the aforementioned challenges in developing socially aware applications. The framework includes an *approach* to model, represent, reason about and manage different types of social context, and a *platform* for acquiring, storing, provisioning and managing social context information to aid the development and operation of socially aware applications. This book reports several important research contributions. **Firstly**, the proposed framework provides an ontology-based *social context model*, including an *upper* social context ontology which can be customised and specialised to form *domain-specific* ontologies. **Secondly**, the framework provides an ontology-based approach to define *rules* for *deriving* and *abstracting* social context information. It also proposes an approach to *inferring* user situations by correlating historical interaction events. **Thirdly**, the framework provides an ontology-based socially aware *access control policy model* and *language* for owners to control access to their information at different levels of granularity. **Fourthly**, the framework also provides a way to model and represent *runtime social interactions* from both the *domain-* and *player perspectives* to support mediated social interactions and manage their adaptation to cope with the changes in user requirements and environments. **Finally**, the framework provides a *platform* for acquiring, storing and provisioning social context information, executing social interaction models and managing their runtime adaptation. This book also presents two *case studies* that validate and evaluate the different functionalities of the framework and its underlying approach and platform.

Bathurst, NSW, Australia                          Muhammad Ashad Kabir
Melbourne, VIC, Australia                                         Jun Han
Melbourne, VIC, Australia                                     Alan Colman
November 2015

# About the Authors

**Ashad Kabir** is a Lecturer in Computing at Charles Sturt University, Bathurst, Australia. He is also an Adjunct Research Fellow in the Centre for Computing and Engineering Software Systems at Swinburne University of Technology, Melbourne, Australia. Prior to joining Charles Sturt, Dr Kabir taught at Deakin University (Melbourne, Australia). He received his PhD degree in Computer Science and Software Engineering from Swinburne University of Technology in 2013. His research interests include context-aware adaptive systems, social context awareness, data/software behaviour mining, smart mobile applications and sensing.

**Jun Han** received his PhD degree in Computer Science from the University of Queensland (Brisbane, Australia) in 1992. Since 2003, he has been Professor of Software Engineering at Swinburne University of Technology (Melbourne, Australia). His primary research focus has been the architecture and qualities of software systems. His current research interests include dynamic software architectures, context-aware software systems, Cloud and service-oriented software systems, software architecture design, and software performance and security. He has published over 200 peer-reviewed articles in international journals and conferences.

**Alan Colman** received his PhD degree in Computer Science and Software Engineering from Swinburne University of Technology (Melbourne, Australia) in 2006. Since 2006, he has been a Researcher and Senior Lecturer of software engineering at Swinburne University of Technology. His primary research focus has been adaptive service-oriented software systems, context-aware software systems, software and Cloud performance prediction and control. He has published over 70 peer-reviewed articles in international journals and conferences.

# Contents

# List of Figures

# List of Tables

# Part I
# Preliminaries

This part of the book consists of the introduction (Chap. 1), application scenarios (Chap. 2), and background and related work (Chap. 3) to provide the required background knowledge and themes for this book.

# Chapter 1
# Introduction

> The most profound technologies are those that disappear. They wave themselves into the fabric of everyday life until they are indistinguishable from it (Mark Weiser) [183].

After introducing the vision of *ubiquitous computing*, also called *pervasive computing*, by Mark Weiser in 1991, over the past two decades, this field evolved through roughly three generations of research challenges. Now, the scientific community articulates next-generation research directions as the quest to attain Weiser's vision continues [76].

## 1.1 Pervasive Social Computing

*Pervasive computing* envisions environments where people are assisted in their everyday tasks by technologies that recede into the background, being invisible yet significantly helpful [159]. To enable such technologies a rapidly growing research area called *"context-awareness"* has emerged, as a technique to make pervasive applications more intelligent and accessible [26, 27, 67]. The term context is commonly understood by those working in pervasive computing, where it is felt that context is "key" in their efforts to disperse and enmesh computation into our lives [137]. The notion of context is much widely appreciated today, which usually refers to information about systems, entities, and their environments. Software applications that adapt their behaviour with the changes of context information (*e.g.*, location, temperature, and time) are called *context-aware applications*. A context-aware application uses context to provide relevant information and/or services to the user, where relevancy depends on the user's task [67].

© Springer International Publishing Switzerland 2016
M.A. Kabir et al., *Pervasive Social Computing*,
DOI 10.1007/978-3-319-29951-8_1

Humans, the centre of pervasive computing, however, are social beings. Hence, the notion of *social context awareness* (in short *social awareness*) can push the field further in achieving the vision of pervasive computing. Recently, it has been rising and attracting attentions of researchers from different communities, including pervasive computing [76] and ambient intelligence [25]. Nevertheless, pervasive computing is moving towards *pervasive social computing* with the pervasiveness of hand-held devices and enormous popularity of social networking websites.

*Pervasive social computing* (PSC) is a novel collective paradigm, derived from pervasive computing, social media, social networking, social signal processing and multimodal HCI [192]. It aims to take advantage of human *social relationships* (a type of *social context*) to enable the fulfilment of users' tasks on the move, ultimately promoting individual well being and social interactivity [41].

Despite the huge prospects of *pervasive social computing* and the extensive work in *context-aware applications*, so far very limited work has focused on *social context-aware applications* (in sort *socially-aware applications*). An application is socially-aware if it uses social context information (*e.g.*, social relationships, social roles, social interactions, situations) to adapt its behaviour [76]. The advent of social media such as online social networks, blogs, and instant messaging, have radically changed the way people interact with each other and share information about their lives and works. Such use of social media platforms produces an unprecedented amount of social context information as people specify their relationships, update their status, share interests and contents. Thus, it is now possible to acquire users' social context information from social media which may be rarely possible to acquire form physical sensors [154]. Such social context information can be exploited to develop various *data-centric* socially-aware applications (where data is the basis of the applications' behaviour). For example, SmartObject considers the users' relationship information to turn on the audio player when friends are present [43]; a socially-aware phone call application can reduce interruptions by allowing a user to filter incoming calls based on her social context information (*e.g.*, relationships with the caller, current situation) [114].

On the other hand, the increased prevalence of advanced mobile devices (the so called "smart" phones) with increasing features, interest has grown in *interaction-centric* socially-aware applications, where the collaborative interactions among persons are based on predefined agreements and constraints, and can be composed with the notion of *interaction-relationships*. Such applications can assist users in their daily activities and ultimately enrich their social interactions and well-being [128]. For instance, a socially-aware telematics application can make travel safe and convenient by allowing drivers to collaborate and interact with each other based on their interaction relationships [115].

Developing such socially-aware applications of distinct focus is a challenge for application developers as they must *define* social context information (*e.g.*, *social roles* and *interaction-oriented social relationships* in a socially-aware telematics application) or *collect* social context information (*e.g.*, *social roles* and *connection-oriented social relationships* in a socially-aware phone call application) from various sources (*e.g.*, Facebook, LinkedIn, Google Calendar), *represent* and *model* such different social context information, *infer* more abstract meaningful context information, and *manage* them in a consistent manner. Therefore, the key requirements for developing socially-aware applications are *modelling*, *managing* and *reasoning about* users' social context information.

## 1.2 Defining Social Context

The notion of *context* has been used in numerous areas, including Pervasive and Ubiquitous Computing, Human Computer Interaction, Computer-Supported Collaborative Work, and Ambient Intelligence [70]. In Ubiquitous and Pervasive Computing area, early works on context-awareness referred to context as primarily the location of people and objects [161]. In recent works, context has been extended to include a broader collection of factors, such as physical and social aspects of an entity, as well as the activities of users [70]. Having examined the definitions and categories of context given by the pervasive and ubiquitous computing community, this section seeks to define our view of social context within the scope of this book. As the definitions of context to pervasive and ubiquitous computing area are also broad, this discussion is intended to be illustrative rather than exhaustive.

Schmidt et al. [163] present a model of context with two distinct categories: human factors and physical environment. *Human factors* consist of three categories: information about the user (*e.g.*, profile, emotional state), the user's social environment (*e.g.*, presence of other people, group dynamics), and the user's tasks (*e.g.*, current activity, goals). *Physical environment* also consists of three categories: location (*e.g.*, absolute and relative position), infrastructure (*e.g.*, computational resources), and physical conditions (*e.g.*, noise, light). This model gives a classification according to specific contextual factors, but does not provide a formal definition. Dey [67] presents a survey of alternative view of context, which are largely imprecise and indirect, typically defining context by synonym or example. Finally, he offers the following definition of context, which is perhaps now the most widely accepted: "*Context is any information that can be used to characterise the situation of an entity. An entity is person, place or object that is considered relevant to the interaction between a user and an application, including the user and the application themselves*". Henricksen [97] relates context to tasks, rather than with respect to interactions between users and applications, as in the definition of Dey. She separates the concepts of context, context modelling and context information. Henricksen argued that context represents a nebulous concept, is difficult to define and bound, where as context models and context information are well defined and understood, and are primary interest in constructing context-aware systems.

Several studies have attempted to define and represent social context from different perspectives. Han et al. [94] define social context as the user's social surroundings, that is to say, the social relationships of the user. Eugster et al. [74] rely on a more restricted definition of social context. They consider distributed objects as peers and the social context of a peer represents its awareness of the existence of other peers. Zheng et al. [191] identify social context as one of the essential elements of the context space for online social interaction. They consider social context as social, cultural, psychological, and emotional influences on online social interactions. Wang et al. [181] analyse the role of the social group in a ubiquitous computing environment as a source of contextual information. They define social context as: *"Information relevant to the characterisation of a situation that influences the interactions of one user with one or more other users"*. Biamino [43] views social context as social aggregations or social groups, and defines social context using 3-tuple expression (¡number of nodes, number of connections between them, nature of relations between the nodes¿) that characterises a social network. Endler et al. [72] introduce the term "situated social context" to enable location-based spontaneous interaction among people and define the term as: *"Situated Social Context of an individual is the set of people that share common spatio-temporal relationship with the individual, which turn them into potential peers for information sharing or interacting in a specific situation"*. Schuster et al. [164] combines the concept of social context with pervasive context and introduce the term "pervasive social context" which they define as: *"Pervasive Social Context of an individual is the set of information that arises our of direct or indirect interaction with people carrying sensor-equipped pervasive devices connected to the same Social Network Service"*.

The term "social context" can have many meanings or definitions, but most of the above works view social context as possible forms of *relationships* and *interactions* among people. Taking this insight, the following interpretations are adopted in this book:

- *Social Context* characterises social milieu[1] of an individual with respect to another individual or group of individuals.
- A *Social Context Model* represents a subset of the social milieu, which we define in terms of social roles, relationships, interactions and situations, of an individual with respect to an another individual or a group. The social context model is employed by a given socially-aware application, is usually explicitly specified by the application developer but may evolve over time.

---

[1] Refers to the social setting or environment in which people live or something happens [36].

- *Social Context Information* is a set of data, gathered from various sources (*e.g.*, social media) or explicitly specified by human, that conforms to a social context model. This provides a snapshot that approximates the state, at a given time, of the subset of the social context encompassed by the model.
- We distinguish social context from the concept of context used in previous research by calling the latter physical context. *Physical context* excludes *Social Context* and mainly refers to the contextual information about systems, entities, and their environments.

## 1.3 Research Challenges

Many of the research efforts in the area of context-aware applications are focused on modelling, reasoning and provisioning context information, so as to reduce the complexity of engineering such systems (see [42] for a survey). These efforts have achieved significant progress in formulating context models which are an important prerequisite for building systems that can respond to changes in their environment. In addition, software architectures, frameworks and platforms have also been proposed for developing and managing context-aware applications (see [148] for a survey).

Existing context models, software architectures and platforms for context-aware applications mostly address contexts of a *physical* nature such as location, time, activity, and so on. Comparatively, there have been only limited works investigating contexts of a *social* nature such as social relationships and social roles. Even though recently some works have attempted to model social context (*e.g.*, [43]) and manage social context (*e.g.*, [121]), they are limited in representing various aspects of social context. Furthermore, there is a lack of support for *modelling* and *reasoning about* different *types* of social context information and for *managing* the acquisition, changes and provision of such information (see Chap. 3 for a detail discussion).

This book explores the concept of *social context* as a means to represent and reason about *social relationships*, *social roles*, *social interactions* and *situations*. It presents a *framework* to provide high-level support for developing socially-aware applications by *provisioning* such different types of social context information and *managing* their runtime changes.

In order to aid the development of socially-aware applications, it is fundamental to understand

- what are the different types of social context and their use in developing socially-aware applications of distinct focus,
- how social context information can be acquired from different sources or can be composed,
- how to model and represent such information,

- how to reason about more abstract and semantically rich social context information based on acquired information, and
- how to model runtime social interactions and manage their adaptation.

Towards this goal, we have formulated three key research challenges which will be discussed in the following three sections, respectively.

### 1.3.1 Consistent Representation of Social Context Information

There are different types of social context information. One type is the user's social relationships which can be categorised into interaction- and connection-oriented relationships. The *interaction-oriented* relationships represent *agreements* and *constraints* regarding collaborative interactions among users, which use in developing interaction-centric socially-aware applications (*e.g.*, the cooperative convoy application).

On the other hand, the *connection-oriented* relationships represent users' relational *ties* which use in developing data-centric socially-aware applications (*e.g.*, the socially-aware phone call application). The connection-oriented relationships can be further categorised as "object-centric" and "people-centric" relationships [121]. The *object-centric* relationship is identified between people who have shown common interests (*e.g.*, like/tag in Facebook) or participated in common activities or become members of similar groups. This type of relationship has been used in applications to infer preferences [93] and incentives of resource sharing [123]. The *people-centric* relationship is a formal and declarative definition of a direct relationship between people. For example, a person identifies other persons as father, supervisor, school friend, etc. This type of relationship can be used in a socially-aware phone call application as identified in [176], the SmartObject application [43], and the application to quantify review quality [127].

A user situation is his/her status or activity or state of affair with respect to surrounding people, which can be acquired from various sources (*e.g.*, schedule description in Google Calendar, status update in OSNs). Such situation information is also important for developing a socially-aware phone call application as identified in  [176]. Thus, the challenge is to consistently *model* and *represent* different types of social context information such as social roles, social relationships, social interactions and situations, to facilitate applications use.

## 1.3.2  *Reasoning About Meaningful Social Context Information*

An application may need social context information that is not directly available from sources but can be derived from basic information. For instance, users may want to filter phone calls based on *situation* categories such as "busy" that may not be acquired from sources but can be inferred from collected data by specifying rules (*e.g.,* meeting or seminar being in busy). Similarly, users may want to filter phone calls based on *relationship* categories such as "family" and "best-friends" that are not provided directly but can be inferred from the semantics of the relationship categories. Thus, there is the need to define and obtain derived relationships (at different abstraction levels) based on the basic relationships (*e.g.,* mother and school-friend) and their semantics (*e.g.,* mother being in family) and attributes (*e.g.,* strength and trust).

To further enhance the services provided by the socially-aware applications, it might be required to infer *situations* based on users' social interaction events. These events can be identified from users' interaction activities in various social interaction platforms (*e.g.,* Facebook, Email). The interaction events have *temporal correlations*. Furthermore, they are associated with users' social context information such as their social relationships and social roles, and thus need to capture in the properties of interaction events. Many of these properties are ontological, *i.e.,* their values have underlying *semantics*. As such, inferring situations from interaction events need to consider semantic matching of interaction event properties and temporal correlations among historical events. Thus, it is required to support *inferring* situations by observing and analysing current and past interaction events, and utilising ontological knowledge about such events.

## 1.3.3  *Managing Access Control and Adaptation*

The user's social context information is inherently sensitive. The scenarios of emerging socially-aware applications require users to share their information for greater benefits but this may also compromise their privacy. For example, allowing a caller to know the status of the callee before calling might reduce interruptions, but may also raise serious concerns regarding the privacy and access control over users' situation and other data [120]. Thus, users should be able to retain control over who has access to their personal information under which conditions. In addition, a user may want to fine-tune the granularity of the answer provided to a given query, depending on the context of that query such as who is asking, what is asked for, and the user's current situation. Therefore, it is necessary to provide a mechanism to support efficient *access* to this social context information while respecting information owners' *privacy*.

Interaction-relationships based *runtime social interaction models* mediate social interactions between users of an interaction-centric socially-aware application. These runtime models typically evolve and many aspects of models such as topology, interaction constraints and non-functional quality properties need to *modify* frequently in response to changes in user requirements and environments. Thus, it is necessary to support *adaptation* in such runtime social interaction models.

## 1.4 Approach Overview

We propose a *framework* to address the aforementioned challenges in designing and implementing socially-aware applications of two different focuses such as data-centric and interaction-centric. The basis of the framework is an approach to *modelling, reasoning about* and *managing* social context information. The framework provides a platform, namely *SocioPlatform* (as illustrated in Fig. 1.1), to aid the development of socially-aware applications by acquiring, reasoning, storing and provisioning different types of social context information, and managing their runtime adaptation.

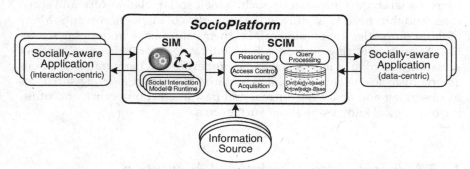

Fig. 1.1: *SocioPlatform* overview

The *SocioPlatform* consists of *social context information management (SCIM)* and *social interaction management (SIM)* components. SCIM supports data-centric socially-aware applications by *acquiring, integrating, classifying* and *storing* social context information from diverse sources such as Facebook, LinkedIn, Twitter and Google Calendar. It provides a number of functionalities including *deriving* social relationships, *deducing* situations from acquired information, and *inferring* situations from users' interaction events. It also provides efficient *access* to social context information while preserving information owners' *privacy*.

SIM provides the *runtime environment* and *adaptation management* for the interaction-centric socially-aware applications. The runtime environment instantiates runtime models and mediates social interactions among collaborative users. SIM supports the *runtime adaptation* of such model to cope with the changes in users' requirements and environments.

## 1.4.1 Social Context Modelling

We adopt an ontology-based approach to modelling and representing social context. Ontology-based approaches have been evaluated as most promising for context modelling in pervasive computing [42]. In order to capture both the general and domain-specific concepts, we propose both the *upper* ontology and *domain-specific* ontologies for different types of social context information such as *social role, social relationship* and *social interaction* and *situation*. The *upper* ontology captures generic concepts, while the *domain-specific* ontology extends the upper ontology to capture the domain-specific concepts. One of the key characteristics of our modelling approach is that we model social context information as *first-class* entities rather than representing them as a generic *link* between people (as in existing approaches such as [178], discussed in Chap. 3). This way of modelling allows us to benefit from description logic (DL) in *classifying* and *reasoning* about social context information at different levels of *abstraction* based on the *properties* of social context.

## 1.4.2 Social Context Reasoning

We adopt an ontology-based approach and use OWL2 DL (a language for encoding ontology) for *deriving, abstracting* and *deducing* social context information (*e.g.*, family, best friend, busy) from acquired information (*e.g.*, father, school friend, meeting). OWL2 DL constructs allow us to specify *reasoning rules* by considering different aspects of social context information such as time-stamp. The main advantage of using OWL2 DL is that a DL reasoner can be used for *executing* reasoning rules and checking *inconsistency* in specification of such rules.

To address the *temporal correlation* aspect in situation reasoning, we propose a *hybrid* approach that combines *ontology-based semantic matching* and *complex event processing* in order to *infer* users' situations from observed data, *e.g.*, users' interaction events. In this regard, we propose an ontology-based interaction event model to capture users' interactions in various social interaction platforms (*e.g.*, Facebook, cooperative convoy), which adopts and extends recent event models and incorporates social context information.

We also propose a *language* to *specify* situations using atomic and complex interaction event patterns, which integrates their *semantic aspect* with *temporal relations*.

### 1.4.3 Social Context Management

We have taken policy-based approach to ensure users' privacy preference in *accessing* their social context information. In this regard, we propose an ontology-based *socially-aware access control policy model*. Our policy model provides intuitive support by considering *social relationship, social role* and *situation* information when defining privacy preferences.

To manage *social interactions* among users of an interaction-centric socially-aware application, we propose an approach to modelling and managing runtime social interactions. We adopt the view of an organisation being a composition structure of dynamic social roles in order to model runtime social interactions. The essences of our approach are the *externalisation* of the interaction relationships from the applications and the *explicit* modelling of such relationships from *domain-* and *player-perspectives*. The *domain-centric social interaction model (DSIM)* captures a *collaborative* view of the interaction relationships among the users/actors, whereas the *player-centric social interaction model (PSIM)* captures an individual's *coordinated* view of all its interactions (across different domains), and thus supports coordination. We *separate* functional and management operations in such runtime models which facilitates their adaptation to cope with the continuous changes in users requirements and environments. We introduce *states* for the runtime models to enable adaptation in a safe manner. We also consider the inherent dependencies between DSIMs and PSIMs, and propose a protocol for adaptation propagation among these models.

## 1.5 Statement and Contributions

This book contends that existing context models, context reasoning and management approach have lacking to address the notion of social context to meet the challenges inherent in developing socially-aware pervasive computing applications. It proposes that the use of a specialised approach to modelling, reasoning about and managing social context, in conjunction with platform support for tasks such as social context gathering, management and provisioning, greatly simplifies the construction of socially-aware applications.

The contribution of this work lies in the development of a conceptual *framework*, and a corresponding software *platform*, that supports design and implementation tasks associated with social context-awareness. At the core of this framework is a novel approach to *modelling, reasoning about* and *managing* social context that allows context to be described at varying levels of abstraction with its semantics, deducing more meaningful and interesting social context information, and managing its acquisition, provisioning and runtime changes. In particular, followings are the original contributions of this work:

- An ontology-based *social context model* including the upper and domain-specific social context ontologies. The *upper* ontology defines and captures generic concepts such as social role, social relationship, social interaction and situation, while the *domain-specific* ontology extends the upper ontology to capture the domain-specific concepts.
- An ontology-based approach to *deriving, deducing* and *abstracting* social context information such as social relationships and situations, from basic acquired information such as social roles and users' profile. A hybrid approach that combines semantic matching and complex event processing to *inferring* users' *situations* from their interaction events. In this regard, we propose both the upper and domain-specific *interaction event ontologies* and a *language* to specify situations.
- An ontology-based socially-aware access control *policy model* and *language* to allow users to specify their privacy preference regarding access to their social context information.
- An approach to *modelling* runtime social interactions from both the domain- and player-perspectives, and *managing* their runtime adaptation.
- *Finally*, a platform, namely *SocioPlatform* for *acquiring* users' social data from various sources, *reasoning about* more useful and interesting social context information, *storing* it into knowledge base and *provisioning* such information while preserving owners' privacy preferences. It also supports to *realise* runtime social interaction models and to *manage* their runtime adaptation.

## 1.6 Book Structure

This book is structured into *three* main parts consisting of *ten* chapters. Part I consists of the introduction (Chap. 1), application scenarios (Chap. 2), and background and related work (Chap. 3) to provide the required background knowledge and themes for this book. Part II presents the approach to developing social context-awareness by presenting the ontology-based approach to modelling and representing different types of social context (Chap. 4), the approach to deriving, deducing, abstracting and inferring social context information (Chap. 5), and the approach to managing privacy in accessing social context information and adaptation of runtime social interaction models

(Chap. 6). Part III discusses the *SocioPlatform* with its implementation details (Chap. 7), case studies (Chap. 8), the evaluation results (Chap. 9), and finally a conclusion recapping the contributions of this work and related topics for future investigation (Chap. 10).

Chapter 2 presents two application scenarios that illustrate two socially-aware applications of distinct focus such as data-centric and interaction-centric, and their associated requirements. The key requirements for developing socially-aware applications are listed by summarising individual requirements of each of the application scenarios. These scenarios are also used as running examples by the remaining chapters of this book. Furthermore, these scenarios are used in case studies to show how the framework supports the design and implementation of different socially-aware applications.

Chapter 3 provides the related background and reviews the related work to analyse the existing approaches to modelling, reasoning about and managing context of physical nature. In addition, the lacking of the recent attempts to modelling, reasoning about and managing social context including runtime adaptation support are also introduced. Furthermore, the relevant work in existing literature is evaluated on the basis of the requirements of developing socially-aware applications as introduced in Chap. 2.

Chapter 4 presents our approach to modelling social context. In particular, it presents an upper and domain-specific ontologies for different types of social context information such as social role, social relationship, social interaction and situation. The *upper ontology* captures the basic concepts, abstracted from the analysis of application scenarios presented in Chap. 2 and the different sources of social context information such as Facebook, LinkedIn, Twitter and Google Calendar. A number of domain-specific ontologies are provided by specialising the concepts in the upper ontology.

Chapter 5 presents our approach to *reasoning about* social context information. An ontology-based approach is proposed to deriving social relationships, and deducing and abstracting situations where OWL2 DL is used to write reasoning rules. A hybrid approach that combines ontology-based semantic matching and complex event processing, is proposed to inferring users' situations from their interaction events. In that regard, a language is proposed to specify situation inference rules.

Chapter 7 served to integrate the theoretical contributions of Chaps. 4–6 into a system architecture and subsequently an implemented platform, namely *SocioPlatform*, incorporating the acquisition, management and querying of social context information, an environment for executing social interaction models and managing their runtime adaptation, and a set of APIs for developers to build socially-aware applications.

Chapter 8 describes two case studies involving the development of two prototypical social context-aware applications that have been discussed in Chap. 2, using our novel approach to *modelling, reasoning about* and *managing* social context information, and the associated *SocioPlatform*. This chapter demonstrates the use and applicability of our framework in developing socially-aware applications. At the same time, it highlights the benefits and strengths of the framework, and also validates the functionalities of the *SocioPlatform*.

Chapter 9 evaluates the functionality of the *SocioPlatform* by conducting a series of experiments using both real data from online social networks and simulated data, as appropriate. This chapter also evaluates the socially-aware applications that have been developed in Chap. 8, using real-life experiments. The results of these experiments demonstrate the real-world applicability and feasibility of developing socially-aware applications using our framework.

Chapter 10 concludes the book by summarising the key *contributions* of the work to the field of *pervasive social computing*, and then discussing some related topics for *future* investigation.

# Chapter 2
# Application Scenarios

In this chapter, we present two application scenarios that illustrate two different types of *social context-aware applications* (in short *socially-aware applications*) and their associated requirements. The objective of this chapter is *twofold*. The *first* objective is to present application scenarios which introduce different kinds of social context information and their use in developing various socially-aware applications. These application scenarios will be used throughout the next chapters to explain the *framework* for social context-aware applications by providing suitable examples. Furthermore, these scenarios will be used in case studies to show how the framework supports the development of various applications. The *second* objective is to motivate and identify key requirements of developing socially-aware applications by analysing these application scenarios.

The chapter is organized as follows. Section 2.1 presents a scenario related to phone call interruptions illustrating the needs and requirements of a *data-centric* socially-aware application which reduces phone call interruptions by exploiting users' social context information, in particular, *connection-oriented social relationships* and *situations*. Section 2.2 presents a cooperative convoy scenario illustrating the needs and requirements of an *interaction-centric* socially-aware application which supports social interactions based on users' *interaction-oriented social relationships*. Section 2.3 generalises the *key requirements* for developing socially-aware applications. Finally, Sect. 2.4 summarises this chapter.

© Springer International Publishing Switzerland 2016
M.A. Kabir et al., *Pervasive Social Computing*,
DOI 10.1007/978-3-319-29951-8_2

## 2.1  A Data-Centric Socially-Aware Application Scenario

In this section, we identify the requirements of developing *data-centric* socially-aware applications (where data drives the applications' behaviour) by analysing the phone call interruptions scenario. Section 2.1.1 discusses the phone call interruptions scenario, while Sect. 2.1.2 analyses the requirements.

### 2.1.1  The Phone Call Interruptions

Mobile phones have the obvious benefit of at the moment communication. Irrespective of time and place, we can expect a phone to ring. But a ringing phone at an inopportune moment can be very disruptive to the current task or social situation. In a survey of 100 senior executives, it was reported that undesirable interruptions constitute 28 % of the knowledge worker's day, which translates to 28 billion wasted hours for companies in the United States alone. It results in a loss of 700 billion dollars per year, considering an average labor rate of $25 per hour for information workers [5]. Studies have also found that undesired disruption causes interrupted users to take up to 30 % longer to complete and commit up to twice the number of errors. Judge Robert Restaino jailed 46 people when a mobile phone rang in his New York courtroom and no one would admit responsibility [1].

Fig. 2.1: Illustrations of phone call interruptions

We witness how often people are interrupted by incoming phone calls which not only disturb the user but also his/her surrounding people (Fig. 2.1 illustrates two scenarios). Mobile phone interruptions have sparked problems that have already been studied extensively, and they are many in number and can be serious in nature (*e.g.*, they cause car accidents [14]). Meanwhile, the burden of managing social norms and patterns implied by mobile phone usage is left to the user. For instance, when one is in a meeting, he/she must remember to switch the phone to silent and decide whether to pick up any incoming call. Many of these interruptions could be avoided or adequately managed, only if the caller could be informed of the current status of the intended callee [120]. For example, if the caller could be informed that the callee is in a meeting, she might decide to call at a better time, thus avoiding or reducing harmful interruptions and possible socially embarrassing situations. On the other hand, the static nature of mobile phone configuration (*e.g.*, reject all incoming phone calls while in a meeting) may lead to communication gaps and socially embarrassing situations [86]. For example, one may not want to miss any incoming call from his/her boss, even though he/she is in a meeting.

Let us consider that Alice, an university graduate student, wants to filter her incoming phone calls as follows: if my status/situation is *meeting* or *seminar*, and (1) a call comes from *friend*, the action is to reject, (2) a call comes from *family*, the action is to reject and forward my status as *Busy*, (3) a call comes from *colleague*, the action is to reject and forward status as meeting or seminar, (4) a call comes from the *supervisor*, the action is to vibrate, (5) if my status is a non-business situation, the action is ring. Alice also wants to make her situation accessible by her colleague when she is in a meeting or seminar.

## 2.1.2 Requirements Analysis

A socially-aware phone call application is a way to minimize mobile phone interruptions that are mostly caused by (1) *unawareness* of each other's (caller and callee) current situation, and (2) a lack of support to allow users to specify their *dynamic* filtering preferences over incoming phone calls. By observing how interruptions are currently handled by users, we might (at least partially) automate interruption management. Recently some studies (*e.g.*, [34, 64]) have tried to identify the context information (*e.g.*, users' situation) that is considered important in deciding whether to initiate phone call. In that regard, some other studies (*e.g.*, [120, 177]) have tried to identify factors that influence the users to share or disclose information about their situations. Some further studies also have focused on identifying actions that are performed currently by users to filter calls (*e.g.*, [86]). Users' social context, in particular, connection-oriented relationships (*e.g.*, father-child, mother-child, husband-wife) and situations (*e.g.*, meeting, seminar, watching a game in a stadium) have shown to have strong social underpinnings in both sharing current status information and filtering incoming phone calls [120, 176, 177].

A socially-aware phone call application that considers both the caller and callee perspectives, need to fulfill the following requirements:

*First*, the application should *acquire* its user's current situation information and allow the user to *share* some of this information with other users. In this regard, the application should also allow its user to specify her *privacy* preferences to retain control over who has access to her situation information under which conditions.

*Second*, the application should allow its user to specify her phone call filtering preferences based on different social context information including *social relationships* and *situations*. When a phone call comes, the application needs to execute these filtering preferences and behaves accordingly. To check the filtering preferences, application needs its user's social context information such as her current situations, her relationships with the caller, and so on. Studies have revealed that users want to define call filtering preferences that apply to all people with certain social relationships (*e.g.*, family, best friends) or social roles rather than explicitly name each person [120, 177]. Thus, it is required to collect, classify, infer and manage different social context information.

## 2.2  An Interaction-Centric Socially-Aware Application Scenario

In this section, we identify the requirements of developing interaction-centric socially-aware applications (where interactions drive the applications' behaviour) by analysing the cooperative convoy scenario. Section 2.2.1 discusses the cooperative convoy scenario, while Sect. 2.2.2 analyses the requirements.

### 2.2.1  The Cooperative Convoy

Two groups of tourists in their two cars hired from two different rental companies want to drive together from Melbourne to Sydney. The car rental companies provide different levels of support to their customers based on the customers' insurance policies, payment, service availability, and so on.

Let us consider that the two cars, Car#1 and Car#2, as depicted in Fig. 2.2, are rented from Budget and AVIS respectively. The Budget Car Rental Company provides a car with a wet-sensor that can detect relevant road conditions and give an alert to reduce speed as necessary. The company also allows access to a Travel Guide Service (TGS) that suggests a possible route to a destination considering the shortest path. However, the service is unable to report real-time traffic information, *e.g.*, road blocks due to road accidents. In contrast, the AVIS Company allows its car to access a Traffic Management Service (TMS) that provides information on traffic conditions ahead, *e.g.*, the

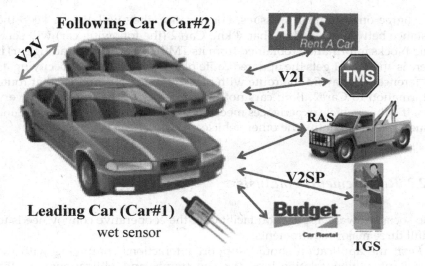

Fig. 2.2: An illustration of cooperative convoy

road is blocked due to accident or any emergency road works. However, both of these car rental companies provide a Roadside Assistance Service (RAS) to their customers. When a vehicle experiences a mechanical issue, its telematics system automatically informs the rental company and RAS, and requests a tow truck if the vehicle is no longer drivable. Information about the vehicle location and the mechanical issue is also sent with the request. Upon receiving the request, the road-side service validates it with the car rental company and takes the necessary steps as defined in the agreement with that company.

Drivers of Car#1 and Car#2 want to form a cooperative convoy to make their travel safe and convenient by collaborating and interacting with each other. In a *cooperative convoy*, a vehicle interacts with other vehicles, service providers and infrastructure systems to make the travel safe and convenient. Through these interactions a vehicle's driver can share information (acquired from the service providers and infrastructure systems) with other vehicles' drivers in performing their tasks. Such interactions are subject to defined agreements and constraints among the entities (*i.e.*, vehicle to vehicle (V2V), vehicle to service providers (V2SP), and vehicle to infrastructure (V2I)).

In the above scenario, we can see that Car#1 and Car#2 have access to different types of services: Car#1 has access to a Travel Guide Service (TGS), while Car#2 has access to a real time Traffic Management Service (TMS). In the cooperative convoy, they decide that Car#1 is the leading car (LC) whilst Car#2 is the following car (FC). The two cars follow the same route chosen by the leading car as it has access to a TGS. In addition, the drivers of both cars agree on a number of issues. For instance, they will always keep the distance between them less than 1 km. Car#2 (the following car) will send road blocks information (obtained from its TMS) to Car#1 (the leading car) if there is any. Car#1 gets the updated route plan from its TGS by specifying its preferences (*e.g.*, avoid the route with blocked road) and notifies that route information to Car#2. Both cars notify each other of their positions every 10 s. If either vehicle experiences mechanical problems (*e.g.*, flat tyre, engine issue) it needs to notify the other vehicle.

### 2.2.2  Requirements Analysis

The socially-aware application facilitating the cooperative convoy needs to fulfill three major requirements:

*First*, the application should support interactions complying with the *agreed* interaction relationships (*i.e.*, constraints and obligations). In the above scenario, these interaction relationships can be clustered into three groups by taking a collaborative view:

- *Interaction relationships between the driver of LC (Car#1) and the Budget Company with its associated services*: The interaction relationships such as getting route plan from the TGS, requesting road side assistance in case of any mechanical problem, and so on, fall into this category.
- *Interaction relationships between the driver of FC (Car#2) and the AVIS Company with its associated services*: The interaction relationships such as getting road blocks information from the TMS, and requesting road side assistance in case of any mechanical problem fall into this category.
- *Interaction relationship between the drivers of LC and FC*: The interaction-relationship between drivers of LC and FC (*i.e.*, their mutual agreements) falls into this category. It includes that FC should send road blocks information to LC if there is any, LC should notify the updated route information to FC, FC follows the same route chosen by LC, both cars notify each other of their positions every 10 s, and in case of any mechanical problem both cars notify each other, and so on.

Thus, a model is required to capture the collaborative view of such interaction-oriented relationships.

*Second*, the application needs to provide a coordinated view of the interactions, and to allow drivers to specify their coordination preferences and to perform the coordination in an automated manner. According to the scenario, each driver is responsible for performing several tasks, for instance, the driver of LC is responsible for notifying route information, current positions, and mechanical problems (if any) to FC. Similarly, the driver of FC should send road blocks information, current positions, and mechanical problems to LC. For the drivers to perform such additional tasks (*e.g.,* forwarding information) may cause distraction and have undesirable consequences. Thus, to facilitate collaboration with less distraction, it is required to provide a coordinated view of the interactions and to allow drivers to specify their coordination preferences.

*Third,* the application needs to support runtime adaptation, as the interaction relationships evolve over time and thus need to *adapt* with the *changes* in requirements and environments. For instance, a third vehicle could join when the convoy is on the way; or the break-down of a following vehicle might result in its leaving the convoy before reaching the destination. A mechanical problem of the leading car may require it to handover the leading car role to one of the following cars. Because of heavy rain, the maximum distance may need to be reduced from 1 km to 600 m.

## 2.3 Requirements for Developing Socially-Aware Applications

The above discussions reveal that there are a number of key requirements for developing socially-aware applications:

Req1   *Modelling Social Context Information*: There are different types of social context information such as interaction- and connection-oriented social relationships, social roles, social interactions and situations. Such social context information need to be modelled and represented consistently with its semantics to facilitate application use. Moreover, a pervasive social computing application assumed to be highly dynamic in the sense that it might require new types of social context information or might introduce new information sources that yield new types of social context, so the social context model should be flexible extensive.

Req2   *Reasoning about Social Context Information*: Application may need social context information that is not directly available from context sources but can be derived from acquired information. For instance, users may want to filter phone calls based on relationship categories such as "family" and "best-friends", and situations such as "busy" that may not be acquired directly from sources but can be inferred from other acquired basic information. Thus, there is the need to define and obtain inferred social context information based on the semantics, attributes and temporal correlations of the acquired basic information.

Req3   *Preserving Privacy in Accessing Social Context Information*: A socially-aware application may require users to share their social context information for greater benefits but this also comprise their privacy. For example, in a socially-aware phone call application, allowing a caller to know the situation of the callee before calling might reduce interruptions, but may also raise serious concerns regarding the privacy and access control over users' status and other data. Therefore, users should be able to retain control over who has access to their personal information under which conditions. In addition, a user may want to fine-tune the granularity of the answer. For instance, an employee may be happy that her boss knows her current status is "at desk". However, she may not be happy for her boss to know that her status is "chatting to friends via instant messaging". Thus, there is a need to provide a privacy policy that should allow users to control access to their information at different levels of abstraction.

Req4    *Acquiring and Managing Social Context Information*: Social media such as online social networks, blogs, and instant messaging, have radically changed the way people interact with each other and share information about their lives and works [184]. The popularity of online social networks such as Facebook, LinkedIn, Twitter and Google+ produce an unprecedented amount of social context information as people specify their relationships, update their status and share contents. Google Calendar also can be a possible source of situation information as people use it to maintain their schedule [126]. Furthermore, users' interaction events in different platforms, *e.g.*, social media, can be exploited to infer their situations. Thus, it is required to *acquire* users' such information from *different sources* and *manage* its changes for up-to-date, accurate and real time *provisioning* of social context information.

Req5    *Modelling Runtime Social Interactions*: Socially-aware applications that support social interactions based on the interaction-oriented relationships (*i.e.*, agreements and constraints) among collaborative actors, need runtime representation of such relationships, called social interaction model. Such runtime social interaction model mediates runtime social interactions between actors. For instance, in the cooperative convoy, to support social interactions between drivers of Car#1 and Car#2 according to their interaction-relationship, a runtime model of such interaction-relationship is required. However, an actor may involve in multiple interaction-relationships and it may have its own view of social interactions related to these relationships. Thus, it is also required to support an individual user to coordinate his/her social interactions by providing a coordinated view of runtime social interaction model.

Req6    *Managing Adaptation in Runtime Social Interaction Models*: Runtime social interaction models typically evolves and many aspects of runtime models such as topology, interaction constraints and non-functional quality properties need to *modify* frequently in response to *changes* in user requirements and environments. Thus, it is necessary to manage the *adaptation* in such runtime social interaction models. For instance, a third vehicle could join when the convoy is on the way; or the break-down of a following vehicle might result in its leaving the convoy before reaching the destination. As a consequence, the runtime social interaction model of convoy needs to be updated.

## 2.4 Summary

In this chapter, we have presented two application scenarios associated with two socially-aware applications of distinct focus such as *data-centric* and *interaction-centric*. These applications need different types of social context information and requires various supports in their development.

*First*, we have presented a phone call interruptions scenario that demands a *data-centric* socially-aware application. This application allows a person to filter incoming phone calls based on her situation and the relationships with the caller. Thus, the application needs *data, e.g.,* connection-oriented social relationships and situations, to provide service to its users. The application also allows a caller to know the status of the intended callee before making the call. In this regard, the application requires to access the callee's situation information while preserving his/her privacy.

*Second*, we have presented a cooperative convoy scenario that demands an *interaction-centric* socially-aware application. This application enables a cooperative convoy by supporting social interactions among drivers and external services, based on their predefined *agreements* and *constraints*, which we refer as *interaction-oriented social relationships*. The application needs a technique to *model* such interaction-oriented relationships. It also requires support to *manage adaptation* in such runtime model to cope with the changes in requirements and environments.

*Finally*, we have identified the key *requirements* for developing socially-aware applications.

# Chapter 3
# Background and Related Work

This chapter presents a review and discussion of related work from various areas within the scope of this book to analyse and position this book work with respect to the existing literature. It covers context modelling techniques, context models, event models, situation specification and reasoning techniques, privacy policy models and access control, context management frameworks and platforms. The review also highlights the principal research areas in which the existing solutions fall short of requirements for social context-aware applications, and motivates the research presented in the following chapters.

The chapter is organised as follows. Section 3.1 gives background information on ontology. Section 3.2 discusses a number of existing context modelling approaches and justifies our decision of choosing the ontology-based approach to modelling social context information. Section 3.3 characterises the existing ontology-based context models, and discusses recent attempts to modelling social context information and their limitations. Section 3.4 explores ontology-based event models, and identifies the common concepts of those models as the basis for our ontology based interaction event model. Section 3.5 discusses existing situation specification and reasoning techniques and their limitations in addressing both the semantic and temporal aspects. Section 3.6 highlights the gaps of existing privacy policy models in fulfilling the requirements for access control over users' social context information. Section 3.7 discusses recent attempts to managing social context information and their limitations in acquiring, reasoning and supporting access to social context information. Section 3.9 motivates the need of a new platform to support collaborative social interactions among users by highlighting the limitations of existing platforms in supporting runtime adaptation. Section 3.10 characterises platforms that support runtime adaptation but are not aimed for collaborative applications, and thus can not be adopted to fulfill our requirements.

© Springer International Publishing Switzerland 2016
M.A. Kabir et al., *Pervasive Social Computing*,
DOI 10.1007/978-3-319-29951-8_3

Finally, Sect. 3.11 summarises the existing work in the field of social context-awareness, highlights a variety of shortcomings, consequently motivates the need of further research, and subsequently positions the contributions of this work.

## 3.1 Ontology Preliminaries

We chronicle the historical definitions of the term ontology and expound on the value of ontology use (Sect. 3.1.1). Later, we give an overview of the development of ontological technologies, especially the standard ontology languages (Sect. 3.1.2). Finally, we discuss the OWL-DL, an ontology encoding language, constructs to illustrate its potentiality in representing knowledge (Sect. 3.1.3).

### 3.1.1 Ontology Definitions

In the Oxford Dictionary [16], an ontology is defined as: *"The science or study of being; that branch of metaphysics concerned with the nature or essence of being or existence; or a theory or conception relating to the nature of being"*. This philosophical definition reflects the essence of ontology: capturing the natural features of realities and relations between realities. The term was borrowed from philosophy and introduced into the knowledge engineering field as a means of *abstracting* and *representing* knowledge. Ontologies are used to build consensual terminologies for the domain knowledge in a formal way so that they can be more easily shared and reused.

Ontologies have been applied in many fields of computer science, such as the semantic Web, information systems, service-oriented computing, and artificial intelligence. Accordingly, the definitions of ontologies have evolved with different and complementary points of view. Some of these definitions stress the *general and intrinsic* properties of ontologies, while others are influenced by the *technical* means of developing ontologies. We will illustrate several typical definitions in both of the perspectives.

Ontology is defined as *"a shared and common understanding of a domain that can be communicated between people and heterogeneous and distributed systems"* [75], and more generally *"a formal, explicit specification of a shared conceptualization"* [88]. Fensel [75] elaborated on the definition of Gruber [88] by saying that *conceptualization* refers to an abstract model of some phenomenon in the world by having identified the relevant concepts of that phenomenon. *Explicit* means that the type of concepts used and the constraints on their use are explicitly defined. *Formal* refers to the fact that the ontology describes what each concept is meant to denote, and specifies formal axioms that constrain the interpretation and well-formed use of these concepts. *Shared* reflects the notion that an ontology captures consensual knowledge; that is, it is not private of some individual, but accepted by a group. This definition describes how the philosophical nature of ontologies could be incorporated into computer science.

Guarino [91] refined Gruber's definition by distinguishing ontologies from conceptualizations formally and logically: *"a logical theory accounting for the intended meaning of a formal vocabulary, i.e., its ontological commitment to a particular conceptualization of the world"*. When this logical theory is used to model a particular aspect of reality—an intended domain—an ontological commitment is specified to capture the very basic ontological assumptions (such as identities and internal structures) about the intended domain. The ontological commitment gives explicit information about the intended nature of the modelling primitives and their a priori relationships for this logical theory. Thus, it constrains a subset of all the possible models of the logical theory by specifying the intended meaning of its vocabulary. These models being constrained are called intended models, which only describe those states of affairs that are compatible with the underlying ontological commitment [92]. Furthermore, Guarino [91] focused on the application side to offer a systematic account of the central role that ontologies played in information systems, leading to the ontology-driven information systems; that is, ontologies 'drive' all aspects and all components of an information system.

Taking the technical aspect, Huhns et al [108] define ontology as *"a computer model of some portion of the world"* [108]. Recently, Tom Gruber [89] again defines ontology as, *"a set of representational primitives with which to model a domain of knowledge or discourse, where the representational primitives are typically classes (or sets), attributes (or properties), and relationships (or relations among class members)"*. This definition provides the representational primitives for modelling information and developing a knowledge base to managing such information. Thus, in this book context, we adopt this definition.

## 3.1.2 Languages for Encoding Ontology

In this section, we give an overview of a number of ontology encoding languages. In particular, we provide a brief introduction of Web Ontology Language (OWL) which is the broadly accepted ontology language, and discuss its strengths over other ontology languages (complied from [31, 107, 134, 138, 169]).

The *Web Ontology Language* (OWL) [169] created based on the DAML+OIL [61], and extends Resource Description Framework (RDF) [39] and Resource Description Framework Schema (RDFS) [46]. Its primary aim is to bring the *expressive* and *reasoning power* of description logic (DL) [35] to the semantic web.

OWL takes the basic fact-stating ability of RDF and the class- and property-structuring capabilities of RDFS and extends them in important ways. OWL can declare classes, and organise these classes in a subsumption ('*subclass*') hierarchy, as can RDFS. OWL classes can be specified as logical combinations (*intersections, unions* or *complements*) of other classes, or as *enumerations* of specified objects, going beyond the capabilities of RDFS. OWL can also declare properties, organise these properties into a '*subproperty*' hierarchy, and provide domains and ranges for these properties, again as in RDFS. The domains of OWL properties are OWL classes, and ranges can be either OWL classes or externally-defined datatypes such as string or integer. OWL can state that a property is *transitive, symmetric, functional*, or is the inverse of another property, here again extending RDFS.

OWL can express which objects (also called '*individuals*') belong to which classes, and what the property values are of specific individuals. *Equivalence* statements can be made on classes and on properties, *disjointness* statements can be made on classes, and equality and inequality can be asserted between individuals.

However, the major extension over RDFS is the ability in OWL to provide restrictions on how properties behave that are local to a class. OWL can define classes where a particular property is restricted so that all the values for the property in instances of the class must belong to a certain class (or datatype); at least one value must come from a certain class (or datatype); there must be at least certain specific values and there must be at least or at most a certain number of distinct values. For example, using RDFS, we can

- declare classes like *Country, Person, Student* and *Australian*;
- state that *Student* is a subclass of *Person*;
- state that *Australia* and *England* are both instances of the class *Country*;
- declare *Nationality* as a property relating to the classes *Person* (its domain) and *Country* (its range);
- state that *age* is a property with *Person* as its domain and *integer* as its range; and
- state that *Peter* is an instance of the class *Australian*, and that his *age* has value *48*.

With OWL, we can additionally

- state that *Country* and *Person* are disjoint classes;
- state that *Australia* and *England* are distinct individuals;
- declare *HasCitizen* as the inverse property of *Nationality*;
- state that the class *Stateless* is defined precisely as those members of the class *Person* that have no values for the property *Nationality*;
- state that the class *MultipleNationals* is defined precisely as those members of the class *Person* that have at least two values for the property *Nationality*;
- state that the class *Australian* is defined precisely as those members of the class *Person* that have *Australia* as a value of the property *Nationality*; and
- state that *age* is a functional property.

Description Logics (DL) [35], and insights from Description Logic research, had a strong influence on the design of OWL, particularly on the formalisation of the semantics, the choice of language constructors and the integration of datatypes and data values. A key feature of Description Logics is that they are logics, *i.e.*, formal languages with well-defined semantics. As such, an OWL ontology may include logical descriptions of classes, properties and their instances. Given such an ontology, the OWL formal semantics (see Sect. 3.1.3) specifies how to derive its logical consequences, *i.e.*, facts not literally present in the ontology, but entailed by the semantics. One advantage of OWL ontologies is the availability of tools that can reason about them.

The expressive power of a language like OWL is determined by the class (and property) constructors supported, and by the kinds of axioms that can occur in an ontology. Of course increased expressive power inevitably means increased computational complexity for key reasoning problems such as entailment. To address this issue, three species of OWL are defined [169]: *OWL Lite, OWL DL* and *OWL Full*.

*OWL Lite* can be used to express taxonomy and simple constraints, such as 0 and 1 cardinality. It is the simplest OWL language and corresponds to description logic $\mathcal{SHIF}(D)$. *OWL DL* supports maximum expressiveness while retaining computational completeness and decidability. The DL in the name shows that it is intended to support description logic capabilities. *OWL DL* corresponds to description logic $\mathcal{SHOIN}(D)$. *OWL Full* has no expressiveness constraints, but also does not guarantee any computational properties. It is formed by the full OWL vocabulary, but does not impose any syntactic constrains, so that the full syntactic freedom of RDF can be used.

These *three* languages are layered in a sense that every legal *OWL Lite* ontology is a legal *OWL DL* ontology, every legal *OWL DL* ontology is a legal *OWL Full* ontology, every valid *OWL Lite* conclusion is a valid *OWL DL* conclusion, and every valid *OWL DL* conclusion a valid *OWL Full* conclusion. The inverses of these relations generally do not hold. Also, every OWL ontology is a valid RDF document (*i.e.*, DL expressions are mapped to triples), but not all RDF documents are valid *OWL Lite* or *OWL DL* documents. Thus, in this work, we use OWL DL for modelling and reasoning about social context information.

### 3.1.3  OWL DL Constructs for Representing Knowledge

OWL DL can form descriptions of classes, datatypes, individuals and data values using the constructs shown in Table 3.1. In this table the first column gives the OWL abstract syntax for the construction, while the second column gives the standard Description Logic syntax. OWL DL uses these description-forming constructs in axioms that provide information about classes, properties and individuals, as shown in Table 3.2. Again, the frame-like abstract syntax is given in the first column, and the standard Description Logic syntax is given in the second column.

A Description Logic knowledge base consists of two parts, namely the TBox and the ABox. The TBox consists of a number of class and property axioms; the ABox consists of a number of individual assertions (see Table 3.2). Here, $C$ refers to a description, $T$ refers to a concrete datatype; $D$ refers to either a description or a datatype. $R$ refers to an object property name, $R_k$ refers to datatype property; $Q$ refers to an object or datatype property where several appearances of $R_i$, $R_j$ in one statement always refer to either both object or both datatype properties; $o$ and $t$ refer to object and concrete values, respectively. A class axiom in the TBox consists of two class descriptions, separated with the GCI (General Class Inclusion, or subsumption; $\sqsubseteq$) symbol or the equivalence symbol ($\equiv$), which is equivalent to GCI in both direction (*i.e.*, $\sqsubseteq$ and $\sqsupseteq$). Similarly, a property axiom consists of two property names, separated with the subsumption ($\sqsubseteq$) or the equivalence ($\equiv$) symbol. A description in the TBox is either a named class ($A$), an enumeration ($\{o_1, \ldots o_n\}$), a property restriction ($\exists R \cdot D, \forall R \cdot D, \exists R \cdot o, \geqslant nR, \leqslant nR$, analogously for datatype property restrictions), or an intersection ($C \sqcap D$), union ($C \sqcup D$) or complement ($\neg C$) of such descriptions (Table 3.1). Individual assertions in the ABox are either class membership ($o \in C_i$), property value ($< o_1, o_2 > \in R_i, < o_1, t_1 > \in U_i$), or individual (in)equality ($o_1 = o_2, o_1 \neq o_2$) assertions (Table 3.2).

Description Logics have a set-based model-theoretic semantics. In an interpretation $\mathcal{I}$, a description $C$ (Table 3.1) is mapped to a subset of the domain $\triangle^{\mathcal{I}}$ and an individual $o$ is mapped to an object of $\triangle^{\mathcal{I}}$ using the mapping function $\cdot^{\mathcal{I}}$. Similarly, a datatype $T$ is mapped to a subset of the concrete domain $\triangle_D^{\mathcal{I}}$ and a literal is mapped to a value in $\triangle_D^{\mathcal{I}}$. An abstract role $R$ is mapped to a binary relation over the abstract domain: $\triangle^{\mathcal{I}} \times \triangle^{\mathcal{I}}$. Similarly, a concrete role R is mapped to a binary relation between the abstract and the concrete domain: $\triangle^{\mathcal{I}} \times \triangle_D^{\mathcal{I}}$. Equivalence of descriptions is interpreted as set equivalence ($C \equiv D$ is interpreted as $C^{\mathcal{I}} = D^{\mathcal{I}}$), subsumption is interpreted as set inclusion ($C \sqsubseteq D$ is interpreted as $C^{\mathcal{I}} \subseteq D^{\mathcal{I}}$), and so on. We refer the interested reader to [35, 140] for a more exhaustive treatment of Description Logic and OWL DL semantics, respectively.

## 3.2 Context Modelling Approaches

One of the major research foci in context-aware computing is on context modelling to reduce the *complexity of engineering* context-aware systems. A number of modelling techniques, such as the key-value based modelling [162], mark-up schema [96], graphical approach [100], object-oriented

| Abstract Syntax | DL Syntax | Semantics |
|---|---|---|
| **Descriptions ($C$)** | | |
| $A$      (URI reference) | $A$ | $A^{\mathcal{I}} \subseteq \Delta^{\mathcal{I}}$ |
| `owl:Thing` | $\top$ | $\texttt{owl:Thing}^{\mathcal{I}} = \Delta^{\mathcal{I}}$ |
| `owl:Nothing` | $\bot$ | $\texttt{owl:Nothing}^{\mathcal{I}} = \{\}$ |
| `intersectionOf`$(C_1\ C_2\ \ldots)$ | $C_1 \sqcap C_2$ | $(C_1 \sqcap D_1)^{\mathcal{I}} = C_1^{\mathcal{I}} \cap D_2^{\mathcal{I}}$ |
| `unionOf`$(C_1\ C_2\ \ldots)$ | $C_1 \sqcup C_2$ | $(C_1 \sqcup C_2)^{\mathcal{I}} = C_1^{\mathcal{I}} \cup C_2^{\mathcal{I}}$ |
| `complementOf`$(C)$ | $\neg C$ | $(\neg C)^{\mathcal{I}} = \Delta^{\mathcal{I}} \setminus C^{\mathcal{I}}$ |
| `oneOf`$(o_1\ \ldots)$ | $\{o_1, \ldots\}$ | $\{o_1, \ldots\}^{\mathcal{I}} = \{o_1^{\mathcal{I}}, \ldots\}$ |
| `restriction`$(R\ \texttt{someValuesFrom}(C))$ | $\exists R.C$ | $(\exists R.C)^{\mathcal{I}} = \{x \mid \exists y.\langle x,y\rangle \in R^{\mathcal{I}}$ and $y \in C^{\mathcal{I}}\}$ |
| `restriction`$(R\ \texttt{allValuesFrom}(C))$ | $\forall R.C$ | $(\forall R.C)^{\mathcal{I}} = \{x \mid \forall y.\langle x,y\rangle \in R^{\mathcal{I}} \rightarrow y \in C^{\mathcal{I}}\}$ |
| `restriction`$(R\ \texttt{hasValue}(o))$ | $R : o$ | $(\forall R.o)^{\mathcal{I}} = \{x \mid \langle x,o^{\mathcal{I}}\rangle \in R^{\mathcal{I}}\}$ |
| `restriction`$(R\ \texttt{minCardinality}(n))$ | $\geqslant n\,R$ | $(\geqslant n\,R)^{\mathcal{I}} = \{x \mid \sharp(\{y.\langle x,y\rangle \in R^{\mathcal{I}}\}) \geqslant n\}$ |
| `restriction`$(R\ \texttt{minCardinality}(n))$ | $\leqslant n\,R$ | $(\geqslant n\,R)^{\mathcal{I}} = \{x \mid \sharp(\{y.\langle x,y\rangle \in R^{\mathcal{I}}\}) \leqslant n\}$ |
| `restriction`$(U\ \texttt{someValuesFrom}(D))$ | $\exists U.D$ | $(\exists U.D)^{\mathcal{I}} = \{x \mid \exists y.\langle x,y\rangle \in U^{\mathcal{I}}$ and $y \in D^{\mathbf{D}}\}$ |
| `restriction`$(U\ \texttt{allValuesFrom}(D))$ | $\forall U.D$ | $(\forall U.D)^{\mathcal{I}} = \{x \mid \forall y.\langle x,y\rangle \in U^{\mathcal{I}} \rightarrow y \in D^{\mathbf{D}}\}$ |
| `restriction`$(U\ \texttt{hasValue}(v))$ | $U : v$ | $(U : v)^{\mathcal{I}} = \{x \mid \langle x,v^{\mathcal{I}}\rangle \in U^{\mathcal{I}}\}$ |
| `restriction`$(U\ \texttt{minCardinality}(n))$ | $\geqslant n\,U$ | $(\geqslant n\,U)^{\mathcal{I}} = \{x \mid \sharp(\{y.\langle x,y\rangle \in U^{\mathcal{I}}\}) \geqslant n\}$ |
| `restriction`$(U\ \texttt{maxCardinality}(n))$ | $\leqslant n\,U$ | $(\leqslant n\,U)^{\mathcal{I}} = \{x \mid \sharp(\{y.\langle x,y\rangle \in U^{\mathcal{I}}\}) \leqslant n\}$ |
| **Data Ranges ($D$)** | | |
| $D$      (URI reference) | $D$ | $D^{\mathbf{D}} \subseteq \Delta_{\mathbf{D}}^{\mathcal{I}}$ |
| `oneOf`$(v_1\ \ldots)$ | $\{v_1, \ldots\}$ | $\{v_1, \ldots\}^{\mathcal{I}} = \{v_1^{\mathcal{I}}, \ldots\}$ |
| **Object Properties ($R$)** | | |
| $R$      (URI reference) | $R$ | $R^{\mathcal{I}} \subseteq \Delta^{\mathcal{I}} \times \Delta^{\mathcal{I}}$ |
| | $R^-$ | $(R^-)^{\mathcal{I}} = (R^{\mathcal{I}})^-$ |
| **Datatype Properties ($U$)** | | |
| $U$      (URI reference) | $U$ | $U^{\mathcal{I}} \subseteq \Delta^{\mathcal{I}} \times \Delta_{\mathbf{D}}^{\mathcal{I}}$ |
| **Individuals ($o$)** | | |
| $o$      (URI reference) | $o$ | $o^{\mathcal{I}} \in \Delta^{\mathcal{I}}$ |
| **Data Values ($v$)** | | |
| $v$      (RDF literal) | $v$ | $v^{\mathcal{I}} = v^{\mathbf{D}}$ |

Table 3.1: OWL DL descriptions, data ranges, properties, individuals and data values [107]

modelling [163], logic-based modelling [145], and ontology-based modelling [58, 180], have been developed. Strang and Linnhoff-Popien [172] described these modelling approaches, which are based on the *data structures* used for representing and exchanging contextual information in the respective systems.

*Key-value based modelling*   The model of key-value pairs is the simplest data structure for context modelling. A key (or identifier) in this type of model corresponds to an attribute of the environment that has a value. This value is usually acquired from sensors or data sources. For example, <Room 31 temperature, 24> is such a <key, value> pair. Key-value models were used by Schilit et al. [162] to manage location information. The model of key-value pairs is easy to manage, but has problems with its expressiveness in representing complex structures.

| Abstract Syntax | DL Syntax | Semantics |
|---|---|---|
| Class($A$ partial $C_1 \ldots C_n$) | $A \sqsubseteq C_1 \sqcap \ldots \sqcap C_n$ | $A^{\mathcal{I}} \subseteq C_1^{\mathcal{I}} \sqcap \ldots \sqcap C_n^{\mathcal{I}}$ |
| Class($A$ complete $C_1 \ldots C_n$) | $A = C_1 \sqcap \ldots \sqcap C_n$ | $A^{\mathcal{I}} = C_1^{\mathcal{I}} \sqcap \ldots \sqcap C_n^{\mathcal{I}}$ |
| EnumeratedClass($A\ o_1 \ldots o_n$) | $A = \{o_1, \ldots, o_n\}$ | $A^{\mathcal{I}} = \{o_1^{\mathcal{I}}, \ldots, o_n^{\mathcal{I}}\}$ |
| SubClassOf($C_1\ C_2$) | $C_1 \sqsubseteq C_2$ | $C_1^{\mathcal{I}} \subseteq C_2^{\mathcal{I}}$ |
| EquivalentClasses($C_1 \ldots C_n$) | $C_1 = \ldots = C_n$ | $C_1^{\mathcal{I}} = \ldots = C_n^{\mathcal{I}}$ |
| DisjointClasses($C_1 \ldots C_n$) | $C_i \sqcap C_j = \bot, i \neq j$ | $C_i^{\mathcal{I}} \sqcap C_j^{\mathcal{I}}\{\}, i \neq j$ |
| Datatype($D$) | | $D^{\mathcal{I}} \subseteq \Delta_{\mathbf{D}}^{\mathcal{I}}$ |
| DatatypeProperty($U$ super($U_1$)...super($U_n$) | $U \sqsubseteq U_i$ | $U^{\mathcal{I}} \subseteq U_i^{\mathcal{I}}$ |
|     domain($C_1$) ...domain($C_m$) | $\geqslant 1 U \sqsubseteq C_i$ | $U^{\mathcal{I}} \subseteq C_i^{\mathcal{I}} \times \Delta_{\mathbf{D}}^{\mathcal{I}}$ |
|     range($D_1$) ...range($D_l$) | $\top \sqsubseteq \forall U.D_i$ | $U^{\mathcal{I}} \subseteq \Delta^{\mathcal{I}} \times D_i^{\mathcal{I}}$ |
|     [Functional]) | $\top \sqsubseteq \leqslant 1 U$ | $U^{\mathcal{I}}$ is functional |
| SubPropertyOf($U_1\ U_2$) | $U_1 \sqsubseteq U_2$ | $U_1^{\mathcal{I}} \subseteq U_2^{\mathcal{I}}$ |
| EquivalentProperties($U_1 \ldots U_n$) | $U_1 = \ldots = U_n$ | $U_1^{\mathcal{I}} = \ldots = U_n^{\mathcal{I}}$ |
| ObjectProperty($R$ super($R_1$)...super($R_n$) | $R \sqsubseteq R_i$ | $R^{\mathcal{I}} \subseteq R_i^{\mathcal{I}}$ |
|     domain($C_1$) ...domain($C_m$) | $\geqslant 1 R \sqsubseteq C_i$ | $R^{\mathcal{I}} \subseteq C_i^{\mathcal{I}} \times \Delta^{\mathcal{I}}$ |
|     range($C_1$) ...range($C_l$) | $\top \sqsubseteq \forall R.C_i$ | $R^{\mathcal{I}} \subseteq \Delta^{\mathcal{I}} \times C_i^{\mathcal{I}}$ |
|     [inverseOf($R_0$)] | $R = (^-R_0)$ | $R^{\mathcal{I}} = (R_0^{\mathcal{I}})^-$ |
|     [Symmetric] | $R = (^-R)$ | $R^{\mathcal{I}} = (R^{\mathcal{I}})^-$ |
|     [Functional] | $\top \sqsubseteq \leqslant 1 R$ | $R^{\mathcal{I}}$ is functional |
|     [InverseFunctional] | $\top \sqsubseteq \leqslant 1 R^-$ | $(R^{\mathcal{I}})^-$ is functional |
|     [Transitive]) | $Tr(R)$ | $R^{\mathcal{I}} = (R^{\mathcal{I}})^+$ |
| SubPropertyOf($R_1\ R_2$) | $R_1 \sqsubseteq R_2$ | $R_1^{\mathcal{I}} \subseteq R_2^{\mathcal{I}}$ |
| EquivalentProperties($R_1 \ldots R_n$) | $R_1 = \ldots = R_n$ | $R_1^{\mathcal{I}} = \ldots = R_n^{\mathcal{I}}$ |
| AnnotationProperty($S$) | | |
| Individual($o$ type($C_1$) ...type($C_n$) | $o \in C_i$ | $o^{\mathcal{I}} \in C_i^{\mathcal{I}}$ |
|     value($R_1\ o_1$)...value($R_n\ o_n$) | $\langle o, o_i \rangle \in R_i$ | $\langle o^{\mathcal{I}}, o_i^{\mathcal{I}} \rangle \in R_i^{\mathcal{I}}$ |
|     value($U_1\ v_1$)...value($U_n\ v_n$)) | $\langle o, v_i \rangle \in U_i$ | $\langle o^{\mathcal{I}}, v_i^{\mathcal{I}} \rangle \in U_i^{\mathcal{I}}$ |
| SameIndividual($o_1 \ldots o_n$) | $o_1 = \ldots = o_n$ | $o_i^{\mathcal{I}} = o_j^{\mathcal{I}}$ |
| DifferentIndividuals($o_1 \ldots o_n$) | $o_i \neq o_j, i \neq j$ | $o_i^{\mathcal{I}} \neq o_j^{\mathcal{I}}, i \neq j$ |

Table 3.2: OWL DL axioms and facts [107]

*Markup scheme based modelling*   Markup-based models use a hierarchical data structure consisting of markup tags with attributes and content. Profiles represent typical markup scheme models. Typical examples are the Composite Capabilities/Preference Profile (CC/PP) and User Agent Profile (UAProf) which are encoded in RDF/S with XML notation [22]. Various other examples can be found in [172].

*Graphical modelling*   The Unified Modelling Language (UML) is also used for modelling context. Various approaches exist where contextual aspects are modelled by using UML, *e.g.*, [167]. Another modelling approach includes an extension to Object-Role Modelling (ORM) by context information presented in [100].

*Object-oriented modelling*   This is based on the concept of objects and relationships between them as in the object-oriented programming paradigm. Rather than using implementation-based concepts like records, object-oriented models provide flexible structuring capabilities by using fully-fledged object-orientation mechanisms such as encapsulation, reusability, and inheritance. Objects are used to represent various types of contextual information (*e.g.*, temperature and location); they encapsulate the operations used for context processing. For example, Hydrogen [105] uses such an object-oriented model.

*Logic based modelling*   Logic-based models have a high degree of formality. Typically, facts, expressions and rules are used to define a context model. A logic based system is then used to manage these terms and allows to add, update or remove new facts. An inference (also called reasoning) process can be used to derive new facts based on existing facts and rules in the systems. The contextual information needs to be represented in a formal way as facts. One of the first approaches was published by McCarthy and Buvac [133]. Ranganathan et al. [146] and Katsiri and Mycroft [119] applied first-order logic to reason with contextual information. Loke [125] took rule-based programming further by representing situations for triggering context-aware actions.

*Ontology based modelling*   Ontologies represent a description of the concepts and relationships. Therefore, ontologies are a very promising instrument for modelling contextual information due to their high and formal expressiveness and the possibilities for applying ontology reasoning techniques. Ontology-based techniques support a vocabulary for context predicates [102], so that the data representations in a system can be shared across different systems, or even retrieved from a storage over the Web. Various context-aware frameworks use ontologies as underlying representations for context models such as CoBrA [20, 57], Gaia [153] and SOCAM [90]. They use ontologies and the tools from the "Semantic Web" to represent and reason about context. A discussion and thorough review of these ontology-based context models can be found in [188].

Strang and Linnhoff-Popien further specify six high level requirements for context-aware systems to evaluate the aforementioned context modelling approaches [172]. These requirements are summarised by Christian [102] as follows:

- *Distributed Composition (dc)*—Context-aware systems are distributed, and thus do not have any central instance responsible for the creation, deployment, or maintenance of data and services, particularly context descriptions. Instead, the composition and administration of a context model and its data varies with notably high dynamics in terms of time, network topology, and source.
- *Partial Validation (pv)*—On the structural as well as on the instance level, there is no single place or point in time where the contextual knowledge is available on one node as a result of distributed composition. This is particularly important because of the complexity of contextual interrelationships, which make any modelling intention error-prone.

- *Richness and Quality of Information (qua)*—The quality of information delivered by sensors varies over time, and the richness of information provided by different kinds of sensors characterizing an entity in an ubiquitous computing environment, may differ. Thus, a context model appropriate for use in ubiquitous computing should inherently support both quality and richness.
- *Incompleteness and Ambiguity (inc)*—The set of contextual information available at any point in time characterizing relevant entities in ubiquitous computing environments is usually incomplete and/or ambiguous, particularly if this information is gathered from sensor networks. This should be covered by the model, for instance by interpolating incomplete data on the instance level.
- *Level of Formalism (for)*—It is always a challenge to describe contextual facts and interrelationships in a precise and traceable way. For instance, carrying out the task "print document on the nearest printer" requires a precise definition of terms used in the task, for instance what "nearest" means. It is extremely important that all the entities share the same interpretation of the data that are exchanged, as well as their underlying meaning.
- *Application to Existing Environments (app)*—From the implementation perspective, it is important for a context model to be applied within an existing infrastructure of ubiquitous computing components.

Table 3.3: Comparison of the different context modelling approaches [172]

| Approach—requirements | dc | pv | qua | inc | for | app |
|---|---|---|---|---|---|---|
| Key-value based modelling | - | - | − | − | − | + |
| Markup schema based modelling | + | ++ | - | - | + | ++ |
| Graphical modelling | − | - | + | - | + | + |
| Object oriented modelling | ++ | + | + | + | + | + |
| Logic based modelling | ++ | - | - | - | ++ | − |
| Ontology based modelling | ++ | ++ | + | + | ++ | + |

Table 3.3 shows the summary of the evaluation of the context modelling approaches based on the above six requirements. The evaluation summary shows that ontology is the most expressive context modelling approach and fulfill most of the requirements of context-aware systems. Furthermore, the ontology-based approach exhibits *four* main technical strengths over other modelling approaches [150, 172, 188]:

1. Ontology promotes knowledge sharing and reuse across different applications and services interacting in a pervasive computing environment.

Subsequently, this promotes interoperability between different applications and devices.
2. Ontological representation allows context-aware systems to use existing logic reasoning mechanism to deduce high level, conceptual context from low level, raw context and handle uncertainty and inconsistency in context.
3. Ontologies can be combined to form a more complex ontology and hence this saves the effort of starting from scratch.
4. Finally, a number of graphical tools, rich languages and inference engines are available to support designing, representing and processing ontologies using computer.

Thus, we adopt the *ontology-based approach* for *modelling* and *reasoning* about social context information.

## 3.3 Ontology-Based Context Models

In the field of general context-aware systems, there has been significant amount of research effort to building domain ontologies for pervasive computing, including CoBrA[20, 57], Gaia [153], GLOSS [65], ASC [173, 174], and SOCAM [90]. However, all of these research aim to model context of a physical nature such as location, time, activity, and so on. None of them attempts to model social context which is the focus of this work. As less relevant, here we do not discuss these context models in details, and refer reader to [188] for a survey and detail discussion.

Recently some research efforts such as [17] and [66], have attempted to adopt and extend the Friend of a Friend (FOAF) [10] ontology to represent social relationships. They extend the *foaf:knows* object property, the only option offered by the FOAF ontology, with sub-properties such as *colleagueOf* and *friendOf*. However, representing relationships using such object property suffers from a lack of *generality* for two main reasons:

1. it does not allow the specification of different attributes such as *strength* and *trust* associated with a relationship; and
2. as a consequence more abstract and rich context information cannot be derived, such as *bosom friend*, *best friend*, and so on.

To overcome these limitations, in our approach, we model social context information, as such social relationships, as *first-class* entities rather than representing them as a generic *link* between people (like aforementioned approaches). This way of modelling allows us to benefit from description logic (DL) [35] in *classifying* and *reasoning* about relationships at different *levels of abstraction* based on the properties of these relationships. Furthermore, in addition to *social relationships*, we also model other types of social context information such as *social roles*, *social interactions* and *situations* (see Chap. 4).

## 3.4 Ontology-Based Event Models

An *event* is something of interest that happens within a particular system or
domain [73]. Events can be compound of other events that build the *complex events*. An *event type* is a specification for a set of event objects that have
the same semantic intent and same structure; every *event object* is considered to be an instance of an event type. A *simple event pattern* is an event
type with or without logical constraints on its attributes/properties/contents, *e.g.*, $E1(attr1 == "zzz"$ and $attr2 > 10$ or $attr3 != 6.5)$. A simple event
pattern $F$ is a stateless truth valued function that is applied to an event object. An event object $e$ matches a simple event pattern $F$ if and only if it
satisfies all attributes of pattern $F$ and logical relationships among those attributes. A *complex event pattern* is a temporal/logical relationships among
two or more simple event patterns. Allen [28] proposed *thirteen* temporal
relationships among events such as $E1$ *during* $E2$, $E1$ *after* $E2$, and $E1$ *coincides* $E2$.

A number of ontology-based models have been proposed for representing events in the Semantic Web. Shaw et al. [166] proposed the Linking Open
Descriptions of Events (LODE) model for publishing records of events as
linked data and gave a comparison of some existing event models including Event Ontology (EO) [144], Event-Model-F [160], DOLCE+DnS Ultralite (DUL) [83], CIDOC-CRM [69] and ABC ontology [122], based on their
main constituent properties like type, time, space, participation, causality,
and composition. Hage et al. [7] proposed the Simple Event Model (SEM) to
model events in various domains such as history, cultural heritage and geography. SEM is designed with a minimum of semantic commitment to guarantee maximal interoperability. The authors also classified the EO, LODE
and CIDOC-CRM event models and highlighted their limitations on the
basis of *four* design choices: domain specificity, focus on classes or properties, scope, and the level of formalisation.

Even though the above existing event models differ significantly in purpose and content, they share a set of common background concepts such as
*event*, *time*, and *place*. We generalise and relate those concepts to form a *core
event ontology* which we extend further to establish our *interaction event ontology* by incorporating social context information and other concepts related
to interaction events (see Sect. 5.4.1).

## 3.5 Situation Specification and Reasoning

A substantial amount of work has been carried out on defining, modelling,
specifying and reasoning about situations. Earlier work on situations from
Dey [67], Henricksen et al. [98] and Loke [125] focused on the concept of situations as combinations of *logical* constraints on context information. More

recent approaches from Jakkula and Cook [110], and Augusto et al. [32] consider *temporal* aspect in situation recognition. Here, we discuss the most relevant works highlighting their focus and approach in contrast to ours. A survey of different situation reasoning approaches with detailed discussions can be found in [189].

Dey [67] took the initiative in considering situations as the abstraction of context that was more influential in triggering applications. He proposed a simple logic formula (only using AND to connect context constraints). Henricksen et al. [98] propose to represent a situation specification in a restricted form of quantifications on predicate logic, which serves to restrict possible values for free variables. Loke presents a declarative approach to representing and reasoning with situations at a high level of abstraction where a situation is characterised by imposing constraints on the output or readings returned by sensors [125].

Wang et al. [180] model low-level context in an ontological model and derived high-level context using both ontology reasoning with description logic and user-defined reasoning that is defined in specific rules in first-order logic. As ontology is a popular approach in modelling context, it is also applied by other researchers such as Ranganathan et al. [147] and Chen et al. [56]. Like those approaches, we use ontology to model interaction events. But unlike us, none of these approaches have considered temporal aspect in their situation recognition.

Temporal information has been incorporated into a few situation specification approaches. Jakkula and Cook [110] use Allen's temporal relations [28] as the basis for defining temporal rules across activities. The rules allow the sequence and overlap of activities to be encoded into a rule base. They compare the predictive accuracy of activities with and without the temporal rules, noticing an improvement when temporal rules are applied. This indicates that temporal information will help with situation recognition, and is desirable for us to include into our interaction event-based situation reasoning approach.

Matheus et al. [132] also consider the temporal factor. In their work, a situation is defined as a set of relations with other objects. Augusto et al. [32] introduce the temporal operators 'ANDlater' and 'ANDsim' in event-condition-action rules, upon which temporal knowledge on human activities can be specified. This allows events that co-occur (ANDsim) and events that happen in a sequence (ANDlater) to be used in reasoning. Therefore, their work indicates that co-occurrence and sequence temporal relations improve situation recognition.

Even though some of the above existing works have considered temporal aspects in situation recognition. None of them support all types of temporal relations excepting Jakkula and Cook [110]. None of the existing works have considered both semantic and temporal aspects in situation specification. Moreover, none of them have considered real-time situation recognition over interaction event streams, even though they all have considered inferring situations from context information acquired from sensors and/or focused on "at the moment" situation recognition over static sensor data. To the best of our knowledge, our work is the first systematic attempt at inferring users' situations considering both *semantic* and *temporal* aspects of *interaction events* coming from social media.

## 3.6  Privacy Policy Models and Access Control

Policy-based access control has been the subject of extensive research over the past decade. Recent research efforts have tried to integrate semantic web technologies both in access control models and policy specifications, thus enabling automated reasoning and policy enforcement over expressive access control specifications. In particular, the ROWLBAC [79] and ReBAC [80] models have provided us with useful insight for our socially-aware access control framework.

Most policy models for social networking applications [53], and even those designed for pervasive computing applications [109] consider either *role* or *relationship* in their access control but not both. While the work [177] is very close to ours in protecting user's social context information, it does not consider *role* in its access control model and therefore is not able to offer the advantages of role based access control. Moreover, the work does not consider obfuscation in supporting the access control at different granularity levels, which is an important aspect for access control [185].

## 3.7  Managing Social Context Information

Socially-aware applications are often designed from scratch by embedding all management functionalities into the application logic, providing an application-specific data representation models, and acquiring data from one or a few specific external sources (*e.g.*, [38, 43]). In all of these cases, social knowledge has been mined in the context of a single application. Some efforts, such as [121, 178], have already recognized the need to externalize the social context management functionalities and have taken steps towards systematically managing users' social context information.

Prometheus [121] collects user's social data from different OSNs and represents it as multi-edged graphs, where vertices correspond to users and edges correspond to interactions between users. The interactions are described with a label (*e.g.*, "football", "music") and a weight specifies the intensity of an interaction, and essentially represents an "object-centric" relationship. Prometheus implements a set of inference functions to answer queries like social strength, proximity, and so on, while enforcing user-defined access control policies. Like Prometheus, PocketSocial [187] also collects social data from different sources. But unlike Prometheus, it represents social data in JSON objects and supports only REST based APIs like Facebook, and does not provide any inference functions. Neither Prometheus nor PocketSocial represent both the *object-* and *people-centric* relationships with their semantics, and as a consequence they are not able to infer richer information or fine-tune the granularity of information access.

On the other hand, Yarta [178] adopts the FOAF ontology in their relationship representation. But Yarta only considers *people-centric* relationships and does not capture the *object-centric* ones. Even though it does consider social context in its policy model, its access control policy does not take into account granularity in information access. Moreover, its policy model is RDF-based which lacks in the generality of OWL DL-based models.

Online social networks (OSNs) like Facebook, LinkedIn and so on, offer their native APIs [11, 13] to access simple and unprocessed social data. These APIs do not provide access to derived relationships like "Best friend" or "Father-Son". Instead, an application must explicitly crawl through the graph to obtain them.

Our work significantly differs from the above noted approaches in that it not only collects users' social relationship information (both object- and people-centric) from multiple sources and stores it in richer ontologies, but also considers the owners' status information and their semantics, allowing information representation and derivation at different levels of abstraction and consequently facilitating fine-grained access control and query processing.

## 3.8 Modelling and Managing Runtime Social Interactions

According to the sociologist Max Weber, "an action is social if the acting individual takes account of the behaviour of others and is thereby oriented in its course" [182]. *Social interaction* refers to the sequence of social action between individuals (or groups) by considering their relationships.

*Social interaction* has been studied in multi-agent systems. In a multi-agent system, agents usually interact in order to achieve better goals of them or the system in which they exist. Kalenka et al. [117] incorporate social concepts within the computer system level paradigm to enhance the agent's interaction performance. Rather than defining social relationships, the work proposes multi-furious social interaction attitudes ranging from self interested to the purely altruistic.

Role-based design has been extensively researched in last few decades and adopted in multiple disciplines (*e.g.*, agent-oriented software engineering (AOSE), distributed systems (DS), object-oriented methodologies (OOM), and so on) as a key concept for modelling and managing *interactions.* In AOSE, many frameworks (*e.g.*, BRAIN [49], Gaia [190], and so on) have been proposed to design role-based software systems using agent paradigm. In their survey paper, Cabri et al. [51] compare the strength of existing AOSE proposals based on some evaluation criteria and showed BRAIN is more expressive compared to other frameworks. The existing proposals in AOSE (including BRAIN), DS (*e.g.*, [129] ) and OOM (*e.g.*, [149]), however, mainly consider up to design phase of software engineering and give no indication of how these roles are to be realized. Even though some of the works (*e.g.*, ROADMAP [113]) further extended to consider runtime/implementation phase by incorporating different interaction language such as AUML [37], they do not consider roles as an implementation entity and provide very limited support for managing runtime adaptation. In such approaches roles are used in the modelling and to inform the design, but disappear as entities during implementation. Thus, they are not suitable for managing adaptations in runtime model.

Compared to the above mentioned frameworks, Role-Oriented Adaptive Design (ROAD) [59] brings a number of design principles that support flexible management and runtime adaptations, which has also been recognized and appreciated in [55]. One of such principles is separation of functional and management operations. This principle is important for facilitating application development and runtime adaptation as the functional operations performed by the actors enable normal interactions while the management operations realize adaptation to the structure and parameters of the model. Thus, we adopt ROAD architectural style for modelling and managing *social interactions* at runtime (see Sect. 6.2).

## 3.9  Platform for Collaborative (Social) Interactions

Most of the approaches in the pervasive computing literature mainly focus on tasks of individual users, and provide very limited support to collaborative tasks of a group of users [157]. Furthermore, existing approaches in developing collaborative pervasive applications (*e.g.*, [45, 48, 54, 71, 156]), and middleware architectures and frameworks for pervasive computing [148] are limited in supporting the dynamic *relationships* between users, which themselves are an important aspect of context. In particular, there is a lack of support for managing the *adaptation* in interaction-relationships in response to *changes* in the requirements and environments.

The need for supporting collaboration in pervasive computing environments has emerged in recent years (*e.g.*, [45, 54]). Such research has focused on collaborative interactions between different types of actors such as user-user and device-device, for various purposes. The SAPERE [54] middleware exploits social network graph to establish collaboration for sharing data among spatially collocated users devices. CoCA [71] is a ontology-based context-aware service platform for sharing of computational resources among devices in a neighbourhood. Both SAPERE and CoCA focus on collaboration among devices, where the social interactions in this work primarily target on collaboration among users. Similar to us, MoCA [156], a middleware architecture for developing context-aware collaborative applications, focuses on collaboration among users. But unlike us, the collaborations among users in MoCA are not based on predefined goals or tasks, rather driven by spontaneous and occasional initiatives. CASMAS [48] and UseNet [45] focus on collaborative activities among users to achieve a common goal like us. But none of them explicitly *model* the interactions among users. Moreover, all of the above approaches lack support for *managing* the dynamicity and complexity of the social interactions as highlighted in this work. The *interaction relationships* between actors and their *adaptations* are not modelled explicitly, and instead are often *hard-coded* directly into the applications. To the best of our knowledge, there is no work to date that addresses the runtime adaptation of *social interaction models* in response to the changes in requirements and environments.

## 3.10 Platform for Runtime Adaptation

Much research has been carried out into middleware support for runtime adaptation in context-aware systems (*e.g.*, MADAM [84] and 3PC [95]) and service-oriented systems (*e.g.*, MUSIC [155] and MOSES [52]). These middleware solutions mainly target the tasks of individual users/applications and have focused on reconfiguring applications' settings (rather than *interaction relationships*) based on physical context information (*e.g.*, place, time)/quality of service requirements (*e.g.*, performance, reliability), rather than interaction relationships. Moreover, their proposed runtime models are application-specific and cannot be used to model *interaction relationships* among collaborative users.

In contrast to these solutions, our adaptation management approach (see Sect. 6.2.2) targets interaction-centric socially-aware applications, and focuses on executing adaptation by explicitly modelling and realising *interaction relationships* using a *social interaction model* and providing an *organiser* interface to change such model. On the other hand, in this book, we do not address the monitoring of environment changes (*i.e.*, physical context information), acquiring and analysing such physical context information to make adaptation decisions. In that sense, our adaptation management approach is not a substitute for existing middleware solutions that manages physical context information, rather can be built on top of those solutions as appropriate, in order to manage *social interactions* and *runtime adaptation* in interaction-centric socially-aware applications.

Some of these existing middleware solutions have a degree of similarity to our approach to managing adaptation. Like MADAM [84] and PCOM in 3PC [95], we have employed both structural and parametric adaptations and has adopted an external adaptation approach where adaptation capabilities of applications are realised by an application-independent middleware. Besides, we provide a management interface to trigger adaptations. Thus, any existing middleware solutions (*e.g.*, MADAM) can be used to detect the changes in environmental context, make adaptation decisions and trigger adaptations in platform. Furthermore, users can explicitly trigger the adaptations as required. Like MUSIC [155] and MADAM [84], our approach provides a model-driven development and middleware support to build applications. Like us, MOSES [52] is a service-oriented architecture centric approach, but its adaptation logic is limited to a predefined set of attributes (*i.e.*, response time, expected execution cost, and expected reliability). However, all of these approaches lack an explicit model of social interactions.

## 3.11 Summary

Despite extensive research on context-aware computing, so far very limited work has focused on social context-aware applications. Research on context-aware computing has largely focused on the development of software *frameworks* and *platforms* that perform task such as the *acquisition* of context information from the sensors, persistent *storage* of the information within servers, *processing* applications queries to access such context information and support *adaptation*. These infrastructures serve an important role, shifting much of the complex functionality onto the middleware, and thereby simplifying the construction of robust applications [106, 148, 151]. As such, this type of framework support is also desirable for developing social context-aware applications.

Recently some research work have attempted to provide the functionalities, as described above, to aid the development of socially-aware applications. However, the diverse characteristics and application domain of such socially-aware applications demand for different types of social context information and functionality of the platform/middleware. In the previous chapter, we have described two socially-aware applications with two different focuses (*i.e.*, data-centric and application-centric) and application domains (*i.e.*, business and travel), and identified a set of requirements for developing such types of applications. In this chapter, we have analysed, examined and reviewed the existing approaches that aims to simplify the development of either social context-aware applications or context-aware applications in general, and provide one or more aforementioned functionalities such as context acquisition, modelling, reasoning and management. A summary evaluation of the examined approaches in this chapter against the requirements for developing socially-aware applications from Chap. 2 is given in Table 3.4. The information in the table show that none of the existing approaches explicitly supports either a singe requirement or collectively all the requirements.

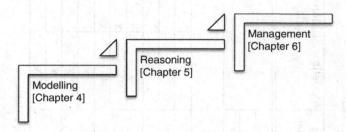

Fig. 3.1: Towards a framework for social-context aware applications

Thus, in this work, we have attempted to explicitly support all the requirements. In a nutshell, there are three essential aspects towards a framework for social context-aware applications, *i.e.,,* social context information *modelling, reasoning* and *management,* where the management includes preserving *privacy* on accessing social context information, *modelling* runtime social interactions and managing their *adaptation,* as shown in Fig. 3.1. Each aspect has its own challenges to address. These challenges and corresponding solutions are discussed in Chaps. 4, 5 and 6, respectively.

Table 3.4: The summary of evaluation of the examined approaches

| Approach | Modelling SCI | Reasoning | Preserving privacy | Acquiring and managing | Modelling SI | Managing adaptation |
|---|---|---|---|---|---|---|
| Prometheus [121] | ~ | ~ | ~ | ~ | | |
| Yarta [178] | ~ | ~ | ~ | ~ | | |
| PocketSocial [187] | ~ | x | x | ~ | | |
| Toninelli et al. [177] | | | ~ | | | |
| Jagtap et al. [109] | | | ~ | | | |
| BRAIN [49] | | | | | ~ | ~ |
| Gaia [190] | | | | | ~ | ~ |
| ROADMAP [113] | | | | | ~ | ~ |
| MoCA [156] | | | | | ~ | x |
| UseNet [45] | | | | | ~ | x |
| CASMAS [48] | | | | | ~ | x |
| MADAM [84] | | | | | x | ~ |
| 3PC [95] | | | | | x | ~ |
| MUSIC [155] | | | | | x | ~ |
| MOSES [52] | | | | | x | ~ |

+ Explicitly supported, ~ Supported to a certain extent, x Not supported, [blank] Not aimed or applicable

# Part II
# Social Context Modelling, Reasoning and Management

This part of the book presents the approach to developing social context-awareness by presenting the ontology-based approach to modelling and representing different types of social context (Chap. 4), the approach to deriving, deducing, abstracting and inferring social context information (Chap. 5), and the approach to managing privacy in accessing social context information and adaptation of runtime social interaction models (Chap. 6).

# Chapter 4
# Social Context Modelling

The social context model provides a basis on which the socially-aware application is developed and executed. This chapter presents an *ontology-based approach* to modelling social context information. We present ontologies for different *types* of social context such as *social role*, *social relationship*, *social interaction* and *situation*. These ontologies allow application developers to specify, represent and interpret users' social context information which drives the behaviour of applications.

The chapter is organised as follows. Section 4.1 presents our modelling approach with its strengths and key features. Section 4.2 presents our *social context upper ontology*. A number of *domain-specific* ontologies are presented in Sect. 4.3 by extending the concepts in the upper-ontology and analysing the application scenarios presented in Chap. 2.

## 4.1 Modelling Approach

We adopt an ontology-based approach to modelling and representing different types of social context information. In computer science, the term *ontology* has numerous descriptions and definitions as we discussed in Sect. 3.1.1. In this work context, we adopt the recent operational definition given by Tom Gruber, *"an ontology defines a set of representational primitives with which to model a domain of knowledge or discourse, where the representational primitives are typically classes (or sets), attributes (or properties), and relationships (or relations among class members)"* [89]. This definition provides us the representational primitives for modelling social context information and developing a knowledge base to managing such information.

© Springer International Publishing Switzerland 2016                    49
M.A. Kabir et al., *Pervasive Social Computing*,
DOI 10.1007/978-3-319-29951-8_4

Ontology-based approaches have been evaluated as most promising for context modelling in pervasive computing [42]. It has two main advantages:

1. It creates a common understanding and knowledge base of context information, thus, promotes re-usability and sharing; *and*
2. It allows context reasoning.

We use OWL2-DL [87], a sub-language of OWL 2, to model social context information. To date, OWL2-DL has been the most practical choice for most ontological applications as it supports maximum expressiveness while retaining computational completeness and decidability [150].

Table 4.1: OWL-DL class constructors

| No. | Constructor | DL syntax | Example |
|---|---|---|---|
| 1 | intersectionOf | $C_1 \sqcap \cdots \sqcap C_n$ | *CollageFriend* $\sqcap$ *UniversityFriend* |
| 2 | unionOf | $C_1 \sqcup \cdots \sqcup C_n$ | *Seminar* $\sqcup$ *Meeting* |
| 3 | complementOf | $\neg C$ | $\neg AtDesk$ |
| 4 | oneOf | $\{x_1\} \sqcup \cdots \sqcup \{x_n\}$ | $\{father\} \sqcup \{mother\}$ |
| 5 | allValuesFrom | $\forall P \cdot C$ | $\forall plays \cdot SocialRole$ |
| 6 | someValuesFrom | $\exists P \cdot C$ | $\exists relates \cdot Person$ |
| 7 | maxCardinality | $\leq nP \cdot C$ | $\leq 2plays \cdot SocialRole$ |
| 8 | minCardinality | $\geq nP \cdot C$ | $\geq strength \cdot \{0.8\}$ |
| 9 | exactCardinality | $= nP \cdot C$ | $= 2relates \cdot Person$ |
| 10 | hasValue | $\ni P \cdot I$ | $\ni plays \cdot father$ |

Table 4.1 presents OWL-DL *class constructors* and its use in representing knowledge about social context information. In particular, the table shows how we can construct new classes from existing named classes, properties and individuals by:

• applying set operators such as intersection, union, and complement on classes (#1, #2 and #3);
• explicitly and exhaustively enumerating the individuals that are members of the new class (#4);
• restricting a property of the class: the range of the property either has all the individuals from a specific class (universal restriction) (#5) or has some individuals in a specific class (existential restriction) (#6);
• restricting the maximum (#7) or minimum (#8) or exact (#9) cardinality of a property;
• specifying a particular value of the property (#10).

Furthermore, we can write a complex expression, namely *reasoning rule*, to represent a new class based on the above basic class constructor (see Chap. 5 for details).

Table 4.2: OWL-DL class semantics

| No. | Name | DL syntax | Example |
|-----|------|-----------|---------|
| 1 | EquivalentTo | $C_i \equiv C_j$ | $HusbandWife \equiv WifeHusband$ |
| 2 | SubClassOf | $C_i \sqsubseteq C_j$ | $MotherChild \sqsubseteq ParentChild$ |
| 3 | DisjointWith | $C_i \sqcap C_j \sqsubseteq \perp$ | $MotherChild \sqcap FatherChild \sqsubseteq \perp$ |

Using OWL-DL *class semantics*, as presented in Table 4.2, we can specify association between classes (named or new class) such as:

*Equivalence*   Individuals of a class are same as individuals to its equivalent class. We also can define a new class using DL expression as an equivalence class which usually referred to as a necessary and sufficient condition. Thus, all **reasoning rules** should be specified as equivalence. If a class $C_j$ is defined using necessary and sufficient condition(s) then we can say that an individual of the class $C_j$ must satisfies the condition(s) and we also can say that any (random) individual satisfies the condition(s) must be a member of the class $C_j$;

*Subclass/Superclass*   Individuals of a subclass are considered as individuals of its superclass. A subclass is more specialised concept of its superclass (**is-a** relationship). We use this association to represent the **granularity** of concepts in ontology, *i.e.*, a subclass is a more fine-grained concept of its superclass (as illustrated in Fig. 4.1). We define an *annotation property*, called *granularityLevel* for explicitly specify the *granularity level* of each concept in an ontology. Section 5.3.2 presents the granularity levels of different situations.

We also can define a new class using DL expression as a subclass which usually imposes **restriction/constraints** and referred to as a necessary condition for the superclass. If a class $C_j$ is described using necessary condition(s), then we can say that an individual of the class $C_j$ must satisfies the condition(s); and

*Disjointness*   Individuals of a class specifically exclude individuals to its disjoint class. Like above, this class could be a primitive class or derived class (*i.e.*, defined using DL expression)

In addition to OWL-DL class constructors and semantics, we can use OWL *object property characteristics*, to specify further association among classes based on their individuals. Properties link two individuals together,

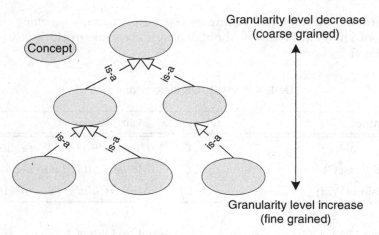

Fig. 4.1: Illustration of granularity levels

Table 4.3: OWL object property characteristics

| Character name | Syntax | Example |
|---|---|---|
| Transitive (P) | $\forall a \forall b \forall c (a \cdot P \cdot b) \sqcap (b \cdot P \cdot c) \Rightarrow (a \cdot P \cdot c)$ | *hasAncestor* |
| Symmetric (P) | $\forall a \forall b (a \cdot P \cdot b) \Rightarrow (b \cdot P \cdot a)$ | *hasSpouse* |
| Asymmetric (P) | $\forall a \forall b (a \cdot P \cdot b) \nRightarrow (b \cdot P \cdot a)$ | *hasChild* |
| Reflexive (P) | $\forall a (a \cdot P \cdot a) \Rightarrow \top$ | *knows* |
| Irreflexive (P) | $\forall a (a \cdot P \cdot a) \Rightarrow \bot$ | *parentOf* |
| Functional (P) | $\forall a \forall b \forall c (a \cdot P \cdot b) \sqcap (a \cdot P \cdot c) \Rightarrow (b = c)$ | *hasHusband* |
| InverseFunctional (P) | $\forall a \forall b \forall c (a \cdot P \cdot b) \sqcap (c \cdot P \cdot b) \Rightarrow (a = c)$ | *hasHusband* |
| InverseOf (P,Q) | $P \equiv Q^- \vDash \forall a \forall b (a \cdot P \cdot b) \Leftrightarrow (b \cdot Q \cdot a)$ | *plays* $\equiv$ *playedBy$^-$* |

*i.e.,* establish binary relations on individuals. As shown in Table 4.3, the OWL property characteristics enrich the meaning of the properties as follows:

- If a property is *transitive,* and the property relates individual a to individual b, and also individual b to individual c, then we can infer that individual a is related to individual c via property P
- If a property P is *symmetric,* and the property relates individual a to individual b then individual b is also related to individual a via property P
- If a property P is *asymmetric,* and the property relates individual a to individual b then individual b cannot be related to individual a via property P
- A property P is said to be *reflexive* when the property must relate individual a to itself

- If a property P is *irreflexive*, it can be described as a property that relates an individual a to individual b, where individual a and individual b are not the same
- If a property is *functional*, for a given individual, there can be at most one individual that is related to the individual via the property. Functional properties are also known as single valued properties. If the property relates individual a to individual b, and also individual a to individual c, then we can infer that individual b and c must be the same individual. It should be noted however, that if *b* and *c* were explicitly stated to be two different individuals then the above statements would lead to an inconsistency
- If a property is *inverse functional* then it means that the inverse property is functional. For a given individual, there can be at most one individual related to that individual via the property
- If a property links individual a to individual b then its *inverse property* will link individual b to individual a

Thus, for modelling social context information, we use the OWL2-DL *class constructors*, *semantics* and *property characteristics* to represent concept hierarchies (*i.e.,* super-class/sub-class relationships), and impose constraints on concepts (*e.g.,* disjoint classes) and their properties (*e.g.,* minimum cardinality). The main advantages of their use is that a *DL reasoner* can be used for (1) *checking* constraints and (2) detecting automatically *inconsistencies* in the *social context information* of the knowledge base.

## 4.2  Social Context Upper Ontology

Despite its intuitive anchoring in everyday life, social context can be very challenging to represent in a formal model. In Sect. 1.2, we define *social context model* as a representation of users' *social roles, social relationships, social interactions* and *situations*. In this section, we use OWL2-DL constructs (as introduced in the previous section) to model such different types of social context.

In order to capture the *general* concepts and incorporate *domain-specific* concepts, we propose both the *upper* and *domain-specific* ontologies. The *upper ontology* captures the basic concepts, abstracted from the analysis of: (1) different types of social context required in various real-world use case scenarios, such as socially-aware phone call application (illustrated in Sect. 2.1.1) and cooperative convoy application (illustrated in Sect. 2.2.1); and (2) different sources of social context information such as Facebook, LinkedIn, Twitter and Google Calendar. This upper ontology can be shared, reused, and adapted to specific domains. It can be customized to represent social context information related concepts in different forms for different domains, applications, even users. It is also extensible to allow for the incorporation of *new* concepts and the *specialisation* of concepts and constraints for a particular domain or application, forming a *domain-specific* ontology.

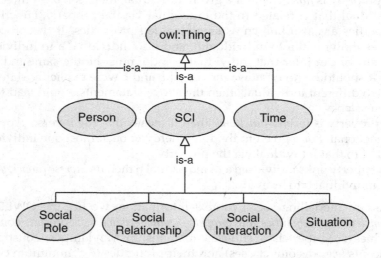

Fig. 4.2: Hierarchies of the core concepts

Our *upper* ontology, called S̲ocial C̲ontext O̲nto̲logy (*SCOnto*), defines four first-class entities, namely, *Social Role, Social Relationship, Social Interaction*, and *Situation*. These entities can be organised into a hierarchy where the root of the hierarchy is the term *SCI*, *i.e.,* social context information, which is the superclass of those four entities and a subclass of the root concept *owl:Thing* (see Fig. 4.2). The concepts *Person* and *Time* are also incorporated as a subclass of *owl:Thing*, as they are associated with social context information.

To define *Person*, we adopt and extend the friend of a friend (FOAF) ontology [10] which describes persons, their activities and their relations to other people and objects. In the FOAF ontology, a literal "status" is used to capture a person's current activity, mood, location, etc. We use the term "situation" which is more general than the term "status" and most frequently used in context-aware computing domain to represent a person's state of affairs. Moreover, to support reasoning over a person's status at different granularity levels we change the type of "status" from *data property* to *class* and rename the term *Status* with *Situation*. We define an object property *hasSituation* which links the *Person* to the *Situation* class (see Fig. 4.3).

To capture a person's situations over different time we incorporate *Time* ontology which connects with the *Situation* using the *hasTimeStamp* object property. The *Time* ontology allows us to capture both the *instant* and *interval* time. We view a person's (social) *situation* as his/her condition or activity or state of affair with respect to surrounding people. For instance,

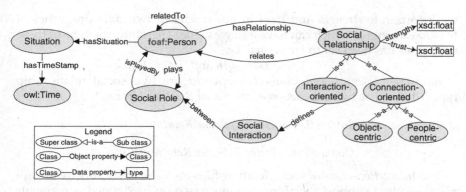

Fig. 4.3: Social context upper ontology (*SCOnto*)

a person's 'meeting', 'seminar', or 'watching game in stadium' situation represents his/her status with respect to surrounding people.

In real-world, a person may have different types of relationships as she plays various roles. To identify a person in such circumstances, we introduce the concept of *Social Role* which *isPlayedBy* the *Person*. The object property *isPlayedBy* is *InverseOf* the property *plays*, *i.e.*,

$$isPlayedBy \equiv (plays^-)$$

The core concept of our model is the *Social Relationship* which is a subclass of *SCI* and *relates* exactly two persons that can be defined in OWL2 using the DL [35] syntax as follows:

$$SocialRelationship \sqsubseteq SCI \sqcap = 2\,relates \cdot Person$$

where those persons should be different individuals and linked with each other through *relatedTo* property. That is, the *relatedTo* object property type should be set to *Irreflexive*, *i.e.*,

$$\{o_i, o_j\} \in relatedTo, o_i \neq o_j, i \neq j$$

and *Symmetric, i.e.*,

$$relatedTo \equiv (relatedTo^-)$$

The *social relationship* can have different properties, can be used to infer more fine-grained relationships. For instance, *trust* in relationships can be measured through mining online social networks, which is used to accept recommendations, make purchase decisions and select transaction partners in the online community [85]. In [186], authors estimate relationship *strength* from users' interaction activity to improve the range and performance of various aspects of online social networks, including link prediction, item recommendation, news-feeds, people search and visualization. As such, we incorporate *strength* and *trust* in our model as two data properties of *Social Relationship*, which can have a *single* value. Therefore, the type of these properties has been set to *Functional*, i.e.,

$$\top \sqsubseteq\ \leqslant 1strength \text{ and } \top \sqsubseteq\ \leqslant 1trust$$

*Interaction-oriented* and *Connection-oriented* are two social relationship types, defined as two subclasses of the *Social Relationship*, i.e.,

$$Interaction\text{-}oriented \sqsubseteq SocialRelationship$$

$$Connection\text{-}oriented \sqsubseteq SocialRelationship$$

The *Interaction-oriented* social relationships are used in socially-aware applications that support social interactions based on predefined agreements and constraints, for example, the cooperative convoy application. An interesting concept for describing and understanding such *interaction-oriented* relationship is *social interaction* as it mediates the interactions between social roles by defining their sequences (called conversations) and associated obligations (*e.g.*, time constraints). A *social interaction* is an interaction *between* exactly two *social roles*, i.e.,

$$SocialInteraction \sqsubseteq\ = 2between \cdot SocialRole$$

On the other hand, The *Connection-oriented* social relationships describe users' relational *ties* which can be further categorized as *People-centric* and *Object-centric* relationships (*i.e., People-centric* $\sqsubseteq$ *Connection-oriented* and *Object-centric* $\sqsubseteq$ *Connection-oriented*). The *Object-centric* relationship is identified between people who have shown common interests (e.g., like/tag in Facebook) or participated in common activities or become member of similar groups. The *People-centric* relationship is a formal and declarative definition of a direct relationship between people. For example, a person identifies other persons as father, supervisor, school friend, etc. Such people-centric and object-centric relationships can be acquired from users' online social networks (OSNs) and can be used by socially-aware applications that exploit social context information to adapt its behaviour, for example, the socially-aware phone call application.

The *SCOnto* model (Fig. 4.3) can be read as follows. A *Person* may have *Social Relationship*(s); each *Social Relationship relates* exactly two Persons, can be classified as *Interaction-oriented* or *Connection-oriented* that can be further classified as *People-centric* or *Object-centric*; thus through a *Social Relationship* that may have a *strength* and a *trust* value, a *Person* is *relatedTo* another *Person*; a *Person plays* a particular *Social Role*; also a *Person* may have a *Situation* that *hasTimeStamp Time*. An *Interaction-oriented* relationship *defines* a set of permitted *Social interaction between* two *Social Roles*.

## 4.3 Domain-Specific Social Context Ontologies

We propose a number of domain-specific ontologies by specialising the upper ontology concepts such as *Social Role*, *Interaction-oriented* relationship, *People-centric* relationship, *Object-centric* relationship and *Situation*. We specialise the social role for *family* and *work* (educational organisation) domains, the interaction-oriented relationship for a *cooperative convoy* domain, the people-centric relationship for *family*, *work* and *friend* domains, the object-centric relationship for *Common interest*, *Living address* and *Following-Follower* domains, and the Situation for *business* and *non-business* domains.

### 4.3.1 *The* Social Role *Ontology*

We consider domain-specific social role ontology for three domains such as family, work and cooperative convoy, as these domain are related to the application scenarios described in Chap. 2. We specialise the *Social Role* class/-concept as *Family Social Role*, *Work Social Role* and *Convoy Social Role* and define them as enumerations/nominals (see Fig. 4.4).

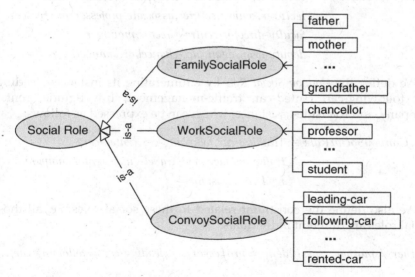

Fig. 4.4: An excerpt of domain-specific *social role* ontology

We define the concept *Family Social Role* by enumerating its instances: father, mother, husband, wife, partner, son, daughter, sister, brother, cousin, uncle, aunt, nephew, niece, grandfather, grandmother, grandson, granddaughter, father-in-law, mother-in-law, brother-in-law, and son-in-law. Combining nominals using the *oneOf* OWL2-DL constructor, we can define the *Family Social Role* enumeration class as follows:

$$FamilySocialRole \equiv \{father, mother, husband, wife, partner, son, daughter,$$
$$sister, brother, cousin, uncle, aunt, nephew, niece,$$
$$grandfather, grandmother, grandson, granddaughter,$$
$$father\text{-}in\text{-}law, mother\text{-}in\text{-}law, brother\text{-}in\text{-}law,$$
$$son\text{-}in\text{-}law\}$$

We define those instances based on our understanding of social role in the family domain and the available family role types in Facebook. Facebook allows people to maintain a family list, where a user can annotate a person in his family list as one of the instances of the *Family Social Role* listed above.

Similarly, we define the *Work Social Role* class for an university domain by enumerating its instances: student, research-assistant, post-doctoral-fellow, lecturer, senior-lecturer, associate-professor, professor, faculty-director, centre-director, manager, dean, deputy-dean, vice-chancellor and chancellor, which can be expressed as follows:

$$WorkSocialRole \equiv \{student, research\text{-}assistant, post\text{-}doctoral\text{-}fellow,$$
$$lecturer, senior\text{-}lecturer, associate\text{-}professor, professor,$$
$$faculty\text{-}director, centre\text{-}director, manager,$$
$$deputy\text{-}dean, dean, vice\text{-}chancellor, chancellor\}$$

We define the *Convoy Social Role* by enumerating its instances: leading-car, following-car, rented-car, traffic-management, travel-guide, rental-company, and roadside-assistance, which can be expressed as follows:

$$ConvoySocialRole \equiv \{leading\text{-}car, following\text{-}car, rented\text{-}car,$$
$$traffic\text{-}management, travel\text{-}guide, rental\text{-}company,$$
$$roadside\text{-}assistance\}$$

We also define the constraint related to these social roles, *i.e.*, all those social roles are different individuals:

$$father \neq mother, \ldots, student \neq professor, \ldots, leading\text{-}car \neq following\text{-}car, \ldots$$

## 4.3.2 *The* Connection-Oriented *Social Relationship Ontology*

The *Connection-oriented* relationships describe users' relational *ties* which we further categorised into *People-centric* (Sect. 4.3.2.1) and *Object-centric* (Sect. 4.3.2.2) relationships.

### 4.3.2.1  The *People-Centric* Social Relationship Ontology

The *People-centric* relationship is a formal and declarative definition of a direct relationship between people. We specialise the *people-centric* relationship (see Fig. 4.5) to propose a fine-grained relationship model for *Family*, *Work* and *Friend* relationships.

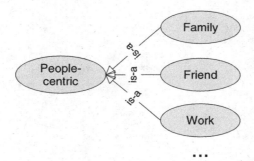

Fig. 4.5: A domain-specific *people-centric* relationship ontology

Family

We rely on Facebook to deduce Family relationships. Facebook allows people to maintain a family list, where a user can annotate a person in his family list as brother, father, uncle and so on, which ultimately indicates the role played by the person being annotated from the user's point of view rather than the specific relationship between the user and that person (as shown in the screenshot of Fig. 4.6). Based on these list of social roles and our understanding of family domain, we classify the *Family* relationship (see Fig. 4.7) as *Parent-Child*, *Parent_in_law-Child_in_law*, *Grandparent-Grandchild*, *Uncle-Nephew*, *Aunt-Nephew*, *Uncle-Niece*, *Aunt-Niece*, *Sibling*, *Cousin* and *Partner*. To provide a fine-grain family relationship model, we further classify the *Parent-Child* relationship as *Father-Child* and *Mother-Child*. The *Father-Child* relationship is further classified to the *Father-Son* and *Father-*

*Daughter* relationships. Similarly, the *Mother-Child* relationship is classified to the *Mother-Son* and *Mother-Daughter* relationships.

Like the *Parent-Child* relationship, we also classify the *Grandparent-Grandchild* and *Parent_in_law-Child_in_law* relationships. We classify the *Sibling* as *Brother-Brother*, *Brother-Sister* and *Sister-Sister* relationships.

To keep the ontology consistent, it is required to define *constraints* related to the associated concepts in the ontology. For instance, a relationship between two persons can not be both the *Father-Son* and *Father-Daughter*,

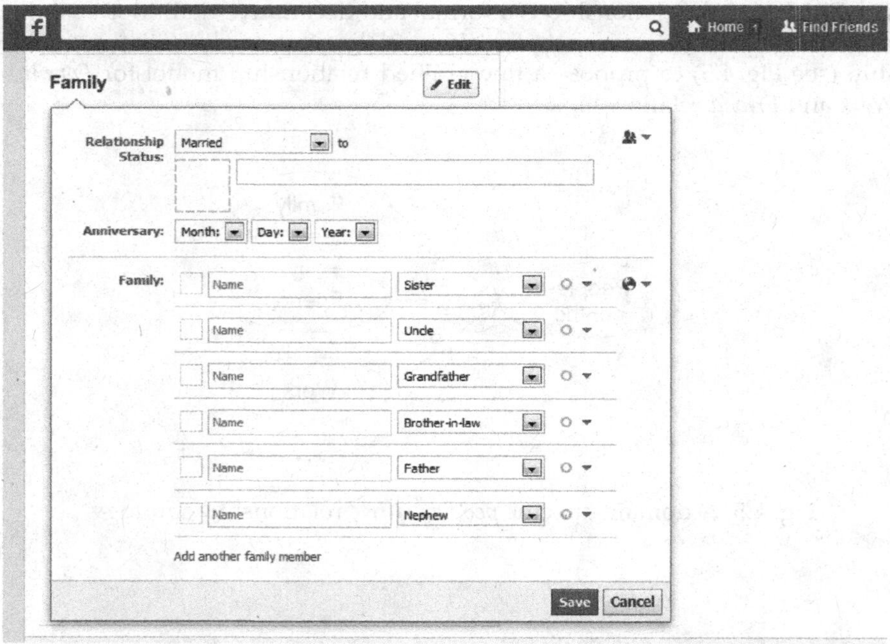

Fig. 4.6: Identifying family member in Facebook

*i.e.*, the *Father-Son* and *Father-Daughter* concepts should be disjoint; a person can have only one father, *i.e.*, a person can have only one type of *Father-Son* relationship with another person who plays the father role. We define those constraints using the OWL2-DL as follows:

$$Father\text{-}Son \sqcap Father\text{-}Daughter = \perp$$
$$Father\text{-}Son \sqsubseteq = 1\,relates(Person \sqcap plays \cdot father)$$

Similarly, we define associated constraints related to the other concepts in the ontology. A complete constraint specification list can be found in Appendix A.2.

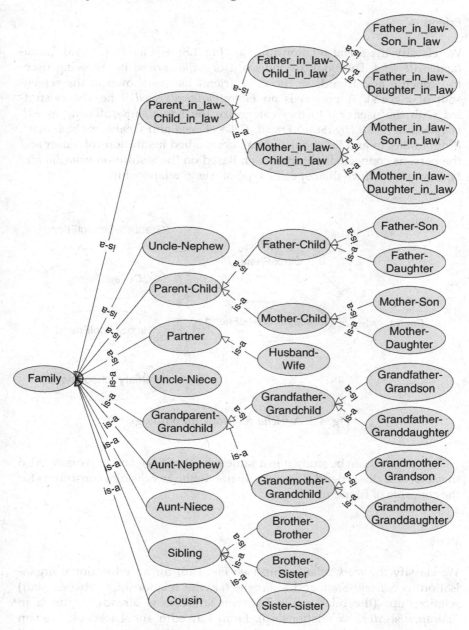

Fig. 4.7: A *family* relationship ontology

Friend

We classify the *friend* relationship (see Fig. 4.8) as *CloseFriend* and *EducationBasedFriend*. Facebook recognises users' *CloseFriend* by allowing users
to explicitly add friends in the close friend list (as shown in the screenshot of Fig. 4.9). A person is an *EducationBasedFriend* if he/she is studied with the user. We further categorize the *EducationBasedFriend* as *PrimarySchoolFriend*, *HighSchoolFriend*, *CollegeFriend* and *GraduateSchoolFriend*.
From LinkedIn and Facebook, we can get studied institutions of a user and
the persons connected with that user. Based on the institution *name/id* and
*type*, we can deduce their specific type of friend relationship.

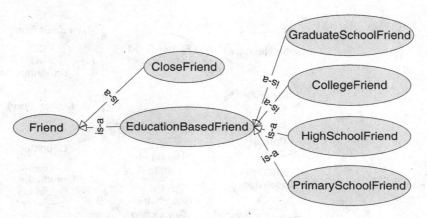

Fig. 4.8: A *friend* relationship ontology

Two persons can be studied in a same school, college and university. Also
they can be a close friend. Thus, we do not define any disjoint constraints for
the concepts of friend ontology.

Work

We classify the *work* relationship (see Fig. 4.10) for an educational organisation as *Student-Staff* and *Colleague* (*i.e.*, the relationship between staff)
relationships (the relationship between students is already captured in
*EducationBasedFriend* relationship). From LinkedIn and Facebook, we can
get the current and the past employment organisations of a user and all
the persons connected with that user. Based on the organisation *name* or
*id* and the *positions* held by them, we can deduce their work relationships.
For instance, if two persons hold any of the staff roles in an organisation,
we can deduce their relationship as being *Colleague*. Based on the specific

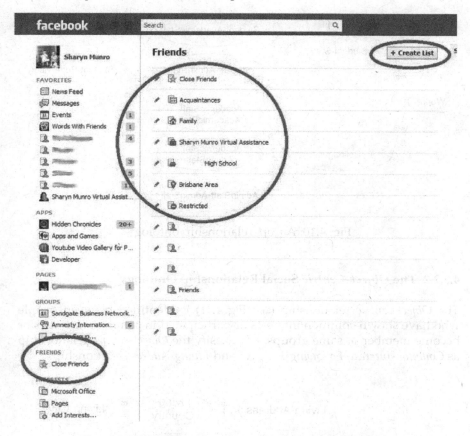

Fig. 4.9: Facebook recognises *close friend* relationship

types of staff roles, we can further classify the relationship as: *AcademicStaff-AdminStaff*, *AcademicStaff-AcademicStaff*, *AdminStaff-AdminStaff*. Similarly, we can classify the *Student-Staff* relationship as *Student-AcademicStaff* and *Student-AdminStaff*. A student can be supervised by an academic staff in relation to his/her project or thesis. To capture such specific relationship, we further classify the *Student-AcademicStaff* as *Student-Supervisor* and *Student-Teacher*.

In an educational organisation, a person can play both an academic staff and administrative staff roles. Also a student can play an academic staff role. For instance, a person can be a professor as well as a faculty dean; a student can be involved in tutoring and/or work as a research assistant. Thus, there is no disjoint constraint on the relevant concepts in the work ontology.

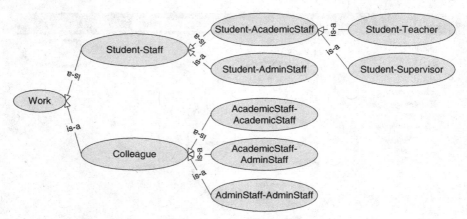

Fig. 4.10: A *work* relationship ontology

### 4.3.2.2  The *Object-Centric* Social Relationship Ontology

The *Object-centric* relationship (see Fig. 4.11) is identified between people who have shown common interests or participated in common activities or become member of same groups. We classify the *Object-centric* relationship as *Common-Interest*, *Following-Follower* and *Living-Address* relationships.

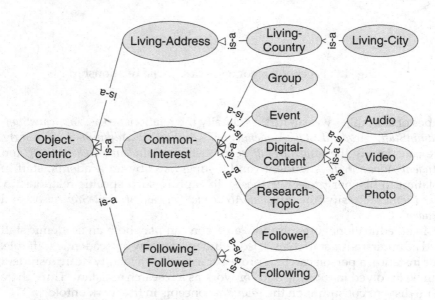

Fig. 4.11: An *object-centric* relationship ontology

*CommonInterest* includes the relationships with person(s) who like the same *Digital-Content* (*e.g.*, those people use "like" to express in Facebook), are members of the same *Group* (*e.g.*, soccer, cricket), are interested in the same *Event* (*e.g.*, conference), or have *CommonResearchInterest* which can be collected from LinkedIn.

From Twitter we can obtain the *Following-Follower* relationship, where the *Following* includes the person(s) whom the user is interested and following, and the *Follower* includes person(s) who are following the user.

*Living-Address* based relationship can be acquired from Facebook or LinkedIn, and further categorized at *Living-Country* and *Living-City* levels.

## 4.3.3  *The* Interaction-Oriented *Social Relationship Ontology*

The *interaction-oriented* relationship is formed between collaborative individuals who are obliged to interact with each other. In some cases, such a relationship is based on an explicit agreement; in other cases, participants behave as though they agree to the relationship without a formal agreement. For example, in the cooperative convoy scenario (discussed in Sect. 2.2.1), when the group of tourists rent the cars from Budget and AVIS, they are often required to sign a rental contract. The contract defines key aspects of the relationship between the customer and the rental company. In another case, the convoy agreements between the drivers of these rented cars is less formal. Figure 4.12 shows the *interaction-oriented* relationships ontology for the cooperative convoy scenario. The concepts hierarchy is represented as follows:

Social Interaction Ontology

The *social interactions* are defined by the *interaction-oriented relationships* between collaborative individuals playing social roles. These interaction-relationships are used to construct *runtime social interaction models* that mediate runtime interactions (see Sect. 6.2). *Social interaction* captures social norms, rules and obligations between social roles, which we represent in terms of *interactions*, *conversations* and *obligations* (see Fig. 4.13).

*Interactions* define permitted atomic message exchange *between* the *social roles*. The properties of an interaction include an identifying *message signature*, a direction of the message (*i.e.*, *fromRole* and *toRole*) and the *interaction type*.

*Conversation* defines an acceptable sequence of interactions defined by temporal constraints in the interaction rule specification language [112]. For

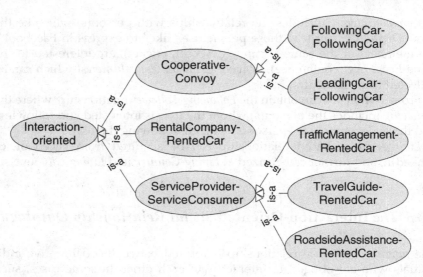

Fig. 4.12: An *interaction-oriented* social relationships ontology for cooperative convoy

instance, a conversation, say $c_1$, relates the interactions $i_1$ and $i_2$ linked with the *intrac1* and *intrac2* object properties respectively, using the sequence type *precedes* (*i.e.*, before); it means that the $i_1$ should occur before $i_2$.

*Obligation* defines *time* constraints in a conversation using an operational parameter. The *operational parameter* includes a parameter *name*, a *time unit* or *distance unit* and a *value*. The obligation with a timer "duration" and a specific operational parameter value, constraint the maximum allowed time duration between the interactions in the associated conversation. For example, an operational parameter value "2min" means that the maximum allowed delay between two interactions is 2 min. On the other hand, the obligation with a timer "period" and a specific operational parameter value, constraint the frequency of the associated conversation. For example, a obligation with a timer "period" and "2min" operational parameter value means that the associated conversation should occur at least once in every 2 min.

In the cooperative convoy scenario, both the leading car and following car need to send their positions to each other in every 10 s. Table 4.4 represents (in Turtle syntax [40]) the $i1$ interaction, *i.e.*, leading car notifies its position to the following car, while Table 4.5 represents the $i2$ interaction, *i.e.*, following car notifies its position to the leading car. Table 4.6 represents the obligation associated with these two interactions, *i.e.*, the position update should be every 10 s.

There are a number *constraints* related to the specification of *social interaction* ontology. A social interaction consists of *at least one* interaction, occurs

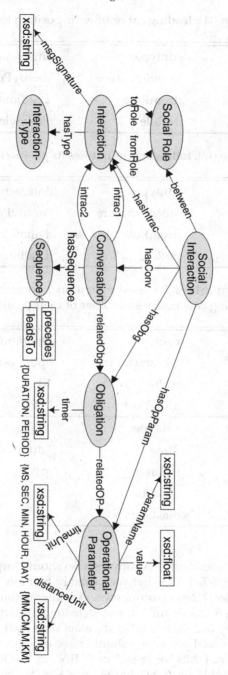

Fig. 4.13: A *social interaction* ontology

Table 4.4: Interaction (i1): leading car notifies its position to the following car

| :i1 | rdf:type | :Interaction |
|---|---|---|
| :i1 | :msgSignature | "notifyPosition" |
| :i1 | :fromRole | :LeadingCar |
| :i1 | :toRole | :FollowingCar |

Table 4.5: Interaction (i2): following car notifies its position to the leading car

| :i2 | rdf:type | :Interaction |
|---|---|---|
| :i2 | :msgSignature | "notifyPosition" |
| :i2 | :fromRole | :FollowingCar |
| :i2 | :toRole | :LeadingCar |

Table 4.6: Obligation (o1) and related operational parameter (p1): both the leading and following cars notify each other of their positions every 10 s

| :p1 | rdf:type | OperationalParameter |
|---|---|---|
| :p1 | :paramName | "posUpdateFreq" |
| :p1 | :value | 10 |
| :p1 | :timeUnit | "SEC" |
| :o1 | rdf:type | :Obligation |
| :o1 | :time | "duration" |
| :o1 | :relatedOP | :p1 |
| :i1 | :hasObg | :o1 |
| :i2 | :hasObg | :o1 |

between *exactly two* social roles. A conversation should impose a sequence—either *precedes* or *leadsTo* [112]—between exactly two interactions linked by the *intrac1* and *intrac2* object properties. An interaction should have exactly *one toRole*, *one fromRole* and *one msgSignature* properties. An obligation should have exactly *one* timer (either *duration* or *period*) and *one relatedOp* property. An operational parameter should have exactly *one paramName, one value* and *one timUnit* ("MS" or "SEC" or "MIN" or "HOUR" or "DAY") or *one distanceUnit* ("MM" or "CM" or 'M" or "KM"). These constraints are represented as follows:

$$Social\text{-}Interaction \sqsubseteq\, \geq 1 \quad hasIntrac \cdot Interaction$$

$$Social\text{-}Interaction \sqsubseteq\, = 2 \quad between \cdot Social\text{-}Role$$

$$Conversation \equiv \{precedes, leadsTo\}$$

$$Conversation \sqsubseteq\, = 1 \quad intrac1 \cdot Interaction$$

$$Interaction \sqsubseteq\, = 1 \quad toRole \cdot Social\text{-}Role$$

$$Interaction \sqsubseteq\, = 1 \quad fromRole \cdot Social\text{-}Role$$

$$Interaction \sqsubseteq\, = 1 \quad msgSignature$$

$$timer \in \{DURATION, PERIOD\}$$

$$Obligation \sqsubseteq\, = 1 \quad timer$$

$$Obligation \sqsubseteq\, = 1 \quad relatedOp \cdot Operational\text{-}Parameter$$

$$timeUnit \in \{MS, SEC, MIN, HOUR, DAY\}$$

$$distanceUnit \in \{MM, CM, M, KM\}$$

$$Operational\text{-}Parameter \sqsubseteq\, \leqslant 1 \quad timeUnit$$

$$Operational\text{-}Parameter \sqsubseteq\, \leqslant 1 \quad distanceUnit$$

$$Operational\text{-}Parameter \sqsubseteq\, = 1 \quad paramName$$

$$Operational\text{-}Parameter \sqsubseteq\, = 1 \quad value$$

## 4.3.4 *The* Situation *Ontology*

A situation ontology is a logical specification and representation of situation related concepts that are of application interest [189]. In this work context, we view situation as a user status with respect to his/her surrounding people. For example, a user's situation is 'meeting', 'seminar' or 'watching game in a stadium' describes his/her status with respect to the surrounding people.

We categorise *situation* as *business* and *non-business* situations considering their use in application scenarios (described in Chap. 2). We further categorise business situation as 'meeting', 'seminar' and 'Lecture', and nonbusiness situation as 'watching game in a stadium' and 'driving in convoy' (see Fig. 4.14).

Most of the business situations are very *formal* and *scheduled*. Such situations of users can be *acquired* from online digital calendar, *e.g.*, Google Calendar—assuming that the users maintain their schedules through the Google calendar, or can be *deduced* from time instant (see Sect. 5.3). This type of situation is very useful for many socially-aware applications. For example, in the socially-aware phone call application, a 'meeting' situation is an important factor for a user to filter an incoming phone call; also this situation is a vital factor for a caller to make decision about the suitable time of making call.

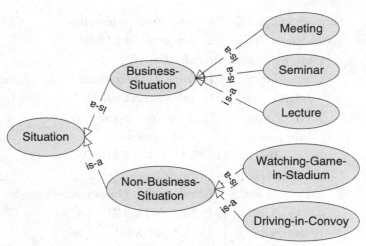

Fig. 4.14: A *situation* ontology

On the other hand, non-business situations are usually *occasional*. Many of such situations can be inferred from users' interaction activities in online social networks. For instance, 'watching game in a stadium' can be inferred from user interactions in Facebook (see Sect. 5.4 for details). This situation can be used to automate mobile settings, *e.g.*, automatically change the ring tone and ring volume in mobile phones, as the stadium environment usually very noisy and a person may prefer to set their phone ring tone volume in a highest level.

We specify a number of constraints in the situation ontology. At the same time, a person can not be in any of the two non business situations. Also, it is not possible to watch game in a stadium and drive, at the same time. These constraints are represented as follows:

$$Meeting \sqcap Seminar \sqsubseteq \bot$$
$$Meeting \sqcap Lecture \sqsubseteq \bot$$
$$Seminar \sqcap Lecture \sqsubseteq \bot$$
$$Watching\text{-}Game\text{-}in\text{-}Stadium \sqcap Driving\text{-}in\text{-}Convoy \sqsubseteq \bot$$

## 4.4 Summary

In this chapter, we have presented an ontology based approach to modelling social context information. We have presented both the *upper* and *domain-specific* ontologies for different types of social context information such as *social role*, *social relationship*, *social interaction* and *situation*. The *upper ontology* specifies general concepts, their semantics and related constraints, while the *domain-specific ontologies* extend and classify general concepts to specify domain-specific concepts, their semantics and related constraints. We use the OWL2-DL, an ontology representation language, for encoding the concepts hierarchies, their disjointness and constraints on the properties of those concepts. One of the benefits of using OWL2-DL is that existing DL-based reasoners can be used for checking *inconsistency* and *integrity* of knowledge.

The key advantages of the ontology-based model are that it is reusable and extensible, and provides a basis for developing a knowledge base to store and manage context information. Furthermore, the ontology-based modelling and OWL-DL based representation provide a basis for composing new concepts and inferring new social context information (see Chap. 5).

# Chapter 5
# Social Context Reasoning

In the previous chapter, we have introduced different types of social context information and present ontologies that represent them. However, some useful social context information in the ontologies (*e.g., Father-Daughter, best friend*) cannot be acquired directly from the possible sources, but can be *derived* from the acquired data. Moreover, new concepts (*e.g., Group Meeting, Busy*), as required by applications, can be *deduced* and *abstracted* from the existing concepts. Furthermore, users' social interactions can be exploited to *infer* their situations which can be used to enhance applications' functionalities.

To address the above requirements, in this chapter, we present our approach to *deriving* different types of social relationships (Sect. 5.2), and *deducing* and *abstracting* situations from acquired information. We also present our approach to *inferring* situations from users' interaction events (Sect. 5.3).

## 5.1 Reasoning Approach

Reasoning is the process of identifying meaningful facts from observed data [42, 189]. There are *four* aspects of reasoning about social context information:

*Structure and Property*    Social context information can be *derived* from a set of other social context information and their properties. For example, a *'best friend'* relationship can be derived from a *'close friend'* relationship and its *trust* property. A person's relationship with another person can be derived from their social roles and gender, for example, a *'Father-Daughter'* relationship between two persons can be derived from a person's corresponding social role, *e.g., 'Father'* and the other person's gender information, here *'female'*.

© Springer International Publishing Switzerland 2016                    73
M.A. Kabir et al., *Pervasive Social Computing*,
DOI 10.1007/978-3-319-29951-8_5

*Composition/Abstraction*     Social context information can be *composed of* or *abstracted from* a set of other social context information. For example, a *'busy'* situation abstracts the *'seminar'*, *'lecture'* and *'meeting'* situations.

*Time-Stamp*     Social context information might be related with a time-stamp, *i.e.,* time of day, duration, frequency. A situation can be *deduced* from the current time-stamp as—it may only happen at a particular time of a day, it may only last a certain length of time, it may only happen a certain times per week. For example, a person have a *lecture* on every Tuesday 9:30 am to 11:30 am till May 30 except public holidays.

*Temporal Correlation*     Social context information can be *inferred* from the temporal correlation of observed facts. For example, a *'watching game'* situation can be inferred from a person's location and consequent message updates in social media such as posting current location as stadium, posting a game related picture and/or commenting on a game performance.

In this book, we address the above four aspects of social context information reasoning. As such, we view reasoning as a process of *deriving, deducing, abstracting* and *inferring* social context information that is of interest to applications. We adopt a specification based technique in our reasoning approach. In the specification based technique, domain knowledge is represented in rules and reasoning engine is applied to infer facts from observed data. There are number of approaches proposed for the specification based technique. These approaches have developed from earlier attempts in first-order logic [147, 180] to a OWL-DL based model [150] that aims to support efficient reasoning while keeping expressive power, to support formal analysis, and to maintain the soundness and completeness of a logical system.

Ontologies have been widely applied [42, 58, 146, 188] for its powerful representation and reasoning capabilities. Ontologies can provide a standard vocabulary of concepts to represent domain knowledge, specifications and semantic relationships of context information defined in formal logic approaches. They can also provide fully fledged reasoning engines to reason on them following rules specified in formal logic approaches. Thus, we adopt an ontology based approach to *deriving, abstracting* and *deducing* social context information considering their *structural/property, composition-al/abstraction* and *time-stamp* aspects. In particular, we use OWL 2 DL [87] to represent and specify reasoning rules.

To date, OWL 2 DL[1] has been the most practical choice for most ontological applications as it supports maximum expressiveness while retaining computational completeness and decidability [150]. OWL-DL class constructors such as *intersectionOf* ($\sqcap$), *unionOf* ($\sqcup$), *complementOf* ($\neg$), *oneOf* ($\{\}$), *allValuesFrom* ($\forall$), *someValuesFrom* ($\exists$), *maxCardinality* ($\leq$), *minCardinality* ($\geq$), *exactCardinality* ($=$) and *hasValue* ($\ni$) can be used to construct new classes/concepts from existing named classes, properties and individuals. OWL-DL class semantics such as *equivalentTo* ($\equiv$), *subclassOf* ($\sqsubseteq$) and

---

[1] For the sake of brevity we use OWL-DL later on.

*disjointWith* ($\sqcap = \perp$) can be used to specify associations between classes (named or a new class). In addition, OWL property characteristics such as *Transitive, Symmetric, Asymmetric, Reflexive, Irreflexive, Functional, Inverse functional* and *InverseOf* can be used to specify further associations among classes based on their individuals. Details of these constructors are discussed in Sects. 3.1.3 and 4.1.

As such, we use the OWL-DL class constructors, semantics and property characteristics to impose constraints on named classes in the ontologies and to specify reasoning/inference rules for defined classes. The main advantages of their use is that a DL reasoner can be used for (1) *executing* inference rules, and (2) *detecting* automatically *inconsistencies* in the specification of those inference rules.

To address the *temporal correlation* aspect in situation reasoning, we propose a *hybrid* approach that combines *ontology-based semantic matching* and *complex event processing* in order to *infer* users' situations from observed data, *i.e.*, users' interaction events. In this regard, we have developed an ontology-based interaction event model to capture users' interactions in various social interaction platforms, which adopts and extends recent event models and incorporates social context information. We also propose a technique to *specify* situations using atomic and complex interaction event patterns, which integrates their *semantic aspect* with *temporal relations*.

## 5.2 Deriving Social Relationships

In this section, we present DL-based reasoning rules to derive different types of family relationship from acquired social context information (Sect. 5.2.1), and to derive new types of friend relationship based on the existing friend relationship types and their properties (Sect. 5.2.2).

### 5.2.1 *Deriving* Family *Relationships*

In Sect. 4.3.2.1, we have presented a *family* relationship ontology that captures different types of family relationships. However, such relationships information cannot be acquired directly from sources, but can be derived based on acquired social roles and gender information. We rely on users' Facebook information to deduce *Family* relationships. Facebook allows people to maintain a family list, where a user can annotate a person in his family list as *brother, father, uncle* and so on, which ultimately indicates the role played by the person being annotated from the user's point of view rather than the specific relationship between the user and that person. For instance, if a user annotates a person in his/her family list as "father", the relationship between them could be a "Father-Son" or "Father-Daughter" relationship, which can be inferred and differentiated by utilising the user's gender information. Some examples are given below:

$$
\begin{aligned}
Father\text{-}Daughter \equiv (\ &\exists relates(Person \sqcap plays \cdot \{father\}) \sqcap \\
&\exists relates(Me \sqcap gender \cdot \{female\})) \\
)\sqcup (\ & \\
&\exists relates(Person \sqcap plays \cdot \{daughter\}) \sqcap \\
&\exists relates(Me \sqcap gender \cdot \{male\}) \\
)&
\end{aligned}
\tag{5.1}
$$

$$
\begin{aligned}
Uncle\text{-}Nephew \equiv (\ &\exists relates(Person \sqcap plays \cdot \{uncle\}) \sqcap \\
&\exists relates(Me \sqcap gender \cdot \{female\})) \\
)\sqcup (\ & \\
&\exists relates(Person \sqcap plays \cdot \{nephew\}) \sqcap \\
&\exists relates(Me \sqcap gender \cdot \{male\}) \\
)&
\end{aligned}
$$

Here, *Father-Daughter* and *Uncle-Nephew* relationships between a user and another person are inferred from the user's *gender* information (a data property of *foaf:Person*) and the related person's social role. *Me* is a subclass of *Person* that specifies the user from whose perspective the relationship is computed.

A complete list of the reasoning rules can be found in Appendix A.1.

### 5.2.2 *Deriving* Friend *Relationships*

In Sect. 4.3.2.1, we have presented a friend ontology that captures different types of friend relationship. Such basic friendship concepts can be used to further derive friendship relationships such as *BestFriend*, *BosomFriend*, *ChildhoodFriend* and *LongtimeFriend*. Figure 5.1 shows the inferred friend relationship ontology. The specialised friend relationships might be of interest to different socially-aware applications. For example, in the socially-aware phone call application, a user might want to filter incoming phone calls or specify her privacy preference based on the "best friend" relationship type.

According to an application requirements, developers can specify *reasoning rules* for deriving such relationships. For instance, a *best* friend could be specified as a specially *close* and *trusted* friend [23]; a *bosom* friend is a very close friend [23], *i.e.*, a *close* friend with a high relationship *strength*, for example, greater than or equal to 0.8; a person is a *childhood* friend if he/she

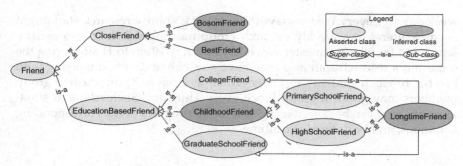

Fig. 5.1: An *inferred friend* relationship ontology

is primary school or high school friend; a person can be identified as a *long time* friend if he/she is a *PrimarySchoolFriend*, *HighSchoolFriend*, *CollegeFriend* and *GraduateSchoolFriend*. We specify these reasoning rules using OWL-DL constructs as follows:

$$BestFriend \equiv CloseFriend \sqcap (trust > \{0.0\})$$
$$BosomFriend \equiv CloseFriend \sqcap (strength \geq \{0.8\})$$
$$ChildhoodFriend \equiv PrimarySchoolFriend \sqcup HighSchoolFriend$$
$$LongtimeFriend \equiv PrimarySchoolFriend \sqcap HighSchoolFriend \sqcap$$
$$CollegeFriend \sqcap GraduateSchoolFriend$$

## 5.3 Deducing and Abstracting Situations

Situation reasoning is the process of identifying situations from acquired information. In this section, we present DL-based reasoning rules to *deduce* situations from acquired information by considering their *time-stamp* aspect (Sect. 5.3.1). The deduced situations are further used to define more *abstract* situations (Sect. 5.3.2).

### 5.3.1 Deducing Situations

In Sect. 4.3.4, we have presented *'meeting'*, *'seminar'* and *'lecture'* situations that are related to the business/office environments. We have argued that most of these situations occur periodically and follow a fixed schedule. For instance, in a university, course lectures are scheduled before starting of each semester, *e.g.*, a teaching staff have a lecture on every Tuesday 9:30 am to 11:30 am; a faculty may run a weekly seminar in a specific time and

week day, *e.g.*, every Wednesday 10:30 am to 11:30 am; a research staff might
need to attend to a weekly research group meeting which is also usually
scheduled for whole semester, *e.g.*, every Monday 10 am to 11 am during the
semester; a research staff also may have a weekly individual meeting with
his/her research students, *e.g.*, every Monday 2 pm to 3 pm; research group
members may go for a group lunch every Thursday. Such *scheduled* situations of a user can be *defined* using *time-stamp* property of the corresponding
situations, and be *deduced* at runtime.

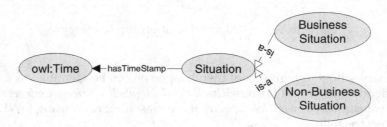

Fig. 5.2: An excerpt of *situation* ontology

Our Situation ontology is linked with *owl:Time* ontology using *hasTime-
Stamp* object property, as shown in Fig. 5.2. Figure 5.3 shows an excerpt of
*owl:Time* ontology [103, 104]. We extend the *owl:Time* ontology by incorporating and defining a number domain-specific concepts such as *Weekends*,
*Weekdays*, *NonBusinessHours*, *BusinessHours*, *WorkingHours*, *LunchHours* and
*Holidays*. These concepts will be used in inference rules to define the aforementioned scheduled situations. We define these concepts based on the general rules in Australia [4]. To define *Holiday* we use the Victorian public
holidays 2013 [6]. However, these can be modified according to the application domains. We define Saturday and Sunday as *Weekends*; Monday to
Friday as *Weekdays*; 9:00 to 16:59 is *BusinessHours* while 9:00 to 11:59 and
13:00 to 16:59 are *WorkingHours*, and 12:00 to 12:59 is *LunchHours*; 17:00 to
23:59 and 00:00 to 8:59 are *NonBusinessHours*. We further categorize *Holidays*
as *NewYearDay* (Tuesday 1 January), *EasterMonday* (Monday 1 April), *Christ-
masDay* (Wednesday 25 December), and so on.

Figure 5.4 shows the inferred concepts hierarchy in the time ontology. The
inference rules of these concepts are represented using OWL-DL as follows:

$$Weekends \equiv \exists inDateTime(DateTimeDescription \sqcap$$
$$(dayOfWeek \cdot \{Saturday\} \sqcup dayOfWeek \cdot \{Sunday\}))$$
$$Weekdays \equiv \exists inDateTime(DateTimeDescription \sqcap$$
$$(dayOfWeek \cdot \{Monday\} \sqcup dayOfWeek \cdot \{Tuesday\}$$
$$\sqcup dayOfWeek \cdot \{Wednesday\} \sqcup dayOfWeek \cdot \{Thursday\}$$
$$\sqcup dayOfWeek \cdot \{Friday\}))$$

(5.2)

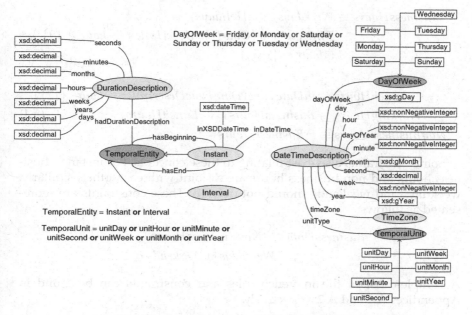

Fig. 5.3: An excerpt of *owl:Time* ontology

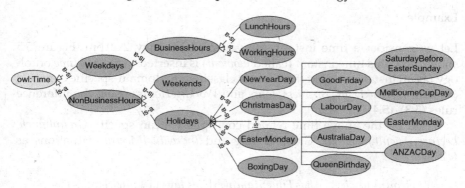

Fig. 5.4: An *inferred owl:Time* ontology

$$Holidays \equiv NewYearDay \sqcup ChristmasDay \sqcup BoxingDay$$
$$\sqcup GoodFriday \sqcup LabourDay \sqcup AustraliaDay$$
$$\sqcup QueenBrithDay \sqcup ANZACDay \sqcup EsaterMonday$$
$$\sqcup MelbourneCupDay \sqcup SaturdayBeforeEasterSunday$$
$$NewYearDay \equiv \exists inDateTime(DateTimeDescription \sqcap$$
$$(year \cdot \{2013\} \sqcap month \cdot \{--01\} \sqcap day \cdot \{---01\}))$$
$$ChristmasDay \equiv \exists inDateTime(DateTimeDescription \sqcap$$
$$(year \cdot \{2013\} \sqcap month \cdot \{--12\} \sqcap day \cdot \{---25\}))$$

$$BusinessHours \equiv Weekdays \sqcap (\neg Holidays) \sqcap$$
$$\exists inDateTime(DateTimeDescription \sqcap (hour \geq \{9\}$$
$$\sqcap hour \leq \{16\}))  \qquad\qquad (5.3)$$

$$LunchHours \equiv inDateTime(DateTimeDescription \sqcap hour \cdot \{12\})$$
$$WorkingHours \equiv BusinessHours \sqcap (\neg LunchHours)  \qquad (5.4)$$
$$NonBusinessHours \equiv \neg BusinessHours$$

Some constraints also exist relating to these concepts. For instance, business hours and non business hours are disjoint with each other; similarly, weekdays and weekends should not overlap. These constraints are represented as follows:

$$BusinessHours \sqcap NonBusinessHours \sqsubseteq \perp$$
$$Weekdays \sqcap Weekends \sqsubseteq \perp$$

A complete list of the inference rules and constraints can be found in Appendices A.1 and A.2 respectively.

## Example

Let us consider a time instant, May 20 2013 Monday 2:30 pm. Figure 5.5 shows how this time instant (called *moment*) is inserted to the *owl:time* ontology (as an instance, called *time*) and is classified to domain-specific concepts (*moment* is *WeekDays*, *BusinessHours* and *WorkingHours*) using the inference rules (5.3)–(5.4).

Based on the above time related concepts, we can specify *GroupLunch*, *Lecture*, *FacultySeminar*, *GroupMeeting* and *IndividualMeeting* situations as follows:

$$GroupLunch \equiv \exists hasTimeStamp(\neg Holidays \sqcap LunchHours \sqcap$$
$$\exists inDateTime(DateTimeDescription \sqcap$$
$$dayOfWeek \cdot \{Thursday\}))$$
$$Lecture \equiv \exists hasTimeStamp(WorkingHours \sqcap$$
$$\exists inDateTime(DateTimeDescription \sqcap$$
$$((hour \cdot \{9\} \sqcap minute \geq \{30\}) \sqcup$$
$$(hour \cdot \{11\} \sqcap minute \leq \{30\}))$$
$$\sqcap dayOfWeek \cdot \{Tuesday\}))$$

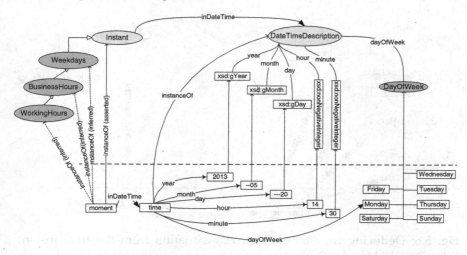

Fig. 5.5: Classifying the time instant (May 20 2013 Monday 2:30 pm) to domain-specific concepts

$$
\begin{aligned}
FacultySeminar \equiv\ & \exists hasTimeStamp(WorkingHours \sqcap \\
& \exists inDateTime(DateTimeDescription \sqcap \\
& ((hour \cdot \{10\} \sqcap minute \geq \{30\}) \sqcup \\
& (hour \cdot \{11\} \sqcap minute \leq \{30\})) \\
& \sqcap dayOfWeek \cdot \{Wednesday\})) \\
GroupMeeting \equiv\ & \exists hasTimeStamp(WorkingHours \sqcap \\
& \exists inDateTime(DateTimeDescription \sqcap \\
& (hour \cdot \{10\} \sqcup (hour \cdot \{11\} \sqcap minute \cdot \{0\})) \\
& \sqcap dayOfWeek \cdot \{Monday\})) \\
IndividualMeeting \equiv\ & \exists hasTimeStamp(WorkingHours \sqcap \\
& \exists inDateTime(DateTimeDescription \sqcap \\
& (hour \cdot \{14\} \sqcup (hour \cdot \{15\} \sqcap minute \cdot \{0\})) \\
& \sqcap dayOfWeek \cdot \{Monday\})) \quad\quad (5.5)
\end{aligned}
$$

## Example

Figure 5.6 shows how Alice's situation is deduced as *individual meeting* on the *moment* time instant using reasoning rule (5.5).

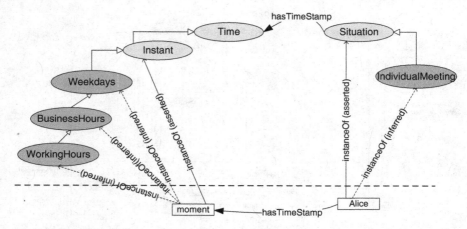

Fig. 5.6: Deducing the *individual meeting* situation from the time instant (May 20 2013 Monday 2:30 pm)

### 5.3.2 *Abstracting Situations*

More abstract *general* situations (in a business domain) can be defined based on the above time-related situations from users' location perspective. For instance, a user's *group lunch, lecture, group meeting* and *faculty seminar* situations can be *abstracted* to '*not at desk*' situation. Usually there are particular places for these activities and they are not held in a person's office or at desk. On the other hand, a person's individual meetings with another person might held in his/her office. Thus, the individual meeting and chatting with friends situations can be abstracted to '*at desk*' situation. The inference rules for these situations are as follows:

$$NotAtDesk \equiv GroupLunch \sqcup Lecture \sqcup Seminar \sqcup GroupMeeting$$
$$AtDesk \equiv IndividualMeeting \sqcup Chatting$$

The *time-related* situations also can be abstracted to define *user-specific* situations. For example, a user might say her status as being '*busy*' when she is in a lecture or group seminar or group meeting or individual meeting or group lunch. Furthermore, user may want to define situations from an application perspective. For example, a user might prefer not to be interrupted by any phone call when she is busy, but she may tolerate only urgent phone call when she is in individual meetings or a group lunch. Identifying and making available users' such situations allow a caller to take decision of her making a phone call. The inference rules for abstracting such situations are given below:

$$Busy \equiv GroupLunch \sqcup Lecture \sqcup Seminar \sqcup Meeting$$
$$PhoneCallNotExpected \equiv Busy$$
$$OnlyUrgentCall \equiv \neg Busy \sqcup GroupLunch \sqcup IndividualMeeting$$

Figure 5.7 shows the concepts hierarchy in the inferred business situation ontology with granularity level. We have set the granularity level for each concept in the ontology as an increasing number from root to leaf nodes. Thus for a given situation, we can answer the situation of a user at different levels of granularity. For instance, for a situation *"IndividualMeeting"* with granularity level 2, we can say that the user is *"Busy"*.

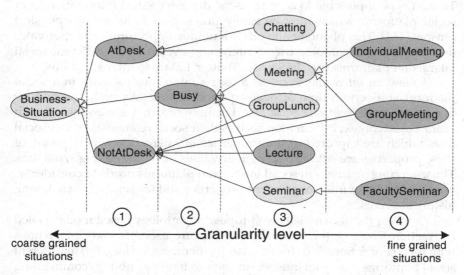

Fig. 5.7: An *inferred business situation* ontology

## 5.4 Inferring Situations from Interaction Events

The advances of internet technologies and the increased prevalence of advanced mobile devices (the so called "smart" phones), have radically changed the way people perform tasks, interact with each other and share information about their lives and works. In order to facilitate such device mediated interactions different social (interaction) platforms or applications have emerged.

Some of the applications are developed for specific tasks, and based on predefined agreements and constraints, *e.g.*, the cooperative convoy application (see Sect. 2.2). Users interactions in these applications generate interaction events.

On the other hand, users' interactions using online social networks, instant messaging and email are open and not based on predefined agreements and constraints. On these platforms people interact with each other in many ways: sharing their interests; tagging, bookmarking and commenting on digital contents such as photos and videos; chatting and sending emails; and posting messages about what they did, what they are currently doing or what their plans are for the (near) future [184]. Thus, it is now possible to acquire users' diverse context information from social platforms which may be rarely possible to acquire from physical sensors [154]. This phenomenon offers a unique opportunity and motivates us to exploit and combine users' interaction events across different social interaction platforms (*e.g.*, Facebook, Twitter, Email) to infer situations.

We view an *interaction event* as a user's interaction/activity in a social platform at a certain time or over a period of time. As such, the interaction events have *temporal correlations*. Furthermore, they are associated with users' social context information such as their social relationships and social roles which are captured in the properties of interaction events. Many of these properties are *ontological*, *i.e.*, their values have underlying semantics. Thus, *inferring situations* in social interaction platforms needs to consider *semantic matching* of interaction event properties and *temporal relations* among historical events.

To address the above issue, we propose an ontology based model, called Interaction Event Ontology (*IntEO*), to capture users' (social) interactions with their connections (*e.g.*, friends, family members, colleagues) in different social platforms where an interaction *refers* to like/promoting/commenting on/sharing/posting a status message, current location, music, photo, video, link, and so on. This interaction also includes chatting in instant messenger, sending email, or any type of mediated interactions.

In order to capture the *general* concepts and incorporate *domain-specific* concepts, we propose both the *upper* and *domain-specific* ontologies. The *upper ontology* captures the general concepts, abstracted from the analysis of possible interaction events in different platforms (see Sect. 5.4.1). This upper ontology can be shared, reused, and adapted to specific domains. It is also extensible to allow for the incorporation of new concepts and the specialisation of concepts and constraints for a particular social platform, forming a *domain-specific ontology* (see Sects. 5.4.2 and 5.4.3). We also propose a *language* to specify situations using atomic and complex interaction event patterns, which integrates semantic aspect of interaction events with their temporal relations (see Sects. 5.4.5 and 5.4.6).

### 5.4.1 Interaction Event Upper Ontology

The *core event ontology* is the basis of our interaction event upper ontology, and is formulated based on the LODE and SEM models (see Sect. 3.4) as they are most recently proposed event ontologies and focus on generality and interoperability. The core event ontology (see upper part of Fig. 5.8), has four key entities/concepts/classes: *Event*, *Time*, *Place* and *Thing*.

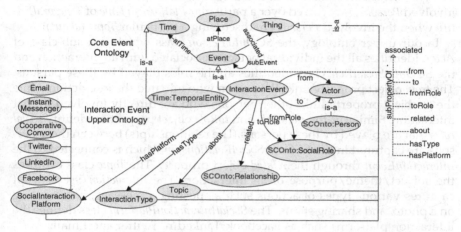

Fig. 5.8: Interaction event upper ontology (*IntEO*)

To model the *interaction event upper ontology* (see lower part of Fig. 5.8), we extend the *core event* ontology with concepts concerning *interaction events* and incorporate our social context ontology (*SCOnto*) (see Sect. 4.2). Our upper ontology defines eight first-class entities, namely, *InteractionEvent*, *Actor*, *SocialRole*, *SocialRelationship*, *Topic*, *InteractionType*, *SocialInteraction-Platform* and *TemporalEntity*. *InteractionEvent* is the core class which extends (specialisation of/sub-class of) the *Event* class in the core event ontology. The upper ontology inherits the *Place* from the core event ontology. To define the *Time* in the upper ontology, we specialise the *Time* class in core event ontology by adopting the *TemporalEntity* class from the *owl:Time* ontology [103]. We extend the *Thing* concept in the core event ontology to define the *Social-InteractionPlatform*, *InteractionType*, *Topic*, *SocialRelationship*, *SocialRole* and *Actor* concepts in the interaction event ontology, where the *SocialRelationship* and *SocialRole* concepts are adopted from the *SCOnto* ontology. We also define the *from*, *to*, *fromRole*, *toRole*, *related*, *about*, *hasType* and *hasPlatform* object properties by extending and specialising the *associated* object property of the core event ontology. These extension and specialisation such as *InteractionEvent* is a *SubClassOf Event*, *Actor* is a *SubClassOf Thing*, and *fromRole* is a *SubPropertyOf associated*, can be represented using OWL-DL as follows:

$$InteractionEvent \sqsubseteq Event$$
$$Actor \sqsubseteq Thing$$
$$fromRole \sqsubseteq associated$$

The upper ontology can be read as follows. An *InteractionEvent* is a communication *from* a *Person* (which is an *Actor*) acting in a *SocialRole* (*fromRole*) *to* another *Person* acting in another *SocialRole* (*toRole*). This *InteractionEvent hasType InteractionType*, is *related* to a *SocialRelationship* that exists among the involved *Persons*, is occurred over a particular *Platform atTime* of *TemporalEntity* when the involved *Persons* are discussing a particular *Topic* (*about*).

In our upper ontology, the *SCOnto:Person* class which is a sub-class of *Actor*, identifies all the individual persons associated with an interaction and the *SCOnto:SocialRole* class identifies all the roles played by these persons. The *from* object property links the person who initiated the interaction while the *to* object property links other persons who are directly involved in that interaction. Similarly, the *fromRole* and *toRole* object properties identify *social roles* that are played by these persons. The relationship(s) between these persons are captured in the *SCOnto:SocialRelationship* which is connected to the *InteractionEvent* through the *related* object property. The *Topic* class captures the subject/theme/purpose of an interaction. The *InteractionType* concept captures various types of actions such as posting a message, commenting on a photo, and sharing status. The *SocialInteractionPlatform* class defines the interaction platforms such as Facebook, LinkedIn, Twitter and Email.

## 5.4.2 Domain-Specific Interaction Event Ontology for Cooperative Convoy

In this section, we present a domain-specific interaction event ontology for the cooperative convoy by adopting and extending the interaction event upper ontology presented in the previous section. In the cooperative convoy (discussed in Sect. 2.2.1), collaborative actors (*e.g.,* drivers of the cars) interact with each other to achieve their goals/objectives. Such message-based interactions are mediated through an interaction-centric socially-aware application.

In such convoy, car drivers identify themselves as a driver of a leading car or a following car. Based on the agreements among these drivers, we can define *interaction relationships* among them in terms of interactions, conversations and obligations. Interactions performed by drivers at runtime may follow some patterns among many possible valid interaction patterns, and some of these patterns might refer to different meaningful situations. By inferring such situations, it might possible to understand drivers' needs and provide services accordingly.

During convoy, drivers may pass through different situations, e.g., 'hungry' and thus need to find a suitable restaurant. One possible interaction pattern to infer this 'hungry' situation would be: *one of the drivers proposing to stop for the Food and other drivers agreed on that, and it is a breakfast, lunch or dinner time.* The cooperative convoy application's functionality can be enhanced based on this situation. For instance, the application can automatically collect nearby restaurants information by invoking a restaurant searching service and recommend those restaurants to drivers.

To infer situations from drivers' interaction activities in a cooperative convoy, first we need to define an interaction event ontology for the cooperative convoy by adopting and extending *IntEO*. Sections 4.3.1 and 4.3.3 present social role and (interaction-oriented) social relationship ontologies, respectively, for the cooperative convoy application. Figure 5.9 shows how we extend the *InteractionType*, *Topic* and *Time* concepts of the *IntEO* for the cooperative convoy application.

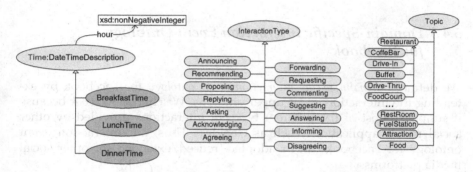

Fig. 5.9: *InteractionType*, *Topic* and *Time* ontologies for the cooperative convoy application

By motivating the usage of John R. Searle's "speech act" [165] which is often meant to refer just to the same thing as the term illocutionary act that John L. Austin had originally introduced to Do Things with Words [33], we define an *InteractionType* ontology for the cooperative convoy application. This ontology provides vocabulary or concepts to classify interactions among collaborative actors. For instance, we can classify the interaction "*convoyBreak*" to stop for the food while driving as a "proposing" interaction type. A positive response of this interaction from other drivers is classified as "agreeing" interaction type, while an negative response is classified as "disagreeing" interaction type. Figure 5.9 shows the interaction types that we use to classify all the interactions in our cooperative scenario.

In the cooperative convoy domain, we classify *Topic* as *food, attraction, restaurant, fuel-station,* and *restroom,* as these are relevant. Time when an interaction takes place is also important to identify situation. For instance, to identify *hungry* situation, breakfast, lunch and diner times are relevant. Thus, we define *BreakfastTime* (between 6 am and 8 am), *LunchTime* (between 12 pm and 2 pm) and *DinnerTime* (between 6 pm and 8 pm) concepts by classifying *Time:DateTimeDescription* concept in the *IntEO*, as follows:

$$BreakfastTime \equiv \exists inDateTime(DateTimeDescription \sqcap (hour \geq \{6\}$$
$$\sqcap hour \leq \{8\}))$$
$$LunchTime \equiv \exists inDateTime(DateTimeDescription \sqcap (hour \geq \{12\}$$
$$\sqcap hour \leq \{14\}))$$
$$DinnerTime \equiv \exists inDateTime(DateTimeDescription \sqcap (hour \geq \{18\}$$
$$\sqcap hour \leq \{20\}))$$

In Sect. 8.3.6.1, we use this domain-specific interaction event ontology for inferring the *'hungry'* situation.

### 5.4.3 Domain-Specific Interaction Event Ontology for Facebook

We define a *domain-specific interaction event ontology* for Facebook by extending the interaction event upper ontology. We choose *Facebook* because it supports most of the different types of interactions provided by other social media applications such as Google+. Thus, our interaction event ontology for Facebook can be adopted/reused/extended for other social media platforms.

#### Interaction Types

Facebook allows users to perform different types of interaction activities. To classify such interactions we extend the *InteractionType* class as shown in Fig. 5.10. Facebook allows users to post various digital contents such as status, current location, life event, photo, photo album, video and music. We classify a user's status posting as having the *PostingStatus* interaction type. In a status, a user can say anything, *i.e.*, whatever on her mind. Thus, it is hardly possible to comprehensively classify all possible status messages. However, in a status update, users generally mention about their current activity, *i.e.*, what they are currently doing or going to do or have already done, their emotion, current affairs, news, and so on [184].

We classify a user's life event, current place, photo, photo album, music and video posting as *PostingLifeEvent*, *PostingCurrentLocation*, *PostingPhoto*, *PostingPhotoAlbum*, *PostingMusic* and *PostingVideo*, respectively. Facebook allows a user to post different types of her life events related to the various

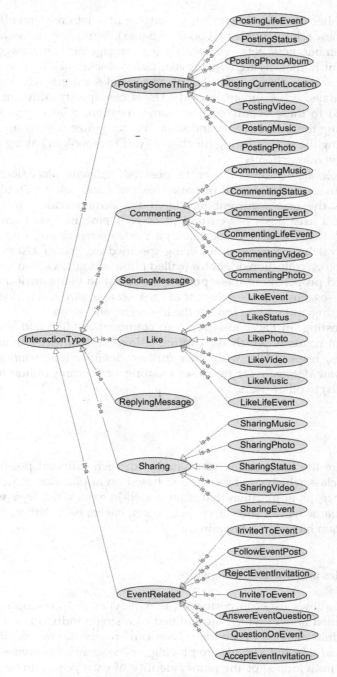

Fig. 5.10: An *InteractionType* ontology

aspects of her life such as work (*e.g.*, starting new job, retirement), education (*e.g.*, new school, published book or paper), family (*e.g.*, new child, new family member, new pet), relationship (*e.g.*, engagement, marriage), home (*e.g.*, bought home), living (*e.g.*, moved, new vehicle), health & well-being (*e.g.*, overcame an illness, quit a habit), and travel & experiences (*e.g.*, return from holidays, achievement, award). Users can specify different properties related to these events such as name, location, related persons, start time, ending time, description and so on. We recognize posting any of such events using life event posting functionality of Facebook as having the *PostingLifeEvent* interaction type.

Facebook also allows a user to post her current place/location by referring to an existing event or page object of Facebook which ultimately represents the user's current location (at a certain scale) and possible activity. If a user posts her current place as "being in a stadium SSS", it represents that the user is located in a particular stadium, *e.g.*, SSS, and possibly watching a game (until being specified explicitly). Users also can post a photo, a collection of photos (called photo album), a video and music. The related properties of these posting are specified using attributes of the above classes. For example, content of the message, physical address of the place, starting and ending time of the life event, and so on.

Like posting, in Facebook users can comment on, like and share various digital contents which we capture using *Commenting*, *Like* and *Sharing* classes, respectively, with their further classification. *SendingMessage* and *ReplyingMessage* refer to a user chatting or sending offline messages (*e.g.*, emails) to other users.

Topic

We capture the main theme associated with such different posting using the *Topic* class which can be extended based on application requirements. For instance, an application that is interested in games, the *Topic* would be different game names such as cricket, soccer, basket ball, with their further classification hierarchy (if required).

Social Roles and Social Relationships

Facebook allows users to perform different types of interaction activities (as explained above) which are notified to a single individual or a group of individual or none ('only me'). User can specify the recipient(s) based on the *social roles* individuals are playing, or the *social relationships* between user and individuals, or the name/identity of each *person*. In Sect. 4.3 we have presented different types of social roles and social relationships which can be adopted and reused to capture social context information related to users' interaction events in Facebook.

### 5.4.4 Examples of Interaction Event

Based on the model described above, an interaction event can be specified using a set of attribute-value pairs. For instance, an interaction event *"in Facebook Bob has posted his current location, MCG Stadium, at 2:30PM and based on Bob's posting preference that post has been notified to all of his connections who are living in the Melbourne area"* can be specified as follows:

```
ie1:InteractionEvent(platform="Facebook",from="Bob",
related=
LivingCity,hasType=PostingCurrentLocation,atPlace="MCG
Stadium",
atTime=TemporalEntity(start=2:30PM,duration=0ms))
```

*At 3:21PM bob posts a photo that has been taken in the stadium and shares it with his close friends*:

```
ie2:InteractionEvent(platform="Facebook",from="Bob",
related=CloseFriend,hasType=PostingPhoto,about="Cricket
Game",
atTime=TemporalEntity(start=3:21PM,duration=0ms))
```

After some time, *at 3:39PM Bob posts a status message in Facebook like "Wow! great 6" or "4" or "out" and shares it with his close friends*:

```
ie3:InteractionEvent(platform="Facebook",from="Bob",
related=CloseFriend,hasType=PostingStatus,about="Cricket
Game",
atTime=TemporalEntity(start=3:39PM, duration=0ms))
```

### 5.4.5 Interaction Event Based Situation Specification

We specify a *situation* (SITU) as a set of interaction event patterns with temporal and/or logical relationships among them, while any information in the event instance(s) can be integrated to the situation description. Our proposed situation specification language comprise five basic elements: (1) Interaction Event Pattern (IEP), (2) Complex Interaction Event Pattern (CIEP), (3) Temporal Operator (TOP), (4) Binary Logical Operator (BOP), and (5) Relational Operator (ROP). The syntax of our situation specification language is shown below.

```
SITU  := CIEP | IEP
CIEP  := (CIEP TOP CIEP) | (IEP TOP IEP) | (CIEP TOP
  IEP) |
        (IEP TOP CIEP) | (CIEP BOP CIEP) | (IEP BOP
  IEP) |
```

```
                (CIEP BOP IEP) | (IEP BOP CIEP) | (NOT CIEP)
IEP    := InteractionEvent(CONST) | (NOT IEP)
CONST := (Attr ROP Value) | (Attr ONTOEQ Value) |
         (CONST BOP CONST) | (CONST) | ()
TOP    := BEFORE | AFTER | COINCIDES | DURING |
FINISHES |
         FINISHEDBY | STARTS | STARTEDBY | MEETS |
  METBY |
         OVERLAPS | OVERLAPPEDBY | INCLUDES
BOP    := AND | OR
ROP    := LT | GT | LE | GE | EQ | NE
```

An *interaction event pattern* (IEP) is defined by imposing *constraints* in the attributes of the interaction event model. Each constraint restricts an attribute's (Attr) value. Our interaction event ontology serves as a vocabulary for domain experts to specify the attributes' values. If an attribute's value refers to an ontological concept, ONTOEQ keyword is used which means that the attribute should be matched semantically. For non-ontological concept, the relational operators (ROP) such as less than (LT), greater than (GT), less than or equal (LE), greater than or equal (GE), equal to (EQ) and not equal (NE) are used to specify constraint. The binary logical operators (BOP) AND and OR can be used to compose multiple constraints in an interaction pattern.

An interaction event can have one of two temporal features: instantaneous/point-in-time (zero duration) or interval-based (duration greater than zero). For *point-in-time*, the correlation between events could only be one of three types: "before", "after" or "coincides". For *interval-based*, as introduced by Allen [28], the correlation types between events become thirteen: "before", "after", "during", "coincides", "meets", "met by", "overlaps", "overlapped by", "starts", "started by", "finishes", "finished by" and "includes". We refer these correlation types as temporal operators (TOP).

A *complex interaction event pattern* (CIEP) correlates two IEPs or complex interaction event patterns using a temporal operator or binary logical operator. CIEP also can be specified by complementing (using NOT) a complex interaction event pattern.

## 5.4.6 Human-Readable Situation Specification Language

An important aspect of situation specification is there readability and user friendliness. Situation specification language presented in the previous section aimed mostly at developers. However, it sometimes needed that these rules are readable and understandable by the domain experts or non-technical persons. Ideally, they should be able to change the rules or even write new ones. Looking at a rule, one should immediately have an idea of what it is about. Thus, we propose a *human-readable situation specification language (SituLang)* which is close to the natural English language.

---

when
[not]{An atomic interaction event $aie_id$ occurred
[in "platform_name"] [which is a message
communication, {type "value"} and|or {from actor "
value"} and|or {from role "value"} and|or {in
place "value"} and|or {to actor "value"} and|or {
to role "value"} and|or {related with "value"
relationship} and|or {discuss about "value"} and|
or {at time "value"} and|or {duration is less than
or equal to | is less than | is greater than or
equal to | is greater than | is equal to | equals
"value"}]}

[and|or]

[not]{A complex interaction event $cie_id$ observed
between $ie_id$ and $aie_id$, where interaction
event $aie_id$ is a message communication, {type "
value"} and|or {from actor "value"} and|or {from
role "value"} and|or {in place "value"} and|or {to
actor "value"} and|or {to role "value"} and|or {
related with "value" relationship} and|or {discuss
about "value"} and|or {at time "value"} and|or {
duration is less than or equal to | is less than |
is greater than or equal to | is greater than |
is equal to | equals "value"}, has occurred"before
"|"after"| "coincides"| "during"|"finishes"|"
finishedby"|"includes"|"meets"|"metby"|"starts"|"
startedby"|"overlaps"|"overlappedby" $ie_id$ [by "
value"|by "value1" and "value2"|between "value1"
and "value2"]}

then
Notify "situation" //or any additional actions

---

The syntax of our human-readable situation specification is shown above, where the word in-between '$' represents variable name, '""' represents fix attribute value, '[' represents optional terms, '{' represents zero or more terms. The symbol '—' represents choice. In this language, a situation is composed of a set of sentences. Each sentence describes either (1) a type of simple interaction event with constraints in its properties, or (2) a complex interaction event which describes a correlation of an interaction event with another already stated simple or complex interaction event.

### 5.4.7 Situation Inference Example

A person's situation, for example, *"watching a game in a stadium"* can be inferred from her interaction activities in Facebook. We can say a person is most likely watching a game in a stadium—*if the person posts her current location "at stadium" and after a while posts something about sports or stadium.* We can specify this situation using our human-readable situation specification language as follows:

```
when
An atomic interaction event IE1 occurred in "
   Facebook" which is a message communication, type "
   PostingCurrentLocation" and in place ''Stadium''
A complex interaction event CIE1 observed between
   IE1 and IE2, where interaction event IE2 is a
   message communication, type "PostingSomeThing" and
   discuss about ''Sports'', has occurred ''after''
   IE1
then
Notify ''Person is watching a game in a stadium''
```

Following the situation specification syntax defined in Sect. 5.4.5, the above situation can be rewrite as follows:

```
IE1 := InteractionEvent(hasType EQ "PostingCurrent
Location" AND
                     atPlace ONTOEQ "Stadium")
IE2 := InteractionEvent(hasType ONTOEQ "PostingSome
Thing" AND
                     about ONTOEQ "Sports")
CIE1 := IE2 AFTER IE1
SITU(Person is watching a game in a stadium) := CIE1
```

Note that in this situation specification rule, we have used the EQ relational operator with the *hasType* property in specifying the *IE1* interaction event pattern (IEP), because *PostingCurrentLocation* is one of the possible primitive values for the *hasType* property (*i.e.,* no further classification of this concept, see Fig. 5.10) and an interaction event of the *PostingCurrentLocation* type will be reported with the *hasType* attribute value equal to *PostingCurrentLocation* (see example *ie*1 in Sect. 5.4.4). Thus, in this case, we do not need to use ONTOEQ for semantic matching. On the other hand, in the *IE*2 pattern we should use ONTOEQ with the *hasType* property as *PostingSomeThing* is not a primitive value and thus semantic matching is required. For instance, *IE*2 pattern has restricted the *hasType* attribute value *PostingSomeThing*, where the *ie*2 and *ie*3 interaction events are reported with the *hasType* attribute value *PostingPhoto* and *PostingStatus*, respectively. Therefore, without semantic matching the inference system cannot identify that the *ie*2 and *ie*3 interaction events match the *IE*2 pattern.

The key benefit of incorporating the *IntEO* in the situation specification language is that it simplifies the situation rules by reducing complexity. For instance, the *IntEO* simplifies the *constraint* in the *IE*2 by allowing us to state *hasType* ONTOEQ *"PostingSomeThing"* in place of

```
hasType  EQ  "PostingPhotoAlbum" OR
hasType  EQ  "PostingLifeEvent" OR
hasType  EQ  "PostingPhoto" OR
hasType  EQ  "PostingMusic" OR
hasType  EQ  "PostingStatus" OR
hasType  EQ  "PostingVideo" OR
hasType  EQ  "PostingSCurrentLocation"
```

This detected situation, *i.e.*, *"Person is watching a game in a stadium"*, can be used by different applications and services. For example, an online ticket selling service can identify a person of interest to notify the schedule of the next tournament; automatically increase phone ring tone volume because of a noisy environment.

## 5.5 Summary

In this chapter, we have presented our *approach to reasoning about* different types of social context information. We have considered *four* aspects of reasoning social context information such as *property, time-stamp, abstraction* and *temporal correlation*.

We have adopted an ontology-based approach and used OWL2-DL for *deriving, deducing* and *abstracting* social context information. We have presented reasoning rules to *deriving* different types of *family* relationships from *social role* and *gender* information. We have shown how to *derive* new types of *friend* relationship from already defined friend relationships and their properties. We have also presented reasoning rules to *deducing situations* considering their time-stamp aspect, and further *abstracting* the deduced situations to define more useful situations.

In related to the *temporal correlation* aspect, we have further presented a novel approach to *inferring* users' situations from their *interaction events* in different social interaction platforms. The novelties of our approach are that we have considered users' *interaction events* in inferring situations, and we have combined the *semantic* and *temporal* aspects of these events in defining and specifying situations. In doing so, we have developed an *interaction event ontology (IntEO)* to capture users' interaction activities in different platforms. To capture both the general and domain-specific concepts, the *IntEO* includes an *upper* interaction event ontology which can be customized and specialised to form *domain-specific* ontologies. As examples, we have presented domain-specific ontologies for Facebook and cooperative convoy application. To allow developers to specify situations based on interaction event patterns and their correlations, we have proposed a *situation specification language* that integrates the *IntEO* with temporal relations, where the *IntEO* serves as a vocabulary for developers to specify the attribute values in an interaction event pattern and consequently simplifies the situation rules. We further proposed a human-readable situation specification language for domain experts, which is close to the natural English language and thus assists non-technical person to understand, define and modify situation specifications.

# Chapter 6
# Social Context Management

In Chaps. 4 and 5, we have presented *ontologies*, description logic based *inference rules* and a situation specification *language* for *modelling* and *reasoning about* different types of social context information. In this chapter, we introduce our approach to *managing* access to such social context information by considering users' *privacy* preferences (Sect. 6.1). We also present our approach to *modelling* runtime social interactions and *managing* their runtime *adaptation* (Sect. 6.2).

## 6.1 Managing Access to Social Context Information

Users' social context information is inherently sensitive. In pervasive social computing environments, users might need to allow others to access their social context information for greater benefits but this may also compromise their privacy. Thus, users should be able to retain control over who has access to their personal information under which conditions. We adopt *policy-based* access control to allow users to control their social context information. In this regard, we propose an *ontology-based* socially-aware access control policy model (*SACOnto*) (Sect. 6.1.1) and a *description logic* based language (Sect. 6.1.2) to represent and specify users' privacy preferences. We also present a mechanism to check the inconsistency in policy specification (Sect. 6.1.2) and to enforce users' policies while accessing their social context information (Sect. 6.1.3).

The main advantages of our approach are that a DL reasoner can used for (1) detecting automatically inconsistencies in the specification of policies, and (2) executing policies.

© Springer International Publishing Switzerland 2016                    97
M.A. Kabir et al., *Pervasive Social Computing*,
DOI 10.1007/978-3-319-29951-8_6

## 6.1.1 A Socially-Aware Access Control Policy Model

We propose an access control policy model to protect the users' social context information based on the context information itself. Thus, our policy model, called Socially-aware Access Control Ontology (*SACOnto*) (see Fig. 6.1), reuses the concepts from the core *SCOnto* model to define under which conditions (i.e. the social context) a given resource is accessible. The accessible resource could be any social context information (e.g. relationship, situation), including the meta-information related to any relationship of a user such as the *numbers* of friends and colleagues.

Studies have revealed that users want to define policies that apply to all people with certain relationships or roles rather than explicitly name each person [120, 177]. Thus in access conditions, we consider both the requester's role and her relationships with the information owner to reflect the way users tend to group similar sets of people when deciding to share resources with other users. Therefore, our model is able to represent existing policy models, such as the popular role-based model [79] and the recently emerged relationship-based model [80], with enhanced capabilities.

In addition, we consider the owner's current situation information which is another important aspect of defining policies [177]. Users typically specify their policies using combinations of the main dimensions driving access control decisions, including

- Who is requesting access and what is her relationship with the owner?
- What role is the requester playing?
- The (current) situation of the owner when the request is made?
- What type of resource is being requested and what are its characteristics?

Our ontological model enables a user (owner) to specify logical relations between the above fundamental elements. In the owner's conceptual model, such aspects as who/what/when dimensions are typically interrelated. Our model (Fig. 6.1) captures these dimensions which can be read as follows: A *Policy*, is defined using a policy id (an instance of the *Policy* class) and a *policyStatement*, *isDefinedBy* an *Owner* which specifies *Access decision* [*Denied* or *Granted* or *GrantedInGL1* (granted in granularity level 1), and so on] for *Requester*(s) who *plays* a *SocialRole*, *relatedTo Owner* and *hasRelationship* with owner named *SocialRelationship*, *asksFor* a *Resource*, when the *Owner hasSituation Situation*.

There are a number of constraints related to the *SCACOnto*. For instance, a policy should have exactly one policy statement; an access decision can not be a member of multiple access types, e.g. both granted and denied. The OWL2-DL representation of these constraints are as follows:

$$Policy \sqsubseteq\, = 1\, policyStatement$$
$$Granted \sqcap Denied \sqsubseteq \bot \tag{6.1}$$

A complete list can be found in Appendix A.2.1.

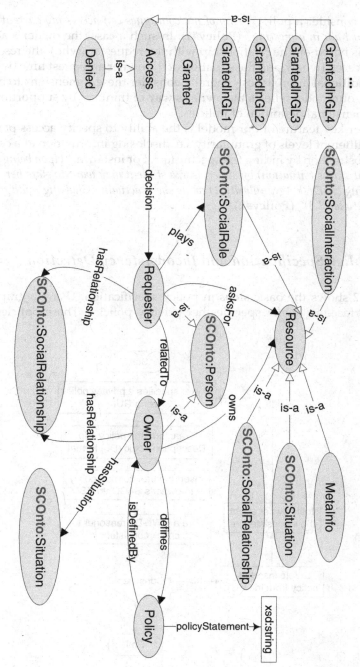

Fig. 6.1: Access control policy model

Let us consider a policy, *"Any of my colleagues can access my current situation when I am in a meeting"* (**Policy#1**). In such a case, the owner's access decision is based on the relationship with the requester (who), the resource being accessed (what), and the situation of the owner at request time (when). While traditional approaches generally consider these dimensions to be orthogonal, our model reflects the owner's way of thinking by supporting the cross-dimensional definition of policies.

Another key feature of our model is the ability to specify access permissions at different levels of granularity, i.e. disclosing information at a certain level of abstraction by hiding the specific fact. For instance, *"Upon being asked the current status (situation) by supervisor, a student may want to state her situation as being 'AtDesk' (granularity 1) while she is actually 'Chatting' with friends (granularity level 3)"* (**Policy#2**).

### 6.1.2  Policy Specification and Inconsistency Detection

Figure 6.2 shows the basic steps in policy specification. Using a graphical user interface, an owner specifies her privacy policies. These policies can

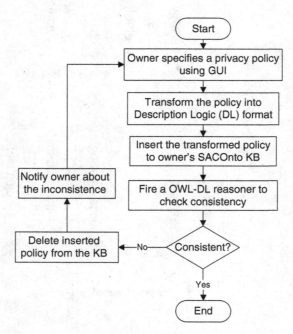

Fig. 6.2: Policy specification steps

then be easily transformed to the Description Logic (DL) format. The template of our policy rule in the DL is defined as follows:

*Denied* / *Granted* / *GrantedInGL*?**n** ≡ *Access* ⊓ ∃*decision*(*Requester* ⊓

∃*hasRelationship*.?**SocialRelationship** ⊓ ∃*asksFor*.?**Resource** ⊓

∃*plays*.?**SocialRole** ⊓

∃*relatedTo*.(*Owner* ⊓ ∃*hasSituation*.?**Situation**))

where bold words with a preceding '?' mark are variables that will be filled based on the owner's privacy preference statements. For example, we can represent the above Policy#1 and Policy#2 as follows:
Policy#1:

*Granted* ≡ *Access* ⊓

∃ *decision*(*Requester* ⊓ ∃*asksFor*.**Situation** ⊓

∃ *hasRelationship*.**Colleague** ⊓

∃ *relatedTo*.(*Owner* ⊓ ∃*hasSituation*.**Meeting**))

Policy#2:

*GrantedInGL1* ≡ *Access* ⊓

∃ *decision*(*Requester* ⊓ ∃*asksFor*.**Situation** ⊓

∃ *hasRelationship*.**Student-Supervisor** ⊓

∃ *relatedTo*.(*Owner* ⊓ ∃*hasSituation*.**Chatting**))

Once the policy is transformed to the DL format, it is inserted into the owner's access control ontology. For instance, Policy#1 and Policy#2 will be inserted into the *SACOnto* as an *equivalent class* of *Granted* class and *GrantedInGL1* class, respectively.

Let us assume that the owner specified another policy, "*An admin-staff can NOT access my current situation when I am in individual meeting*" (Policy#3), which can be represented in DL format as follows:
Policy#3:

*Denied* ≡ *Access* ⊓

∃ *decision*(*Requester* ⊓ ∃*asksFor*.**Situation** ⊓

∃ *hasRelationship*.**AcademicStaff-AdminStaff** ⊓

∃ *relatedTo*.(*Owner* ⊓ ∃*hasSituation*.**IndividualMeeting**))

The *AcademicStaff-AdminStaff* relationship (used in Policy#3) is a subclass of *Colleague* (used in Policy#1) and the *IndividualMeeting* (used in Policy#3) is a subclass of *Meeting* (used in Policy#1). However, Policy#1 grants the access and Policy#3 denies the access, where the *Granted* and *Denied* classes are *disjoint* with each other (according to the constraint 6.1). Thus, Policy#3 makes the owner's *SACOnto* KB inconsistent as it violates the disjoint constraint by overlapping with Policy#1. During the policy specification process, if such inconsistency occurs the inconsistent policy will be rejected and deleted, and the owner will be notified.

### 6.1.3 Policy Enforcement in Accessing Social Context Information

When an access request or query comes from an user's application which basically corresponds to invoking a function from the query APIs (see Sect. 7.1.5), some facts about the context of the query are temporarily inserted into the *SACOnto* knowledge base to get the access decision based on the information owner's privacy preferences. The following steps describe this process.

1. Identify the individual (who requests information) of the *SCOnto:Person* class as an individual of the *Requester* class, say *John*
2. Insert an individual, say *resourceIns*, into the requested resource class such as *MetaInfo* or *Situation* or *SocialRelationship* or any of their subclasses
3. Insert an individual, say *accessRequestResult*, into the *Access* class
4. Link the inserted *Requester* individual, i.e. *John*, to the *Resource* individual, i.e. *resourceIns*, using *asksFor* object property
5. Link the inserted *Access* individual, i.e. *accessRequestResult*, to the *Requester* individual, i.e. *John*, using *decision* object property

After that a DL reasoner is fired which classifies the individual of *Access* class to one of its subclasses, i.e. *Denied*, *GrantedInGL1*, and so on, based on the defined policies. The query processing manager considers this result to answer the query.

Let us consider a scenario, *"Alice, who is a graduate student, specifies her privacy policy as Policy#2. John who is the supervisor of Alice requests the current situation of Alice while Alice is chatting with her friend via instant messaging"*. The process of checking Alice's privacy preferences regarding that request by following the above mentioned steps are: (1) Specify *John* as an individual of *Requester* class, (2) insert an individual, namely *resourceIns*, to the *Situation* class, (3) insert an individual, namely *accessRequestResult*, to the *Access* class, (4) link *John* to the *resourceIns* using *asksFor* object property, and (5) link *accessRequestResult* to *John* using *decision* object property. Finally, the DL reasoner is fired which classifies the *accessRequestResult* as an individual of *GrantedInGL1* (one of the subclasses of *Access* class), which means that in the above scenario Alice allows John to know her current situation at granularity level 1. Thus, in this case, John will get a reply from the query processing module about Alice's current situation as 'AtDesk' (instead of 'Chatting').

## 6.2 Modelling and Managing Social Interactions

There are three major requirements of developing an interaction-centric socially-aware application for facilitating social interactions (as identified in Sect. 2.2.2):

- *First*, the application should support social interactions complying with the agreed interaction relationships, i.e. constraints and obligations.
- *Second*, to facilitate collaboration, the application needs to provide a coordinated view of the interactions.
- *Third*, the application needs to support runtime adaptation as the interaction relationships evolve over time, and need to adapt with the changes in requirements and environments.

In Sect. 4.3.3, we have presented an *interaction-oriented relationship ontology* and a *social interaction ontology*, which allow us to capture different types of *interaction-oriented social relationships* between collaborative actors and their associated *agreements* and *constraints*. In this section, we present an approach to modelling *runtime social interactions* where the runtime models are built based on the information captured in the ontologies. The runtime models *enforce* agreements and constraints while *mediating* social interactions between actors. Such *agreements* and *constraints*, and thus models, are also subject to change. To address this issue, we present an approach to *managing adaptation* in such runtime models.

A promising approach to support *runtime changes* is to develop adaptation mechanisms that leverage software models, referred to as *models@run.time* [44]. Runtime models provide *"abstractions of runtime phenomena"* [82]. That is, the *models*[1] should represent the system and should be *linked* in such a way that they constantly *mirror* the system and its current *state* and *behaviour*; if the system changes, the representations of the system—the models—should also change, and vice versa. A runtime model can be seen as a *live* development model that enables dynamic evolution and the realisation of software design [44].

To fulfill the aforementioned requirements of developing interaction-centric socially-aware applications, we propose an approach to modelling *social interactions @run.time* (Sect. 6.2.1), and a technique to perform *runtime adaptation* in a consistent manner (Sect. 6.2.2).

---

[1] Through out this section *model(s)* refers to *runtime model(s)*.

## 6.2.1 *Modelling Social Interactions*

*Role* based approaches have been increasingly used in software system design and implementation. Roles, in different variations, have been applied in many fields such as computer supported collaborative works, role based access control, multi-agent systems, and object modelling [193]. In the access control domain, the notion of roles has been used to represent a set of responsibilities and privileges associated with a particular position within an organisation [158]. In CSCW and group-aware applications, the notion of role has been used to provide a natural abstraction for representing users without requiring prior knowledge of their individual identities [62, 124]. In multi-agent systems, the concept of role has been used as an abstraction for representing an entity's behaviour [50], where a role specifies a functional behaviour of an agent.

We have taken a role based approach to model social interactions as it has been evaluated as being very useful in modelling entities, their relationships, functions and interactions [51]. Our approach utilises the notion of roles for functional abstractions. Among the many different approaches to role modelling [171], one common way to develop a role based model is to use organisational concepts [60]. According to Daft [63] *"organisations are social entities that are goal directed, deliberately structured, and coordinated activity systems, linked to the environment"*. A similar view has taken by Rollison [152], who says *"organisations are artifacts, that are goal directed social entities with structured activities"*. Organisations are typically viewed as a managed network of roles that decompose the abstract functions of the organisation into descriptions that can be performed by role players (e.g. people, subsystems, other organisations). Organisation theory addresses the structuring of organisations in order to more effectively achieve those goals (e.g. [101]). The structure defines how the organisation is composed, i.e. what units it consists of and what are the relationships or the connections between these units.

We adopt the view of organisation as a composition structure of dynamic relationships between social roles in order to *model* runtime social interactions. *Role Oriented Adaptive Design (ROAD)* [59] introduces such an organisational structure to define self-managed software composites. In this work, we use ROAD and further extend it to define adaptable runtime social interaction models. ROAD defines roles or positions of a composite. Players can come and play these roles. We enrich the *interactions* in ROAD with the new constructs of *obligation* and *conversation*. We specialise the ROAD composite structure (meta model) from the *domain* and *player* perspectives. To provide a collaborative view of runtime social interactions among actors, we propose a *domain-centric social interaction model (DSIM)* (Sect. 6.2.1.1). To facilitate collaboration, the applications need to provide a coordinated view of the interactions, allow a user to specify his/her coordination preferences and perform the coordination in an automated manner. To address this requirement, we further propose a *player-centric social interaction model (PSIM)* (Sect. 6.2.1.2).

### 6.2.1.1 Domain-Centric Social Interaction Model

The *Domain-centric Social Interaction Model* (DSIM) provides a structure of the relationships among social roles associated with a particular domain or environment such as a company, a cooperative convoy, and so on. The DSIM grouped the social interactions (stored in the social interaction ontology) from a domain perspective. Figure 6.3 shows the meta-model of the DSIM, which adopts and extends the ROAD meta-model for creating adaptive software. The *DSIM meta-model* comprises four key elements: *social role*, *social relationship*, *player*, and *organiser role*. To visualise the structure of the social interaction model, we define a set of graphical notations (see Fig. 6.4).

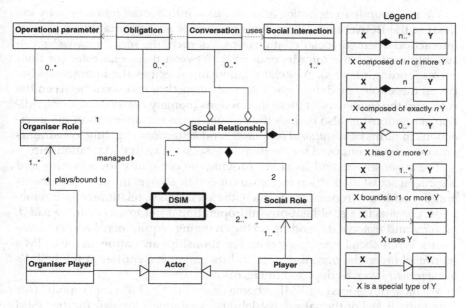

Fig. 6.3: Meta-model of DSIM

A *social role* (called *functional role* in ROAD) defines and represents expected functional interactions of a participating actor.[2] Social roles are loosely-coupled elements and are modelled as first class entities, and as such they are separated from their players who play those roles. An *interaction-oriented social relationship* (called *contract* in ROAD) is an association between *two* social roles, which defines and represents the *social interactions* (called *interactions* in ROAD) between them.

---

[2] We use the term *"actor"* and *"player"* interchangeable throughout this book.

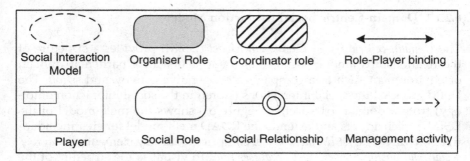

Fig. 6.4: Graphical notations for representing social interaction model

We incorporate *conversation* and *obligation* into a *social relationship* by extending the ROAD *contract*, as these constructs are important to represent interaction-oriented social relationships. As such, the *social relationship* can suitably captures the interdependencies between the social roles (or their corresponding players). A social relationship specifies the interactions between these roles by defining what *social interactions* can occur between the roles and the sequences of these interactions (namely *conversations*). In addition, a relationship also defines the *non-functional* requirements of the interactions in terms of *operational parameters* and *obligations* (e.g. time constraints on interactions) imposed on the players associated with that relationship.

The *organiser role* and its *player* provide the capability for *managing* and *adapting* a social interaction model to cope with *changes* in the requirements and dynamic environments. As such, the social roles, relationships, interactions, conversations, obligations and operational parameters can be *added*, *modified* and *removed* depending on the changing requirements and environments. While social roles, players and relationships are entities at the DSIM's *functional* layer, the organiser role and its player are entities at the DSIM's *management* layer, as depicted in Fig. 6.5.

We have developed an XML schema based on the DSIM meta-model (see Appendix E.1). For the sake of readability, we define a *template* for the DSIM (see Fig. 6.6) by using a pseudo notation based on the DSIM XML schema. In this notation, the terms in boldface represent the XML tags in our schema. Social interactions among users (in an interaction-centric socially-aware application) are designed using the *DSIM template*.

To illustrate the domain-centric social interaction model, we use the cooperative convoy application scenario, introduced in Sect. 2.2.1, as an example. In that scenario, there are three domains that need to be modelled, namely, the two car rental companies (Budget and AVIS) and the cooperative convoy.

The Budget rental company allows travel guide and roadside assistance services, and the company has its own policies and constraints to use these services through the telematics system in the cars rented from them. These

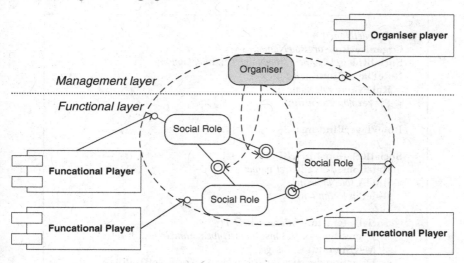

Fig. 6.5: Separation of *functional* and *management* aspects

constraints and policies are captured in the domain-centric social interaction model of the Budget, called *BudgetDSIM*, as shown in Fig. 6.7. This model comprises four social roles (Rented Car, Rental Company, Travel Guide and Roadside Assistance), four interaction-centric social relationships (R2, R3, R4 and R5), and one organiser role. These relationships represent the interaction constraints and agreements (as specified in the scenario) among the social roles. For instance, R2 (*RentedCar-TravelGuide*) relationship represents that *"upon receiving a route request from a rented car, travel guide should send a route notification by 15 seconds"*. Figure 6.8 shows the representation of this agreement which consists of two social interactions (*i7* and *i8*), one conversation (*c1*) and one related obligation (*o3*). The *i7* social interaction represents the route request from rented car to travel guide, while the *i8* represents the route notification from travel guide to rented car. The *c1* conversation imposes the sequence related constraints between these two social interactions, while *o1* imposes time related obligation.

The Budget company is the owner of this runtime model and controls it through the organiser role. The customer, e.g. the tourist group, who rents Car#1 plays the rented car role through the telematics system of that car. The roadside assistance service (e.g. RACV.com.au) and the travel guide service (e.g. travelguide.org) play the roadside assistance and travel guide roles respectively. A complete description of the *BudgetDSIM* is presented in Appendix C.1.2.

On the other hand, the AVIS company allows access to traffic management and roadside assistance services. Like Budget, we also model the domain-centric runtime social interactions for AVIS, called *AVISDSIM*, as

```
DSIM modelName{
  OrganiserRole orgRoleName;
  SocialRole roleName`1, roleName`2,...,roleName`n;
  RolePlayerBinding b`1{
    RoleName roleName`n;
    PlayerplayerIdentity;
  };
  RolePlayerBinding b`2{...},...b`n{...};

  SocialRelationship relID`1{
    RelationshipName rel`name;
    RoleA roleName`m;
    RoleB roleName`n;

    SocialInteraction interactionID`1{
      //message format msg`name(type:paramName,...)
      MsgSignature message;
      Direction direction;//RoleAToRoleB or RoleBToRoleA
      InteractionType type`name;//any string (optional)
      RelatedObligation obgID`n;
    };
    SocialInteraction interactionID`2{...},...,interactionID`n{...};

    OperationalParam opParamID`1{
      OPParamName param`name;//any string
      OPParamValue value;//any non-negative number
      TimeUnit tUunit;//MS, SEC, MIN, HOUR or DAY
      DistanceUnit dUnit;//MM, CM, M or KM
    };
    OperationalParam opParamID`2{..},...,opParamID`n{...};

    Obligation oblID`1{
      Timer timer;//either DURATION or PERIOD
      RelatedOperationalParam opParamID`n;
    };
    Obligation oblID`2{...},...,oblID`n{...};

    Conversation conID`1{
      SocialInteractionX interactionID`m;
      SocialInteractionY interactionID`n;
      Sequence sequence`type;//leadsTo or precedes
      RelatedObligation obgID`n;
    };
    Conversation conID`2{...},...,conID`n{...};
  };
  SocialRelationship relID`2{...},...,relID`n{...};
};
```

Fig. 6.6: A template for the domain-centric social interaction model (DSIM)

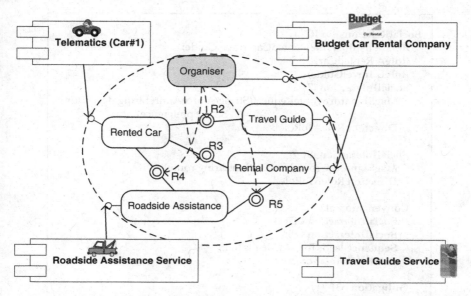

Fig. 6.7: Budget domain-centric social interaction model (*BudgetDSIM*)

shown in Fig. 6.9. It also consists of four social roles. Unlike Budget, it does not have a travel guide role. However, it has a traffic management role. There are four interaction-oriented social relationships, i.e. R6, R7, R8 and R9, among these roles, which represent agreements and constraints among social roles, according to the specification in the scenario. The AVIS company plays the organiser role of this runtime model as the company is the owner of this model. The customer, e.g. the tourist group, who rents Car#2 plays the rented car role through the telematics system of that car. The roadside assistance service (e.g. RACV.com.au) and the traffic management service (e.g. VicRoad.org) play the roadside assistance and traffic management roles respectively. A complete description of the *AVISDSIM* is presented in Appendix C.1.3.

Like Budget and AVIS, the interaction-relationship between the drivers of Car#1 and Car#2 is modelled from a domain perspective, called *ConvoyD-SIM*, as shown in Fig. 6.10. According to their agreements, it consists of two social roles: *LeadingCar (LC)* and *FollowingCar (FC)*, and their interactions are captured in the *R1 (LeadingCar-FollowingCar)* relationship. The Car#1 plays the *LeadingCar* role, while the Car#2 plays the *FollowingCar* role. Car#1 is also designated to play the organiser role of the *ConvoyDSIM*.

Figure 6.11 shows a partial notational description of *ConvoyDSIM*. It includes description of the *i1* social interaction, and its associated obligation (*o1*) and operational parameter (*p1*), which represents the agreement

```
SocialRelationship R2{
  RelationshipName RentedCar-TravelGuide;
  RoleA RentedCar;
  RoleB TravelGuide;
  SocialInteraction i7{
    MsgSignature routeRequest(String sourceAddr, String destAddr,
                              String preference);
    Direction RoleAToRoleB;
  };
  SocialInteraction i8{
    MsgSignature routeNotification(String route);
    Direction RoleBToRoleA;
  };
  Conversation c1{
    SocialInteractionX i7;
    SocialInteractionX i8;
    Sequence leadsTo; // i7 leadsTo i8
    RelatedObligation o3;
  };
  Obligation o3{
    Timer DURATION;
    RelatedOperationalParam p3;
  };
  OperationalParam p3{
    OPParamName maxTimeDelay;
    OPParamValue 15;
    TimeUnit SEC;
  };
  ......
};
```

Fig. 6.8: A partial description of *R2* relationship in *BudgetDSIM*

*"following car should send a position update to the leading car every 10 seconds"*.
The complete description of *ConvoyDSIM* is presented in Appendix C.1.1.

### 6.2.1.2 Player-Centric Social Interaction Model

In addition to the common view of a domain-centric social interaction
model, a player may have its own perception or view of the domain with respect to the role(s) it plays and the interactions it participates in that domain.
Moreover, a player may operate in different domains. Thus, we also model
the social interaction from a player's perspective, namely *Player-centric Social Interaction Model* (PSIM). The PSIM provides an overall view of all the

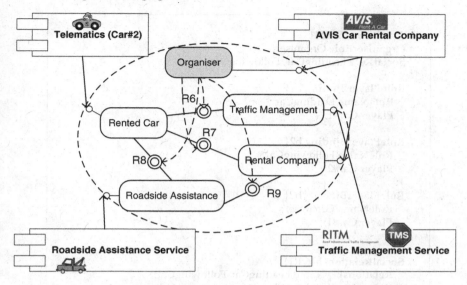

Fig. 6.9: AVIS domain-centric social interaction model (*AVISDSIM*)

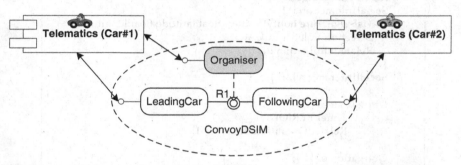

Fig. 6.10: Convoy domain-centric social interaction model (*ConvoyDSIM*)

interactions of an individual across different domains and allows coordination of its interactions across these domains.

As presented in the previous section, the *R1* interaction-relationship of *ConvoyDSIM* captures the agreements between LC and FC in terms of their social interactions. But some of these interactions are driven by or depend on their interactions with other associated domains (i.e. Budget and AVIS). For instance, when the road block information is received from the traffic management service (TMS), FC should immediately forward it to LC. Likewise, when the route information is received from the travel guide service, LC should forward it to the LC. However, in some cases the driver may want to carry out these activities automatically with less or no explicit human intervention. For example, the driver of FC may want to forward the

```
DSIM ConvoyDSIM{
   OrganiserRole Organiser;
   SocialRole LeadingCar, FollowingCar;

   RolePlayerBinding b1{
      RoleName LeadingCar;
      Player Car#1;
   };
   RolePlayerBinding b2{
      RoleName FollowingCar;
      Player Car#2;
   };
   RolePlayerBinding b2{
      RoleName Organiser;
      Player Car#1;
   };

   SocialRelationship R1{
      RelationshipName LeadingCar-FollowingCar;
      RoleA LeadingCar;
      RoleB FollowingCar;
      SocialInteraction i1{
         MsgSignature notifyPosition(float:latitude,float:longitude);
         Direction RoleBToRoleA;
         RelatedObligation o1;
      };
      SocialInteraction i2{..},...;

      Obligation o1{
            Timer PERIOD;
            RelatedOperationalParam p1;
      };
      Obligation o2{...};

      OperationalParam p1{
         OPParamName posUpdateFreq;
         OPParamValue 10;
         TimeUnit SEC;
      };
      OperationalParam p2{...};
};
```

Fig. 6.11: A partial description of the convoy domain-centric social interaction model (*ConvoyDSIM*)

road block information to LC as soon as it is received from the TMS. The player-centric model addresses these issues by introducing the coordinator role which allows player to coordinate (automatically or manually) his/her social interactions.

Like DSIM, the PSIM is also a structured composition of social roles. Like a DSIM, a PSIM contains *social roles*, *players* and an *organiser role*. In PSIM, however, all social roles are played by the actor[3] in question and are connected with the *coordinator role* through the *role-centric relationships*. Thus, in addition, it contains a *coordinator role* and *role-centric relationships*. Therefore, the PSIM meta-model comprises of five key elements: *social role*, *coordinator role*, *role-centric social relationship*, *player*, and *organiser role*. Figure 6.12 shows the meta-model of PSIM. Like DSIM, we also define a template for the PSIM (see Fig. 6.13) based on the PSIM meta-model.

The *coordinator role* is a means of achieving inter-domain coordination, i.e. interactions in one domain can be used for interactions in another domain. In the cooperative convoy scenario, drivers relate their interactions in their own rental company with each other in their cooperative convoy. For instance, Car#2 should send road blocks information to Car#1 when Car#2 receives that information from the traffic management service. The *coordinator role* provides a position to the player/user in question for coordinating his/her social interactions across multiple domains. A user (driver) can coordinate interactions explicitly through the application's user interface or he/she may define some rules or use an intelligent application to coordinate his/her interactions on behalf.

A *role-centric relationship* is the *aggregation* of all the relationships associated with a particular *social role* in a *DSIM* model, but localised in the player-centric model. Algorithm 1 presents the aggregation procedure of computing a role-centric social relationship for a particular social roles in a domain-centric social interaction model. The algorithm takes an instance of a runtime DSIM model and a social role name, say $r$, of that model from which perspective the role-centric relationship needs to be computed. First, it creates an empty instance of social relationship. After that, it invokes the management operation *getAllRel4Role* to get all the relationships connected with the target social role $r$. Finally, the algorithm adds these relationships to the empty social relationship instance which represents the role-centric social relationship for the social role $r$.

Figure 6.14 shows the player-centric social interaction models of Car#1 and Car#2, called *Car#1PSIM* and *Car#2PSIM* respectively, and how they relate to the domain-centric models (i.e. *BudgetDSIM*, *ConvoyDSIM* and *AVISDSIM*). According to the cooperative convoy scenario, Car#2 plays the *FollowingCar* role in *ConvoyDSIM* and *RentedCar* role in *AVISDSIM*. Thus, the *Car#2PSIM* contains *FollowingCar* and *RentedCar* social roles and their associated role-centric social relationships, i.e. *Rr3* and *Rr4*. The *Rr4* is the

---

[3] Person with an application.

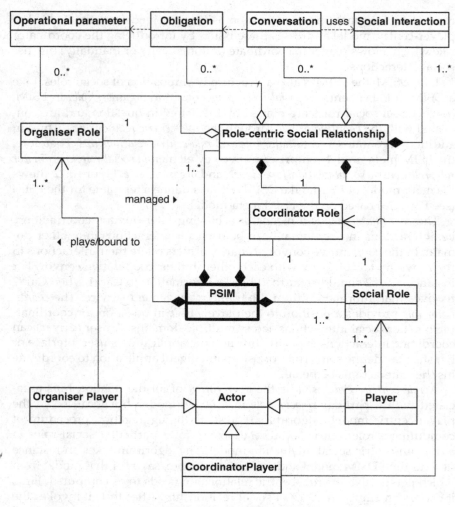

Fig. 6.12: Meta-model of PSIM

role-centric social relationship of *RentedCar* social role in *AVISDSIM*. There-
fore, *Rr4* is the *aggregation of R6, R7* and *R8* social relationships in the *AVIS-
DSIM*. The *Rr3* and *Rr4* connect the *Coordinator Role* to the *FollowingCar* and
*RentedCar* roles respectively. Similarly, *Car#1PSIM* consists of *LeadingCar* and
*RentedCar* social roles and their associated role-centric social relationships,
i.e. *Rr1* and *Rr2*, which connect these social roles to the *Coordinator Role*.

A *player/actor* plays social role(s) in different *DSIM* through its *PSIM*. For
instance, the Car#1 plays *RentedCar* role in *BudgetDSIM* and *LeadingCar* role

```
PSIM modelName{
    OrganiserRole orgRoleName;
    SocialRole roleName`1, roleName`2,...,roleName`n;
    CoordinatorRole coordRole;//single instance
    RolePlayerBinding b`1{...},...,b`n{...};
    RoleCentricSocialRelationship relID`1{
        RelationshipName rel`name;
        RoleA coordRole;
        RoleB roleName`i;
        SocialInteraction interactionID`1{...},...,interactionID`n{...};
        OperationalParam opParamID`1{..},...,opParamID`n{...};
        Obligation oblID`1{...},...,oblID`n{...};
        Conversation conID`1{...},...,conID`n{...};
    },relID`2{...},...,relID`n{...};
};
```

Fig. 6.13: Template for the player-centric social interaction model (PSIM)

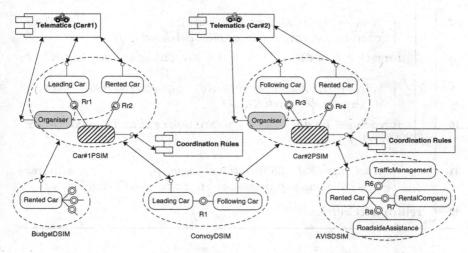

Fig. 6.14: Player-centric social interaction models of Car#1 and Car#2

in *ConvoyDSIM* through the *Car#1PSIM*. Similarly, the Car#2 plays *Rented-Car* role in *AVISDSIM* and *FollowingCar* role in *ConvoyDSIM* through the *Car#2PSIM*.

In the PSIM, the *coordinator* (role and player) does the most important work as it performs actions on behalf of the player based on his/her preferences. These *preferences* or *coordination rules* are player specific and can be defined using *Event-Condition-Action* (ECA) rules. For instance, the Car#2

---

**Algorithm 1:** ComputeRoleCentricRel (*dsim*,*r*)

**Data:** *r* is a social role and *dsim* is a domain-centric social interaction model

**Result:** a role centric relationship, *roleCentricRel*, for the social role *r*

**begin**

1    *roleCentricRel* ← *empty* /* create an empty relationship */

2    *relList* ← *getAllRel4Role*(*dsim*,*r*)            /* all social relationships connected to the social role *r* */

3    **foreach** *rel* ∈ *relList* **do**     /* *rel* is a relationship in the *relList* */

4       **foreach** *i* ∈ *rel* **do**      /* *i* is an interaction in *rel* */

5         *roleCentricRel.addInteraction*(*i*)          /* adding interaction *i* into *roleCentricRel* */

6       **foreach** *c* ∈ *rel* **do**     /* *c* is a conversation in *rel* */

7         *roleCentricRel.addConversation*(*c*)        /* adding conversation *c* into *roleCentricRel* */

8       **foreach** *o* ∈ *rel* **do**      /* *o* is an obligation in *rel* */

9         *roleCentricRel.addObligation*(*o*) /* adding obligation *o* into *roleCentricRel* */

10      **foreach** *p* ∈ *rel* **do**    /* *p* is an operational parameter in *rel* */

11        *roleCentricRel.addOperationalParam*(*p*)        /* adding operational parameter *p* into *roleCentricRel* */

12    **return** *roleCentricRel*

---

driver's preference of automatically forwarding road block information, received from traffic management service, can be represented using the following ECA rule:

### 6.2.1.3  Mediating Runtime Social Interactions

*Social interaction models (SIMs)* are not just a modeling or design-time construct, and they are also *runtime* entities that *mediate* runtime interactions

```
Coordination-Rule "Preference of the Car#2 driver"
when OnNotificationReceived //Event
then
  if (?receivedNotification == notifyRoadBlock)
  //Condition
  do  FC.notifyRoadBlock //Action
```

between actors. Interactions among an actor,[4] its player-centric social interaction model (PSIM), and the relevant domain-centric social interaction models (DSIMs) are loosely coupled and use a messaging style. A runtime social interaction model/composite acts as a message *router* (see Fig. 6.15) that (1) receives messages from an actor, (2) evaluates conditions specified in associated relationships, and (3) passes the messages to another actor or a social interaction model (as a player) or notifies the actor(s) in case of any condition violation. For the PSIM, all the incoming and outgoing messages are intercepted by the *coordinator role* which is played by the person's *coordination application*. The coordination application coordinates messages on behalf of the person based on his/her preferences.

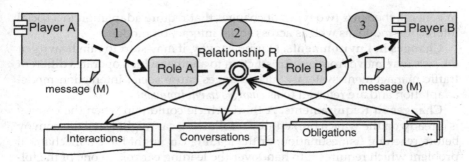

Fig. 6.15: Message based interaction via a runtime social interaction model

## 6.2.2 Managing Runtime Adaptation

Social interaction models (i.e. PSIMs and DSIMs) *externalise* users' interaction relationships from the applications, as depicted in Fig. 6.16. However, the requirements of such applications are subject to continuous *change*. Thus, both the PSIMs and DSIMs need to be managed and adapted to ensure the

---

[4] Person with an application.

proper functioning and evolution of the applications in which the social interaction models play a part. Moreover, the PSIMs are *dependent* on the DSIMs. Thus, the adaptation/modification in a DSIM should be propagated to the related PSIMs. In this section, we discuss the management and runtime adaptation of social interaction models to cope with the different types of changes.

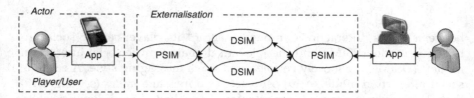

Fig. 6.16: Externalisation of users' interaction-relationships from applications

### 6.2.2.1  Types of Changes

In general, there are two types of changes that require adaptation in a social interaction model as well as across social interaction models.

**Changes in Environments.** During convoy, it may start to rain heavily or the cars may move from one jurisdiction to another which operates different traffic management systems. Such changes cause social interaction model adaptation and are referred to as *changes in environments*.

**Changes in Requirements.** A third vehicle could join when the convoy is already on the way; a broken-down following car might leave the convoy before reaching its destination; or the leading car might have a mechanical problem which requires it to handover the leading car role to one of the following cars (assuming multiple following cars). Such situations also cause adaptation, and are referred to as *changes in requirements*.

### 6.2.2.2  Adaptation in a Social Interaction Model

Runtime adaptation, often called dynamic adaptation, is a widely used term and is extensively studied in multiple disciplines. In pervasive computing, this term is used to denote any kind of modification at the running phase of the system [116]. In general, such runtime adaptation can be classified into two categories: *structure* (compositional) adaptation and *parameter* adaptation [135]. The adaptation in a social interaction model to cope with the changes in user requirements and environments also can be of these two types: *structural* (compositional) and *parametric*.

We achieve *structural* adaptation in two ways:

*Modifying topology*  Adding and removing social roles, players and relationships are carried out. For instance, a third vehicle could join the convoy when it is already on the way, or a broken-down leading car leaves the convoy before reaching the destination. These situations lead to the addition or removal of roles, players and relationships in the *ConvoyDSIM*.

*Modifying the binding between a social role and its player*  The same social role can be played by different players at different times. The binding between the role and the players is dynamic. For instance, in the *AVISDSIM*, the traffic management role can be played by different traffic management systems in the convoy at different times as the vehicle moves from one jurisdiction to another. Also due to a mechanical problem of the leading car (Car#1), the *Car#1PSIM* needs to unbind from the leading car role in the *ConvoyDSIM* and one of the following cars can be assigned to play the leading car role by binding that car's PSIM to the leading role in the *ConvoyDSIM*.

We achieve *parametric* adaptation by *modifying relationships* where adding, removing or updating interactions, obligations, conversations and operational parameters are carried out. For instance, in the *ConvoyDSIM*, the *maxDesiredDistance* parameter value may be reduced, say from 1 km to 600 m because of heavy rain.

### 6.2.2.3 Management Operations and Adaptation Rules

The organiser role provides the management capability of a *runtime social interaction model*, in short *runtime model*. The principle of separation between a role and its player is also applied to the organiser role. The organiser role is internal to a runtime model and allows its player to manage both the *structure* and *parameters* of the runtime model. The organiser role presents management rights over its runtime model, for example, to a person who owns the composite.

The organiser role exposes a management interface that contains methods for *manipulating* the *structure* (see Table 6.1), *parameter* (see Table 6.2) and *state* (see Table 6.3) of the runtime model. Operations manipulating the structure of a runtime model can be divided into two categories: Modifying topology—management operations those modify the topology of the runtime social interaction model by *adding* or *removing* social roles or social relationships, Modifying bindings—management operations those binds or unbinds a player to or from a social role belong to this category. The organiser interface also provides methods for acquiring information related

to the *structure*, *parameter* and *state* of the runtime social interaction model
(see Table 6.4), and subsequently allows the organiser player to monitor the
runtime model and perform adaptation safely.

By playing the organiser role, a *human* can perform adaptation manually
using a graphical interface. On the other hand, automatic adaptation can be
defined and performed through a *computer program* or an *agent* or a set of
predefined adaptation *rules*, as a player of organiser (depicted in Fig. 6.17).
For example, the *maxDistance* parameter value can be reset to 600 m using
the following Event-Condition-Action (ECA) rule:

```
adaptation-rule "Update maximum distance"
when
  EnvironmentChangeEvent(name=="RainingStatusValue-
                                      Changed")//Event
then
  if(rainingStatus == HEAVY_RAIN) //Condition
  callMethodInOrgInterface("updateOperationalParam("R1",
  maxDesiredDistance,600m)") //Action
```

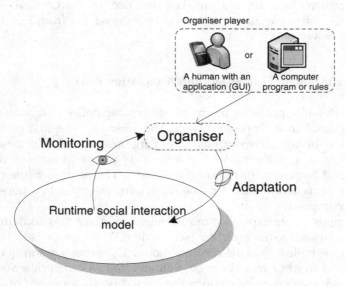

Fig. 6.17: Organiser player and adaptation

Table 6.1: Operations provided by the *organiser role* to manipulate *structure* of the runtime model

| Category | Operation name | Description |
|---|---|---|
| Modifying topology | addSocialRole | Adds a social role to a runtime model |
| | deleteSocialRole | Deletes a social role from a model |
| | addRelationship | Adds a relationship between two roles |
| | deleteRelationship | Deletes a relationship between two social roles |
| Modifying bindings | bindRolePlayer | Binds a player to a role |
| | unbindRolePlayer | Unbinds a player from a role |

Table 6.2: Operations provided by the *organiser role* to manipulate *parameter* of the runtime model

| Category | Operation name | Description |
|---|---|---|
| Modifying relationships | addInteraction | Adds an interaction to a relationship |
| | addObligation | Adds an obligation to a relationship |
| | addConversation | Adds a conversation to a relationship |
| | addOPParam | Adds an operational parameter in a relationship |
| | deleteInteraction | Deletes an interaction from a relationship |
| | deleteObligation | Deletes an obligation from a relationship |
| | deleteConversation | Deletes a conversation from a relationship |
| | deleteOPParam | Deletes an operational parameter from a relationship |
| | updateInteraction | Updates an interaction in a relationship |
| | updateObligation | Updates an obligation in a relationship |
| | updateConversation | Updates a conversation in a relationship |
| | updateOPParam | Updates an operational parameter value in a relationship |

Table 6.3: Operations provided by the *organiser role* to manipulate *state*

| Category | Operation name | Description |
|----------|----------------|-------------|
| | setRoleState | Sets a state to a social role |
| Setting state | setRelationshipState | Sets a state to a social relationship |
| | setSIMState | Sets a state to a runtime model |

Table 6.4: Operations provided by the *organiser role* to *monitor* a runtime model by acquiring information

| Category | Operation name | Description |
|----------|----------------|-------------|
| | getRoleList | Returns a list of role names in a SIM |
| Structure related | getRelationshipList | Returns a list of relationship names in a SIM |
| | getAllRel4Role | Returns a list of relationship associated with a role |
| | getRelationship | Returns a relationship name between two roles |
| | getInteractionList | Returns a list of interactions in a relationship |
| Parameter related | getConversationList | Returns a list of conversations related to an interaction |
| | getObligationList | Returns a list of obligations related to a conversation or an interaction |
| | getOPParam | Returns an operational parameter related to an obligation |
| | getRoleState | Returns the state of a social role |
| State related | getRelationshipState | Returns the state of a social relationship |
| | getSIMState | Returns the state of a SIM |

### 6.2.2.4  Social Interaction State and Safe Change

To perform adaptation in a safe manner without affecting the message flow and loss of messages, we maintain the state of each entity, i.e. the social role, social relationship and social interaction model as a whole. Figure 6.18 shows the states and their transitions. When a social interaction model is deployed all of its entities enter into the *Idle* state. When a conversation (i.e. sequence of social interactions) is started, the associated social roles and relationship move to the *Active* state and remain there until the conversation completes. A (runtime) social interaction model (i.e. DSIM or PSIM) enters into the *Active* state when any of its social role or relationship becomes *Active* and remains there until all of its roles and relationships become *Idle*. When an adaptation operation (structural or parametric) starts, the corresponding entity enters to the *Reconfiguration* state and remains there until the adaptation completes.

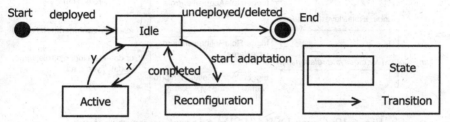

For Social Role and Relationship, x = started conversation, y = completed conversation

For Social Interaction Model, x = exist at least one active role or relationship,
y = no more active role and relationship

Fig. 6.18: State machine for Social Role, Social Relationship and SIM Composite

The time when a change cannot be made is the moment when the entity is in *Active* state. For instance, an adaptation operation cannot be performed in a social role or relationship when a conversation (request/response) associated with these entities is in progress. In that case, the adaptation request will be buffered and executed in the future after the entities enter into the *Idle* state.

### 6.2.3 Adaptation Across Social Interaction Models

As stated in Sect. 6.2.1.2, a PSIM provides a coordinated view of all the interactions of an individual across different domains, and an individual plays roles in multiple domains/DSIMs through her PSIM. Thus, an adaptation in a DSIM should be propagated to its corresponding PSIMs. Figure 6.19 shows a basic protocol for such adaptation propagation. In this protocol, the DSIM organiser triggers the adaptation in a PSIM by invoking the following methods: *triggerRoleAcquisition*, *triggerRoleRelinquishment* and *triggerUpdateRelationship*.

The adaptation across social interaction models has *three* aspects:

*Binding a player to a social role in a DSIM*   When a player binds to a role in a DSIM, her PSIM should add that role and its role-centric relationship.

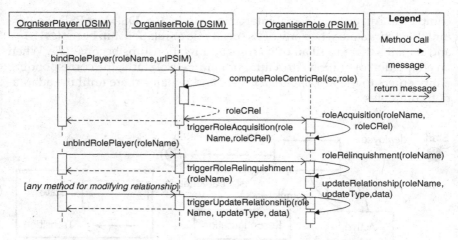

Fig. 6.19: Cross-DSIM/PSIM adaptation propagation

Thus, for the *bindRolePlayer* request, the DSIM invokes *computeRoleCentri-cRel* method to compute the role-centric relationship of a particular social role which is the aggregation of all the relationships associated with that social role in the DSIM (see Algorithm 1). Then the DSIM invokes the *triggerRoleAcquisition* method in the PSIM organiser with the social role and its role-centric relationship, as parameters. The PSIM organiser executes the *roleAcquisition* method to adapt its structure by adding a social role and relationship based on the received information.

The *roleAcquisition* method (see Algorithm 2) first adds a social role based on the received information. After that it checks the *state* of the coordinator role using the *getRoleState* management method. When the coordinator role enters into the *Idle* state which is the safe state to perform adaptation, the state of the coordinator role is set to the *Reconfiguration*. In this state, the coordinator role does not accept any incoming message and thus, it is safe to perform adaptation. A relationship between the added social role and the coordinator role is added based on the received information. Once the adaptation is completed, the state of the coordinator role is set back to the *Idle* state.

For instance, to add a new car, say Car#3, as a following car in the *ConvoyDSIM*, the *ConvoyDSIM* organiser player invokes (using organiser interface) the following management methods:

- *addSocialRole* ("FC2")—to add another following car role to the *ConvoyDSIM*,
- *addSRelationship*("LC", "FC2", *relName*)—to add a relationship between the LC and FC2 social roles,

- *addInteraction, addConversation, addObligation and addOperational-Param*—to add functional and non-functional information to the relationship as required, and
- finally, *bindRolePlayer*—to bind the third vehicle to the FC2 role.

Because the *bindRolePlayer* is invoked, the *ConvoyDSIM* (as part of the cross adaptation process) computes the role-centric relationship of the FC2 (say Rr5) using Algorithm 1 and invokes the *triggerRoleAcquisition* method in *Car#3PSIM* with *FC2* and *Rr5* as parameters. As a result, the *Car#3PSIM* updates its structure by adding the FC2 role and the *Rr5* role-centric relationship between the FC2 and Coordinator roles.

*Unbinding a player from a social role in a DSIM*    When a player is unbound from the DSIM, her PSIM should be adapted by removing that role and its role-centric relationship. Thus, for the *unbindRolePlayer* request the DSIM invokes the *triggerRoleRelinquishment* method with the social role name as the parameter. The PSIM organiser executes *roleRelinquishment* method to adapt its structure by removing the social role, and the relationship between that social role and the coordinator role, when those entities are in *Idle* state (i.e. safe to delete).

The *roleRelinquishment* method (see Algorithm 3) invokes the *getRelationship* management operation to get the relationship name between the target social role and the coordinator role. Then, it checks the state of the relationship (using the *getRelationshipState* management method) and waits until it enters to the *Idle* state which is the safe state to perform adaptation. Once the relationship enters into the *Idle* state, the state of the relationship is set to *Reconfiguration*. After that the adaptation is performed by removing the relationship, unbinding player from the target social role, and finally removing the social role.

For instance, if the leading car (Car#1) breaks-down, the *ConvoyDSIM* organiser player invokes (using the organiser interface) the *unbindRolePlayer* method to unbind *Car#1PSIM* from the LC. As a consequence, the *ConvoyDSIM* (as part of the cross adaptation process) invokes the *triggerRoleRelinquishment("LC")* method in *Car#1PSIM*. As a result, the *Car#1PSIM* updates its structure by removing the LC role and the relationship between the LC and Coordinator roles.

*Updating a social relationship in a DSIM*    All the updates in a relationship and/or a social role in a DSIM should be propagated to the corresponding PSIM(s). Thus, for any modification request in a relationship (i.e. to add, delete or update an interaction, conversation or obligation),

---

**Algorithm 2:** roleAcquisition (*r*, *rel*, *url*)

---

**Data:** *r* is a social role name, *rel* is a relationship, *url* is an endpoint
       URL of role *r* in DSIM
**begin**

1 | *addSocialRole*(*r*)                              /* adding a social role */
2 | *bindRolePlayer*(*r*, *url*)
3 | *crState* ← *getRoleState*("*CoordinatorRole*")
  | /* checking until *CoordinatorRole* enters into *Idle*
  |     state                                                         */
4 | **while** *crState* ≠ *Idle* **do**
5 |     *wait*()                              /* wait for some time */
6 |     *crState* ← *getRoleState*("*CoordinatorRole*")
7 | *setRoleState*("*CoordinatorRole*", *Reconfiguration*)      /* Setting
  | *CoordinatorRole* state as *Reconfiguration* so that
  | adaptation can be performed safely */

8 | *addRelationship*(*r*, "*CoordinatorRole*", *rel*)                 /* adding a
  | relationship (*rel*) between roles *r* and *CoordinatorRole*
  | */

9 | *setRoleState*("*CoordinatorRole*", *Idle*) /* adaptation complete
  | so set back the state to *Idle* */

---

---

**Algorithm 3:** roleRelinquishment (*r*)

---

**Data:** *r* is a social role name
**begin**

1 | *relName* ← *getRelationship*(*r*, "*CoordinatorRole*")      /* getting
  | the relationship name between the role *r* and
  | *CoordinatorRole* */
2 | *relState* ← *getRelState*(*relName*)
  |  /* checking until relationship *relName* enters into
  | *Idle* state */
3 | **while** *relState* ≠ *Idle* **do**
4 |     *wait*()                              /* wait for some time */
5 |     *relState* ← *getRelState*(*relName*)
6 | *deleteRelationship*(*relName*) /* deleting the relationship
  | from the composite */
7 | *unbindRolePlayer*(*r*) /* unbind the player from the role
  | *r* */
8 | *deleteSocialRole*(*r*)                    /* delete the role *r* from the
  | composite */

---

the DSIM organiser invokes the *triggerUpdateRelationship* method in the PSIMs which are bound to the associated social roles in that relationship. Then the PSIM organiser executes the *updateRelationship* method to reflect the changes.

The *updateRelationship* method (see Algorithm 4) invokes the *getRelationship* management operation to get the target relationship name which needs to be updated. After that, it checks the relationship state and waits until the relationship enters into the *Idle* state. When the relationship enters into the *Idle* state which is the safe state to perform adaptation, the state of the relationship is set to the *Reconfiguration*. Based on the update request such as *addInteraction*, *deleteConversation*, *updateOperationalParam*, and so on, the relationship is modified. Once the adaptation is completed, the state of the relationship is set back to the *Idle* state.

For instance, assume that during convoy it is started raining heavily, and as a consequence the adaptation rule defined in Sect. 6.2.2.3 is fired or the *ConvoyDSIM* organiser player (using organiser interface) invokes the *updateOperationalParam(R1,maxDesiredDistance,600m)* method in *ConvoyDSIM* to change the *maxDesiredDistance* parameter value from 1 km to 600 m. Both the *Car#2PSIM* and *Car#3PSIM* are related to the R1 relationship. Thus, the *ConvoyDSIM* (as part of the cross adaptation process) invokes the *triggerUpdateRelationship* method in *Car#2PSIM* and *Car#3PSIM* to update the *maxDesiredDistance* value in both of these PSIMs.

## 6.3 Summary

In this chapter, we have presented our approach to *preserving privacy* in accessing social context information and to *managing runtime adaptation* in social interaction models.

We have proposed a way to preserving owners' privacy by allowing the owners to fine-tune the granularity of information access and to specify access control policies. In this regard, we have presented an ontology-based socially-aware access control policy *model* and *language* for owners to control access to their information. Our policy model provides intuitive support by considering social role, social relationship and situation information when defining *privacy preferences*, and allowing owners to fine-tune the *granularity* of accessing information.

We have also presented a way of managing *runtime adaptation* in social interaction models. Our *explicit* modelling of social interactions from *domain-* and *player-perspectives*, and *separation* of *functional* and *management*

**Algorithm 4:** updateRelationship($r$,$updateType$, $data$)

---

**Data:** $r$ is a social role name related to the relationship that needs to be updated, $updateType$ is the type of updates in the relationship such as $addInteraction$, $deleteConversation$, and so on (any of the operations listed in Table 6.2 under category of modifying social relationship), $data$ is the information that needs to be updated

**begin**

1    $relName \leftarrow getRelationship(r,"CoordinatorRole")$    /* getting the relationship name between role $r$ and $CoordinatorRole$ */

2    $relState \leftarrow getRelState(relName)$
     /* checking until the relationship $rel$ enters into $Idle$          */

3    **while** $relState \neq Idle$ **do**

4      |   $wait()$                  /* wait for some time */

5      |   $relState \leftarrow getRelState(relName)$

6    $setRelState(relName, Reconfiguration)$        /* setting relationship $relName$ state to the $Reconfiguration$ so that the adaptation can be performed safely */

7    **if** $updateType = "addInteraction"$ **then**

8      |   $addInteraction(relName,data)$

9    **else if** $updateType = "addObligation"$ **then**

10     |   $addObligation(relName,data)$

11    **else if** $updateType = "addConversation"$ **then**

12     |   $addConversation(relName,data)$

13    **else if** $updateType = "deleteInteraction"$ **then**

14     |   $deleteInteraction(relName,data)$

15    **else if** $updateType = "deleteObligation"$ **then**

16     |   $deleteObligation(relName,data)$

17    **else if** $updateType = "deleteConversation"$ **then**

18     |   $deleteConversation(relName,data)$

19    **else if** $updateType = "updateInteraction"$ **then**

20     |   $updateInteraction(relName,data)$

21    **else if** $updateType = "updateConversation"$ **then**

22     |   $updateConversation(relName,data)$

23    **else if** $updateType = "updateObligation"$ **then**

24     |   $updateObligation(relName,data)$

25    **else if** $updateType = "addOperationalParam"$ **then**

26     |   $addOperationalParam(relName,data)$

27    **else if** $updateType = "updateOperationalParam"$ **then**

28     |   $updateOperationalParam(relName,data)$

29    **else if** $updateType = "deleteOperationalParam"$ **then**

30     |   $deleteOperationalParam(relName,data)$

31    $setRelState(relName, Idle)$    /* adaptation complete so set back the state to $Idle$ */

operations facilitate the management of dynamic interaction relationships between collaborative persons, and support adaptation in such runtime models to cope with the continuous changes in requirements and environments. The adaptation in a runtime social interaction model (i.e. DSIM or PSIM) can be *structural* and *parametric*, and realised through the management (organiser) interface of the runtime model. The inherent dependencies between runtime models, i.e. DSIMs and PSIMs, are maintained and kept consistent through coordinated cross-model adaptation (i.e. adaptation propagation).

# Part III
# Platform Implementation, Case Studies and Evaluations

This part of the book discusses the *SocioPlatform* with its implementation details (Chap. 7), case studies (Chap. 8), the evaluation results (Chap. 9), and finally a conclusion recapping the contributions of this book and related topics for future investigation (Chap. 10).

# Chapter 7
## *SocioPlatform* Architecture and Implementation

In Chaps. 4 and 5, we have presented the *modelling* of and *reasoning* about different types of social context information, whilst Chap. 6 has showed how we manage the *privacy* in accessing social context information and support the *adaptation* in runtime social interactions. These three chapters have collectively presented the *models*, *languages* and *techniques* underlying the *framework* for developing socially-aware applications. In this chapter, we present a platform, called *SocioPlatform*, to provide high-level support for developing socially-aware applications by *acquiring*, *reasoning*, *storing* and *provisioning* different types of social context information, and *managing* their runtime adaptation.

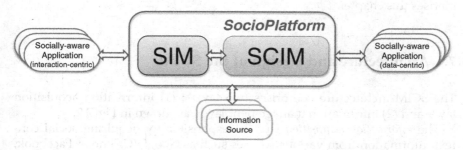

Fig. 7.1: *SocioPlatform* overview

The *SocioPlatform* can be divided into two main parts: *Social Context Information Management (SCIM)* and *Social Interaction Management (SIM)*, as shown in Fig. 7.1. Collectively these two parts provide support to building socially-aware applications of two different focuses, *data-centric* and *interaction-centric*.

*Social Context Information Management (SCIM)* supports *data-centric* socially-aware applications (e.g., the socially-aware phone call application)

© Springer International Publishing Switzerland 2016
M.A. Kabir et al., *Pervasive Social Computing*,
DOI 10.1007/978-3-319-29951-8_7

by *collecting* social context information (SCI) from different sources, *reasoning* about more meaningful SCI (as required by the applications) based on collected SCI, *storing* SCI into a knowledge base, and supporting *access* to such SCI while considering information owners' *privacy* preferences. SCIM also provides functionality to infer situations from users' interaction events in social media and interaction-centric socially-aware applications (e.g., cooperative convoy application). SCIM acquires interaction events from social media, while SCIM receives interaction events in interaction-centric socially-aware applications from SIM (see Sect. 7.4.5).

*Social Interaction Management (SIM)* provides the *runtime environment* and *adaptation management* for the interaction-centric socially-aware applications (e.g., the cooperative convoy application). In our approach, the agreements between collaborative users in a socially-aware application are captured in the social interaction ontology and stored in the SCIM knowledge base. The information in the ontology is used to create both the domain-centric social interaction models (DSIMs) and player-centric social interaction models (PSIMs) (see Sect. 7.4.4). SIM provides *runtime environment* for the application to instantiate these models. These instantiated runtime models *mediate* social interactions among collaborative users according to their agreements. SIM also supports the *runtime adaptation* of such models to cope with the changes in users' requirements and environments.

The rest of this chapter is organised as follows. Section 7.1 presents the architecture and design of the SCIM followed by its prototype implementation in Sect. 7.2. The SIM architecture and design is presented in Sect. 7.3, while its prototype implementation is presented in Sect. 7.4. Section 7.5 summarises this chapter.

## 7.1 Architecture and Design of the SCIM

The SCIM architecture comprises two layers: (1) information acquisition layer and (2) information management layer, as shown in Fig. 7.2.

The *information acquisition layer* is responsible for acquiring social context information from various sources such as Google Calendar, Facebook, LinkedIn, Twitter and other social media. A common interface, called *information acquisition interface,* is provided so that different adapters can be built based on that interface to collect data from various sources. Section 7.1.1 describes this interface. The *acquisition module* is responsible for managing and operating adapters to fetch raw data from the different sources, make the data consistent (i.e., remove irrelevant data, integrate data of interest, and so on) and store it into the knowledge base (see Sects. 7.1.2 and 7.1.3 for the details discussion).

The *information management* layer is responsible to store users' social context information as acquired and to preserve their privacy when accessing

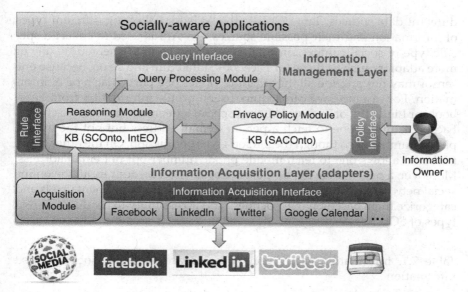

Fig. 7.2: Architecture of the social context information management (SCIM)

this information. This layer consists of three main modules: (1) *Reasoning module*—classifies users' social data that is collected by the information acquisition layer, stores it into the *SCOnto* knowledge base, and provides a reasoning functionality to infer abstract social context information that is of applications interest; (2) *Privacy policy module*—provides a policy interface (Sect. 7.1.4 provides details) to allow users to specify and manager their privacy preferences, and supports policy enforcement in accessing users' social context information; and (3) *Query processing module*—allows different applications to access users' social context information and provides a query interface (Sect. 7.1.5 provides details) so that application developers can build applications without the need to deal with the details of information representation schema and management.

## 7.1.1 Information Acquisition Interface

We propose a set of information acquisition application programming interfaces (APIs) to collect and store information relevant to the concepts defined in the ontologies where a specific type of information can be collected from different sources. These APIs decoupled the information representation and management from the underlying information acquisition process. They provide a common interface to implement various adapters for different data sources. Table 7.1 lists the APIs for collecting different types of information and their possible sources. An API is used to collect a specific type of social context information and can be implemented by one or more adapters such as those for Facebook, LinkedIn, and so on, because one sensor may not provide all the attribute values of a particular type of information. For instance, we can acquire users' profile information from Facebook, or LinkedIn, or Twitter. Without special agreement and service charge, Facebook allows one to fetch a person's email address but not the mobile phone number even though the person gives permission. On the other hand, LinkedIn allows one to fetch mobile phone number but not email address. Moreover, a person may not be a user of or have an account in, all the online social networks (OSNs). Thus, we analyse some of the prominent OSNs and categorize them based on their richness and accessibility to acquire different types of SCI.

Table 7.1: Information acquisition APIs for accumulating social context information

| No | Acquisition APIs | Adapters |
|----|------------------|----------|
| 1 | getProfile(...) | Facebook, LinkedIn, Twitter |
| 2 | getStatusUpdate(...) | Facebook, LinkedIn, Twitter, Google Calendar |
| 3 | getEventBasedRel(...) | Facebook, LinkedIn, Twitter |
| 4 | getWorkRelationships(...) | Facebook, LinkedIn |
| 5 | getEducationRelationships(...) | Facebook, LinkedIn |
| 6 | getLivingAddrBasedRel(...) | Facebook, LinkedIn |
| 7 | getGroupInterestBasedRel(...) | Facebook, LinkedIn |
| 8 | getFamilyRelationships(...) | Facebook |
| 9 | getResearchTopicBasedRel(...) | LinkedIn |
| 10 | getFollowingFollowerRel(...) | Twitter |
| 11 | getDigitalContentBasedRel(...) | Facebook |
| 12 | getInteractionEvent(...) | Facebook, LinkedIn, Twitter |

As reported in Table 7.1, we can acquire a person's profile, status and event based relationship information from Facebook, LinkedIn or Twitter. Google Calendar can also be a possible source of situation information as people use it to maintain their schedule [126]. The relationships based on work, education, living address and group interest can be acquired from Facebook or LinkedIn. A person's family, research topic, and following-follower relationships can be collected from her Facebook, LinkedIn, and

Twitter accounts, respectively. In Facebook, people usually share various digital contents such as photos, audios and videos, and other Facebook users express their impression (e.g., like, dislike) about these contents. Thus, we can acquire the digital content based relationships from Facebook.

In the following two sections, we describe how the raw social data can be collected from different sources and integrated to create a consistent representation of social context information.

## 7.1.2 Designing Adapters to Fetch Raw Data

Online social networks have the potential to act as social data sources, providing us the opportunity to access user's social context information. In this research, we consider a number of social data sources such as Facebook, LinkedIn, Twitter and Google Calendar, and have built adapters for them by implementing the information acquisition APIs (as listed in Table 7.1).

Facebook provides a Facebook Query Language (FQL)[1] for fetching data from individual tables in their system. Thus, we cannot fetch all the data of our interest using a single request. Furthermore, fetching information is a time consuming task and has a high network overhead (see Sect. 9.2.1). We have taken into account this issue in designing the adapter for Facebook and tried to minimize the number of data fetching requests to the lowest level without compromising the data of interest. For Facebook, we require three fetch requests to collect people-centric relationships: (1) fetch user profile data, (2) fetch classified relationships (i.e., relationships under the built-in and user defined classifications), and (3) fetch all connections in the friend list.

In Facebook, the general friend list also includes people who are already classified as family members or colleagues. Thus, to remove duplication, we compare the connections in the friend list with the connections in the classified relationship lists, and remove the connections which are already classified. The result of that process gives us a list of friends/connections who belong to a general friend category. Furthermore, we match the user's profile with its friends' profiles to deduce more specialized relationships such as university friend (if they studied in a same institution), colleague (if they work in a same organization), living address based friend (if they live in a same city), and so on.

Similarly, we have designed adapters for LinkedIn, Twitter and Google Calendar by implementing the APIs as shown in Table 7.1.

---

[1] https://developers.facebook.com/docs/reference/fql/.

### 7.1.3 Fetching and Processing Raw Data for Consistent Social Context Information

The *acquisition module* (see Fig. 7.2) is responsible for *fetching* raw social data from diverse sources, *processing* and *storing* it into knowledge base. The acquisition module keeps the list of the available adapters and their implemented APIs. After a certain time interval, which is configurable, the acquisition manager executes the fetching and processing steps to update the knowledge base with users' recent social context information. The frequency for such information update, however, is not the same for all types of social context information. For instance, a user's situation information may need to be updated more frequently compare to his/her family relationship. To fulfil that requirement, we allow users to schedule the execution of different acquisition functions listed in Table 7.1. Moreover, it is also possible to trigger the execution of these functions manually (i.e., on demand).

After fetching raw social data, the *acquisition manager* processes the data before storing it into the knowledge base. To keep social context information consistent, raw data fetched from the various sources needs to be further processed, e.g., performing *cross* integration among the data from different sources. The data processing depends on the types of raw social data and their possible sources. For instance, we fetch a user's situation information from her schedule on Google Calendar and her status updates in Facebook, LinkedIn and Twitter. To identify users' current "situation" more accurately, we integrate the data fetched from these sources based on their update timestamp, and select the most related and recent update as users' current situation.

### 7.1.4 Policy Interface

Table 7.2 lists the set of *Policy APIs* that allow users' applications to *add*, *delete*, *retrieve* and *update* their privacy policies.

To visualize all the specified policies to an user, the application first invokes the *getAllPolicyIDs* operation which returns a list of policy IDs. For each of these IDs, the application invokes *getPolicyStatement* to retrieve the associated policy statement. To add a new policy to the user's *SACOnto* knowledge base, the application invokes the *addPolicy* operation and passes a policy statement as a string. The *deletePolicy* operation receives a policy ID and delete the associated policy. The *updatePolicy* operation replaces an existing policy with a new policy statement.

Table 7.2: Policy APIs for managing users' privacy policies

| No | Policy APIs | Description |
|----|-------------|-------------|
| 1 | getAllPolicyIDs() | Returns all the specified policy IDs as a list |
| 2 | getPolicyStatement(pID) | Returns *pID* policy statement as a string from the *SACOnto* knowledge base |
| 3 | addPolicy(P) | Adds a policy statement *P* to the *SACOnto* knowledge base and returns its policy ID |
| 4 | deletePolicy(pID) | Deletes the *pID* policy from the *SACOnto* knowledge base |
| 5 | updatePolicy(pID,P) | Replaces the *pID* policy with the new policy statement *P* |

## 7.1.5 Query Interface

The query interface provides a set of basic query APIs to allow applications to access both context and meta-context information. These functions or APIs can be further used to build more complex social inferences or queries. These APIs can be divided into two main categories: (1) APIs for querying social context information (listed in Table 7.3) and (2) APIs for querying meta-context information (listed in Table 7.4).

*APIs for querying social context information (No. 1 to No. 19):* In this category, the first seven (i.e., No. 1 to No. 7) APIs are boolean functions, and among those No. 7 is the most generic function. It takes a relationship type R and two person ids as input and checks whether the relationship R exists between these two persons. Other six APIs, i.e., No. 1 to 6, are a specialized type of the No. 7 API, which check the existence of a particular type of relationship between two persons A and B. For example, the No. 1, 2 and 3 APIs check the existence of a *colleague*, *friend* and *family* relationships respectively. The No. 8 and 9 APIs find an individual person based on his/her phone number and email id, respectively. The No. 10 to 13 APIs return a list of persons with whom an individual A has a particular type of relationship. Among those the No. 13 API is the most generic function as it can answer the query on any relationship type R for an individual A. The No. 10, 11, and 12 APIs are a specialized type of No. 13 API, defined for a particular type of relationship, i.e., close friend, bosom friend and best friend, respectively. The No. 14 and 15 APIs return

Table 7.3: Query APIs for accessing social context information

| No | Query APIs | Description |
|----|-----------|-------------|
| 1 | isAColleagueOfB(A,B) | Boolean function that checks whether a person A is a colleague of B |
| 2 | isAFriendOfB(A,B) | Checks whether person A is a friend of B |
| 3 | isAFamilyOfB(A,B) | Checks whether person A is a family member of B |
| 4 | isAandBLivingSameCity(A,B) | Checks whether person A and B are living in a same city |
| 5 | isAandBLivingSameCountry(A,B) | Checks whether person A and B are living in a same country |
| 6 | isAHasRelationshipWithB(A,B) | Checks whether person A has any relationship with B |
| 7 | isRelRExistBetAandB(R,A,B) | Checks whether a relationship R exists between A and B |
| 8 | getPersonByPhoneNum(phNum) | Returns a person's id whose phone number is *phoneNum* |
| 9 | getPersonByEmailID(emailID) | Returns a person's id whose email address is *emailID* |
| 10 | getCloseFriends(A) | Returns close friends list of person A |
| 11 | getBosomFriends(A) | Returns bosom friends list of person A |
| 12 | getBestFriends(A) | Returns best friends list of person A |
| 13 | getAllRelatedPersonsByR(A,R) | Returns all related by the relationship R |
| 14 | getStrengthOfRel(A,R) | Returns the strength value of the relationship R |
| 15 | getTrustOfRel(A,R) | Returns the trust value of the relationship R |
| 16 | getAllRelationshipsName(A,B) | Returns a list of relationships name between person A and B |
| 17 | getRelByGranularity(A,B,gLevel) | Returns the name of a relationship between person A and B at *gLevel* granularity |
| 18 | getSituation(A) | Returns current situation of person A |
| 19 | getSituAtGranularity(A,gLevel) | Returns current situation of person A at *gLevel* granularity |

Table 7.4: Query APIs for accessing meta-context information

| No | Query APIs | Description |
|----|-----------|-------------|
| 20 | getNumberOfFriends(A) | Returns person A's number of friends |
| 21 | getNumberOfConnections4R(A,R) | Returns person A's number of connections for a relationship name R |
| 22 | getNumberOfRelationships(A,B) | Returns a number of relationship types between A and B |

an attribute value of the relationship R such as strength and trust. The No. 16 API returns all the types of relationship between two persons while the No. 17 API returns the relationship type at a certain granularity level. The No. 18 and 19 APIs are defined to access a person's current situation information. The No. 18 API returns the exact situation while the No. 19 API returns the situation information at a certain granularity level.

*APIs for querying meta-context information (No. 20 to No. 22):* In this category, the No. 20 and 21 APIs return the number of an individual's connections in a specific type of relationship. The No. 20 API returns the number of connections in a friend relationship, while the No. 21 API is a generic API as it allows one to input the name of the relationship type. The No. 22 API returns the number of relationships between two persons.

## 7.1.6 Rule Interface

Table 7.5 lists the set of *Rule APIs* that can be used to develop a graphical user interface application which can be used by the domain experts to *add*, *delete*, *retrieve* and *update* reasoning rules, e.g., situation specification rules for inferring situations from interaction events.

To obtain all the specified reasoning rules, the application first invokes the *getAllRuleIDs* operation which returns a list of rule IDs. For each of these IDs, the application invokes *getRule* to retrieve the associated rule. To add a new rule to the reasoning module, the application invokes the *addRule* operation and passes a rule as a string. The *deleteRule* operation receives a rule ID and delete the corresponding rule. The *updateRule* operation replaces an existing rule with a new rule.

Table 7.5: Rule APIs for managing reasoning rules

| No | Rule APIs | Description |
|----|-----------|-------------|
| 1 | getAllRuleIDs() | Returns all the rule IDs as a list |
| 2 | getRule(rID) | Returns the rule with ID *rID* as a string |
| 3 | addRule(R) | Adds a rule *R* to the reasoning module and returns its rule ID |
| 4 | deleteRule(rID) | Deletes the *rID* rule from the reasoning module |
| 5 | updateRule(rID,R) | Replaces the *rID* rule with the new rule *R* |

## 7.2 SCIM Prototype Implementation

We have implemented a SCIM prototype, in Java 2 Platform Standard Edition (J2SE). The following sections present the details of this implementation.

### 7.2.1 *Implementing Ontologies*

We have used the Protégé tool[2] to create the *SCOnto*,[3] *SACOnto*[4] and *IntEO*[5] ontologies. Figure 7.3 shows a screenshot of the concepts in the *SCOnto* ontology (left panel), the *granularity* specification of the *Chatting* concept, the inference rules for the *Father-Daughter* and *Busy* concepts, and the semantic description of the *Relationship* concept (from top to bottom in the right panels). *SCOnto* contains 126 classes, 8 object properties, 39 data properties and 619 axioms.

Users' privacy policies are stored in their *SACOnto* knowledge base. The policy statement is formatted in Manchester OWL syntax [15] and stored as a string. The Manchester OWL syntax has been designed for writing OWL-DL class expressions in natural language. Figure 7.4 shows a screenshot of the *SACOnto* ontology and Policy#1 written in Manchester OWL syntax. *SACOnto* contains 168 classes, 15 object properties, 41 data properties and 667 axioms.

The Protégé screenshot in Fig. 7.5 shows the concepts (left panel) and object properties (top right panel) in the *IntEO* ontology. *IntEO* contains 144

---

[2] http://protege.stanford.edu/.

[3] http://www.ict.swin.edu.au/personal/akabir/1.0/ontologies/
SCOnto.owl.

[4] http://www.ict.swin.edu.au/personal/akabir/1.00/ontologies/
SCACOnt.owl.

[5] http://www.ict.swin.edu.au/personal/akabir/1.0/ontologies/IntEO.
owl.

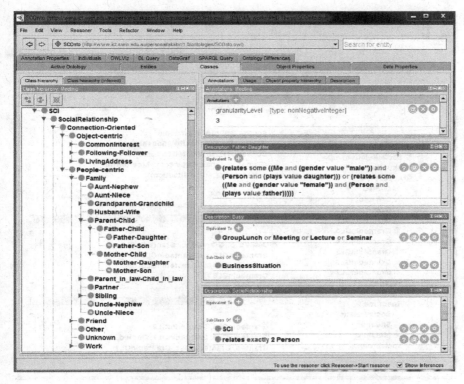

Fig. 7.3: A screenshot of *SCOnto* in Protégé

classes, 19 object properties, 38 data properties, 48 individuals and 623 axioms.

## 7.2.2 Implementing Adapters

We have written *adapters* for Facebook, LinkedIn, Twitter, and Google calendar using restfb 1.6.7,[6] linkedin-j 1.0.415,[7] twitter4j 2.2.4,[8] and gdatacalendar 2.0,[9] respectively, to fetch users' social data. These adapters implement the information acquisition APIs and are managed by the *acquisition manager* module.

---

[6] http://restfb.com/.

[7] http://code.google.com/p/linkedin-j/.

[8] http://twitter4j.org/en/index.html.

[9] http://code.google.com/p/gdata-java-client/.

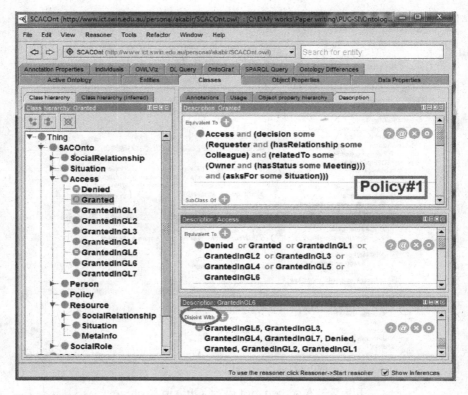

Fig. 7.4: A screenshot of *SACOnto* and an example of formatting policy (Policy#1) in Manchester Syntax [15], using Protégé

We follow the OAuth 2.0[10] protocol for authorization in fetching users' social data. OAuth is an open standard protocol which allows users to share their private resources (e.g., profiles, friend lists) stored on one site with another site without having to hand out their credentials, typically supplying tokens instead of user name and password. Each token grants access to a specific site (e.g., Facebook) for specific resources (e.g., friend list and/or status updates) and for a defined duration (e.g., the next 2 h).

We have created applications (see Fig. 7.6), called *SCIMiddlewareF*, *SCIMiddle wareL*, *SCIMiddlewareT* and *SCIMiddlewareG*, on Facebook, LinkedIn, Twitter, and Google respectively. Through these applications SCIM acquires access tokens and gets authorization from users to fetch their social data from those sites.

---

[10] http://oauth.net/2/.

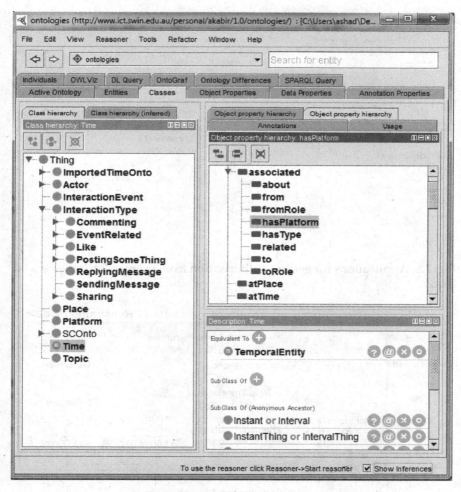

Fig. 7.5: A screenshot of *IntEO* in Protégé

### 7.2.3 *Implementing Rule APIs and Reasoning Module*

The *reasoning module* implementation has three main aspects: (1) implementation of the description logic based reasoning component, (2) implementation of the rule management APIs and (3) implementation of the situation inference component, as shown in Fig. 7.7.

The *DL based reasoning* component employs DL reasoners (listed in Sect. 7.2.4) to execute reasoning rules, described in Sects. 5.2.1, 5.2.2 and 5.3.1, for reasoning about different types of social context information such as friend relationships, family relationships and situations. The *rule*

Fig. 7.6: Applications for getting authorisation from users to fetch their social data

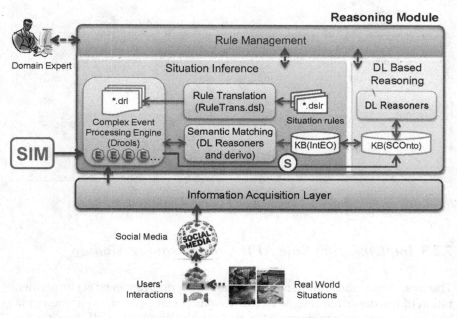

Fig. 7.7: Reasoning module implementation

*management* component implements the *rule management APIs* (described in Sect. 7.1.6) which allow domain experts to *add*, *delete*, *retrieve* and *update* the reasoning rules corresponding to the situation inference component and the DL based reasoning component.

The *situation inference* component combines *complex event processing (CEP)* and *semantic matching* in order to infer users' situations at (near) real time from their *interaction events*. The *information acquisition layer* collects *interaction events* from the different social interaction platforms such as Facebook, Email, and instant messaging. The *rule translation* unit translates *situation rules* specified by the domain experts or application developers, to the executable format that compliant with the CEP engine.

The *complex event processing* engine is responsible for identifying situations by checking the situation specification rules (SSRs) defined by domain experts or application developers, and for inserting the identified situation into the *SCOnto* knowledge base. We employ the open source software Drools 5.5,[11] which includes Drools expert and Drools fusion, for implementing the CEP engine. There are many advantages of using Drools. *Firstly*, Drools provides an integrated platform for processing events, executing rules, and checking temporal correlation among events. *Secondly*, the Drools engine is implemented based on the RETE algorithm [81]. RETE is an efficient pattern matching algorithm which is asymptotically independent from the number of events or facts that is being inserted to the rules engine as long as the number of rules matched by these events are fixed. The RETE algorithm allows the Drools engine to maintain a working memory of the results of partial rule matches across time. Re-evaluation of each condition in the rules is no longer necessary, as the engine knows which conditions might possibly change for each event, and only those are re-evaluated. This improves the efficiency of the situation reasoning platform (see experimental result in Fig. 9.5). *Thirdly*, Drools supports user-defined functions in its rule language. This enables us to realise the constraints with *ONTOEQ* in the interaction event patterns using a function call. For example, the following constraint in the *IE2* interaction event pattern

*hasType ONTOEQ "PostingSomeThing"*

is realised as

*semanticMatching(hasType,"PostingSomeThing")*

The domain expert specifies situation rules by following the human-readable situation specification language (*SituLang*), described in Sect. 5.4.6. The *rule translation* unit automatically translates the situation rules (*\*.dslr*) specified in the *SituLang* to the Drools executable format (*\*.drl*). We have written a rule translation scripts (see Appendix D), namely *RuleTrans.dsl*, using the language construct provided by the Drools. For instance, Fig. 7.8 shows the transformed watching game situation rule (presented in Sect. 5.4.7) in the Drools executable format. The rule in this figure also presents how we realise and implement *ONTOEQ* of our situation

---

[11] http://www.jboss.org/drools/drools-fusion.html.

specification language and support the semantic matching of the interaction event attributes in complex event processing for inferring situations.

```
global IEventKB kbIns; // an instance of the IntEO KB
rule "Watching Game"
   when
      $IE1:InteractionEvent(hasType=="PostingCurrentLocation" &&
                            eval(kbIns.semanticMatching(atPlace,"Stadium")),
                            personaName:fromp,place:atPlace)
      $CIE1:InteractionEvent(eval(kbIns.semanticMatching(hasType,"PostingSomeThing")) &&
                             eval(kbIns.ontologicalMatch(about,"Sports")) &&
                             has occurred "after" IE1)
   then
         kbIns.notifySITU("Person"+personName+" is watching game at the "+place);
end
```

Fig. 7.8: The Drools executable format of the *Watching game* situation rule

The CEP engine uses the *semantic matching* functionality to match event patterns (in situation rules) with incoming interaction event streams. The *semantic matching* is an ontological query on the *IntEO*. Figure 7.9 presents the implementation of the semantic matching function in Java. It is a *boolean* function and returns *true* if the value of the *attrValue* parameter is a *subclass* (in the *IntEO*) of the value of the *constant* parameter. Like the query processing module, we have used the *derivo 1.0*[12] SPARQL-DL query engine with the DL reasoners for implementing the semantic matching function.

```
private static OWLOntologyManager manager; //an IntEO manager
private static OWLReasoner reasoner; //an instance of OWL reasoner,
                                     //e.g.,Pellet or TrOWL or HermiT
private static QueryEngine engine; //an instance of the SPARQL-DL query engine

public static boolean semanticMatching(String attrValue, String constant) thr
      // Create an instance of the SPARQL-DL query engine
      engine = QueryEngine.create(manager, reasoner, true);
      String q  =  "PREFIX sc:<http://www.ict.swin.edu.au/Ontology/IEonto#>" +
                   "ASK {\n" +
                      "SubClassOf(sc:"+attrValue+", sc:"+constant+")" +
                   "}";
      Query query = Query.create(q);
      //Execute the query and generate the result set
      QueryResult result = engine.execute(query);
      return result.ask();
}
```

Fig. 7.9: Implementation of the *semantic matching function*

At runtime, the CEP engine continuously receives users' *interaction events* from social media and/or SIM, and incrementally matches the *interaction event patterns* specified in the *situation rules*. The engine invokes the *semantic*

---

[12] http://www.derivo.de/en/resources/sparql-dl-api/.

*matching function* if it is stated in the situation rules. Once a rule is matched, the situation is identified and inserted into *SCOnto*. The socially-aware applications use these situations to provide services to the users.

### 7.2.4 Implementing Policy APIs and Privacy Policy Module

We have implemented a set of *Policy APIs* (as listed in Table 7.2) that allow users' applications to add, delete, retrieve and update their privacy policies. The *privacy policy module* (see Fig. 7.2) implements these APIs. We have used the OWL API 3[13] to implement a knowledge base for *SACOnto*, and to manage this knowledge base, i.e., adding, deleting and updating privacy policies.

The application developer can develop a web-, mobile- or desktop-based graphical user interface based on these APIs for users to manage their policies. To visualize all the specified policies to an user, the application first invokes the *getAllPolicyIDs* operation which returns a list of policy IDs. For each of these IDs, the application invokes *getPolicyStatement* to retrieve the associated policy statement. These two operations are basically queries over the *SACOnto* knowledge base. Thus, like query APIs, we have used SPARQL-DL (see Sect. 7.2.5 for details) to represent queries related to these operations. To add a new policy to the user's *SACOnto* knowledge base, the application invokes the *addPolicy* operation and passes a policy statement as a string. The *addPolicy* function (see Fig. 7.10 for a Java code snapshot) implements the steps described in Sect. 6.1.2. We have used the DLQuery parser in OWL API 3 to convert the string policy statement into an OWL-DL class expression. Finally, we insert the expression into the knowledge base. For the *deletePolicy* operation, first we delete the policy expression from its equivalent class which is a subclass of the *Access* class. Then, we delete the pID individual from the *Policy* class and its link to the policy statement. For the *updatePolicy* operation, we follow the steps of the *deletePolicy* operation followed by an *addPolicy* operation.

The *privacy policy module* also implements the *executePolicy* function that follows the steps described in Sect. 6.1.3. This function checks users' privacy preferences and returns the access decision. To implement this function, we have used reasoners compliant with the OWL2 DL. In particular, for evaluation purposes, we have incorporated five different DL reasoners: Pellet

---

[13] http://owlapi.sourceforge.net/.

```
public String addPolicy(String strPolicy){
    //transform policy into class expression
    OWLClassExpression owlPolicy = parseClassExpression(strPolicy);
    OWLClass decisionClass = getDecisionClass(strPolicy);
    // adding policy as an equivalent class of the corresponding decision class
    OWLEquivalentClassesAxiom ax = datafac.getOWLEquivalentClassesAxiom
                                          (decisionClass,owlPolicy);
    manager.addAxiom(SACOnto, ax);
    String pID = getPolicyID(strPolicy);
    // checking consistency
    boolean consistent = reasoner.isConsistent();
    if(!consistent){
    // adding policy makes SACOnto inconsistent, thus delete policy and return null
        deletePolicy(pID);
        return null;
    }
    else {//adding policy makes SACOnto consistent, thus return policy id
        return pID;
    }
}
```

Fig. 7.10: A Java code snapshot for the *addPolicy* function

2.3.0,[14] HermiT 1.3.5,[15] TrOWL 0.8.1,[16] Fact++ 1.5.2[17] and RacerPro 2.0.[18] We have also used these reasoners in checking inconsistency during policy specification, executing reasoning rules (see Sect. 7.2.3) and applications' queries (see Sect. 7.2.5).

## 7.2.5 *Implementing Query APIs and Query Processing Module*

The *query processing module* (see Fig. 7.2) implements the query APIs (described in Sect. 7.1.5) to answer applications' queries. We adopt a description logic (DL) based query language, namely SPARQL-DL [168], for query processing and have used the *derivo 1.0* SPARQL-DL query engine with the above mentioned DL reasoners. Recently, SPARQL-DL was introduced as a rich query language for OWL 2, which is a distinct subset of SPARQL (a RDF based language), tailored to ontology specific queries. Therefore, different aspects of context such as the existence of a relationship, granularity level of a current situation, and so on, can be answered easily in a simpler fashion. For example, queries related to the No. 1 and No. 19 APIs in Table 7.3 can be formatted in SPARQL-DL as follows:

```
No.1# isAColleagueOfB(A,B)
PREFIX sc:<http://www.ict.swin.edu.au/Ontology/SCOnto#>
```

---

[14] http://clarkparsia.com/pellet/.

[15] http://hermit-reasoner.com/.

[16] http://trowl.eu/.

[17] http://owl.man.ac.uk/factplusplus/.

[18] http://www.racer-systems.com/products/racerpro/.

```
ASK{
    PropertyValue(A, sc:hasRelationship, ?rel1)
    PropertyValue(B, sc:hasRelationship, ?rel2)
    SameAs(?rel1,?rel2)
    DirectType(?rel1, sc:Colleague)}


No.19# getSituAtGranularity(A,gLevel)
PREFIX sc:<http://www.ict.swin.edu.au/Ontology/SCOnto#>
SELECT ?situ{
        PropertyValue(A, sc:hasSituation, ?situIns)
        DirectType(?situName, ?situIns)
        Annotation(strictSubClassOf(?situName,?situ),
                    sc:granularityLevel, gLevel)}
```

The codification of the No. 19 query operation in Java is shown in Fig. 7.11.

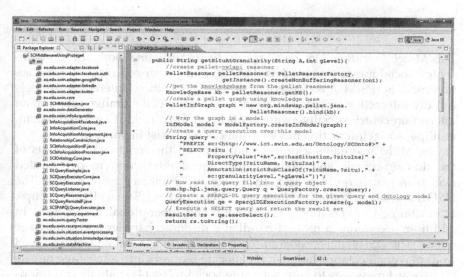

Fig. 7.11: A Java code snapshot in Eclipse that implements *getSituAtGranularity(A,gLevel)* operation

## 7.3 Architecture and Design of the SIM

The *Social Interaction Management (SIM)* architecture comprises two main modules: the *Model Execution Module (MEM)* and the *Management Module (MM)*, as shown in Fig. 7.12. The next two sections describe these two modules in details.

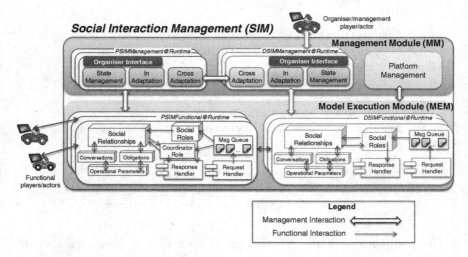

Fig. 7.12: Architecture of the *social interaction management (SIM)* platform

## 7.3.1  *The Model Execution Module*

The *Model Execution Module* supports to instantiating both the domain-centric social interaction models (DSIMs) and player-centric social interaction models (PSIMs). As described in Sect. 6.2.1, these interaction models capture interaction-oriented relationships among collaborative actors in an interaction-centric socially-aware application. Therefore, at a given moment, multiple social interaction model instances may exist in parallel.

The MEM maintains a representation of all the functional elements of the domain-centric and player-centric social interaction models, called *DSIMFunctional@runtime* and *PSIMFuctional@runtime*, respectively. The *DSIMFunctional@runtime* represents Social Roles, Social Relationships, Interactions, Conversations, Obligations and Operational Parameters. In addition, it contains a request handler, a response handler and a message queue. The *DSIMFunctional@runtime* is able to (1) handle requests received from players (i.e., applications); (2) allocate requests into a message queue; (3) forward messages to corresponding social roles; (4) evaluate conditions (i.e., conversation and obligation) specified in the relationships; (5) send request to relevant social roles and then to players.

The *PSIMFuctional@runtime* contains all the components of the *DSIM-Functional@runtime*. In addition, it contains a special type of social role, called the *coordinator role*. The *PSIMFuctional@runtime* bounds to one or more social roles in the *DSIMFunctional@runtime*(s). In the *PSIMFuctional@runtime*, all the incoming messages first forwarded to the *coordinator role*. After evaluating conditions specified in the relationships, the request message is forwarded to the *coordinator player*. The message is processed further based on the decision of the coordinator player. For instance, generate a reply message and send it to the player from where the message has come.

Both the *PSIMFuctional@runtime* and *DSIMFuctional@runtime* maintain the *state* of their corresponding entities such as social roles, social relationships and the composite (as a whole). As the message passes through these entities, the state is changed according to the *state machine* described in Sect. 6.2.2.4.

## 7.3.2 *The Management Module*

The *Management module* supports the runtime adaptation of the instantiated social interaction model. Thus, the *management components*, called *DSIM-Management@Runtime* and *PSIMManagement@Runtime*, are instantiated for each of the *DSIMFunctional@Runtime* and *PSIMFunctional@Runtime*. Both of these management components implement basic management operations provided by the organiser interface. In Sect. 6.2.2.3, we have discussed these operations and classified them as *structure*, *parameter* and *state* related operations. The *In Adaptation* sub-component of the management component implements the *structure* and *parameter* related management operations, while the *State Management* sub-component implements *state* related operations.

In addition to these sub-components (i.e., *In Adaptation* and *State Management*), the management component contains the *Cross Adaptation* sub-component which supports the adaptation across social interaction models and implements the algorithms described in Sect. 6.2.3. The *Cross Adaptation* sub-component of the *DSIMManagement@Runtime* implements the *computeRoleCentricRel* algorithm, while the *Cross Adaptation* sub-component of the *PSIMManagement@Runtime* implements the *triggerRoleAcquisition*, *triggerRoleRelinquishment* and *triggerUpdateRelationship* algorithms. Moreover, the interactions between the *Cross Adaptation* sub-components of *DSIMManagement@Runtime* and *PSIMManagement@Runtime* follow the adaptation propagation protocol described in Sect. 6.2.3.

The *Management module* also supports the platform-level management, i.e., to *create*, *retrieve*, *delete*, *deploy* and *undeploy* social interaction models dynamically. These APIs, as listed in Table 7.6, allows a user to perform administration level management. The *platform management* component implements these APIs.

Table 7.6: Platform level management APIs

| No | APIs | Description |
|----|------|-------------|
| 1 | createDSIM(...) | Creates a DSIM |
| 2 | createPSIM(...) | Creates a PSIM that contains only a coordinator role |
| 3 | deleteModel(...) | Deletes a social interaction model |
| 4 | deployModel(...) | Deploys a model in the platform |
| 5 | undeployModel(...) | Undeploys a running model from the platform |
| 6 | getModel(...) | Returns the xml descriptor of a model |
| 7 | uploadModel(...) | Uploads a model descriptor file |

## 7.4 SIM Prototype Implementation

The *Social Interaction Management (SIM)* prototype can be divided into three main parts: the *Deployment Layer*, *Functional Interaction Layer* and the *Management Layer*, as shown in Fig. 7.13. Collectively these three parts provide the *runtime environment* for supporting *mediated* social interactions and its *adaptation* in interaction-centric socially-aware applications.

The *Model Execution Module* belongs to the *Functional Interaction Layer*, while the *Management Module* belongs to the *Management Layer*. These two layers together are called the *SIM-Core*. One of the key consideration behind the *SIM-Core* implementation is to have a runtime environment that is independent of the underlying deployment environment. The main reason for this design principle is to make the *SIM-Core* reusable among an array of different deployment technologies. Besides, the deployment technologies and standards may evolve over time. For example, apart from *SOAP/Web services* [20, 21], which is the currently supported technology, other alternative technologies such as *Remote Method Invocation (RMI)* [130, 143], *RESTful Services* [77, 141], *XML/RPC* [29], *Mobile Web services* [170] do exist. Therefore, it is important to have *SIM-Core* implemented in a deployment-technology neutral manner.

As discussed in Sect. 6.2.1, we adopt and extend the Role Oriented Adaptive Design (ROAD) approach [59] in modelling social interactions. Therefore, it is a logical choice to adopt the ROAD implementation for realising and implementing the SIM platform. Moreover, the current ROAD implementation considers the aspect of independently implementing the *runtime* environment from the underlying *deployment* environment, which is an important requirement to implement the *SIM-Core* as discussed above.

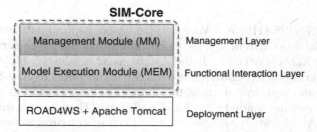

Fig. 7.13: Layers of the *social interaction management (SIM)* prototype

The current ROAD implementation[19] provides a *runtime* environment, called the *ROADfactory* [18], and a *deployment* environment, called the *ROAD4WS* [118]. However, we could not employ the ROAD implementation directly for several reasons. *Firstly,* The *ROADfactory* supports the instantiation and management of the ROAD composites (the *DSIMs* and *PSIMs* in our case), involving *roles* (*social roles* in our case), *contracts* (*social relationships* in our case) and message routing among different roles based on declarative *interaction terms* and contractual rules. However, it does not have the concept of the *obligation* and *conversation* and their realisation in the message routing mechanism. Moreover, the *state machines* for the composite and its elements are not implemented. *Secondly,* the *ROADfactory* was not implemented to recognise the *domain-centric* and *player-centric* views of the ROAD composite. *Thirdly,* the *management operations* (organiser role interface) provided by the *ROADfactory* are limited, in particular, the state, obligation, conversation, operational parameter and cross adaptation related management operations are not supported. Furthermore, the *ROADfactory* does not provide support for the *platform level management*.

We address these limitations in implementing the corresponding modules of the *SIM-Core* by adopting and extending the *ROADfactory*. In particular, the *first* and *second* limitations are addressed in implementing the *model execution module* (Sect. 7.4.1), while the *third* limitation is addressed in implementing the *management module* (Sect. 7.4.2).

---

[19]  http://www.swinburne.edu.au/ict/success/research-projects-and-grants/role-oriented-adaptive-design/implementations.html.

The *ROAD4WS* [118] is a Web service based deployment container for the *ROADfactory*. Currently, it supports only the SOAP/Web services technology. The *ROAD4WS* extends the *Apache Axis2 runtime* [2, 142] to support the service composite deployment, which is in addition to Axis2's existing service deployment. Importantly, the changes are introduced as extensions, and no changes are made to the Axis2 code base. This ensures the compatibility with Axis2 code base. The extension is implemented as another layer on top of Axis2, has additional capabilities beyond the behaviour of Axis2-core [111].

In summary, the *ROAD4WS* is a deployment environment for the *ROADfactory* and supports SOAP message based interaction among the players/actors. As our implementation of the *SIM-Core* adheres to the *ROADfactory* architecture, we can adopt the *ROAD4WS* without any major modification for the deployment of the *SIM-Core*. The details are discussed in Sect. 7.4.3.

Section 7.4.4 presents a tool to compose DSIMs and PSIMs from social interaction information in *SCOnto* KB in SCIM, while Sect. 7.4.5 shows how SIM generates and provides *interaction events* to SCIM.


## 7.4.1 Implementing the Model Execution Module

The *Model Execution Module (MEM)* maintains the functional elements of the runtime models. The main classes associated with the MEM are shown in Fig. 7.14. The element types *DSIMFunctional@Runtime*, *PSIM-Functional@Runtime*, *social role*, *social relationship*, *obligation rule*, *conversation rule*, *operational parameter* and *player binding* are maintained by the MEM. These are called the functional element types of the runtime models. During runtime, new elements of these types can be added, existing elements can be modified or removed. A runtime model connects multiple role-players and mediates interaction among these players by routing messages from one player to another player. That is, an interaction between players are realised as a message flow between them.

The implementation of the *Model Execution Module (MEM)* uses JAXB 2.0 [19] and XML Schema [24]. The DSIM and PSIM models are loaded to the MEM as JAXB 2.0 bindings. JAXB helps the generation of classes and interfaces of runtime models automatically using an XML schema. The XML Schema-based implementation also facilitates change to the model.

JAXB 2.0 supports the translation of an XML representation to Java Classes and vice versa. These processes usually are known as *unmarshalling* and *marshalling* [136, 139]. Correspondingly, two classes for *Unmarshalling* and *Marshalling* have been implemented. In the process of *unmarshalling*, an XML document is converted to Java content objects or a tree of objects. Conversely, the *marshalling* is the reverse process that converts a tree of Java

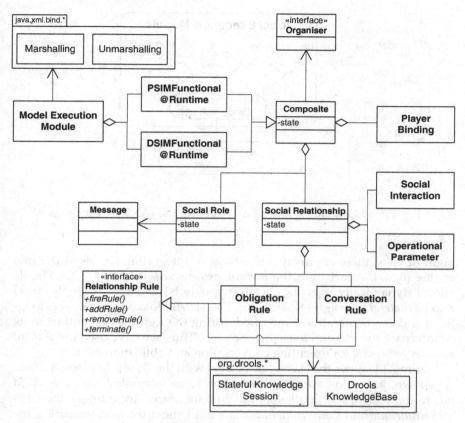

Fig. 7.14: Class Diagram: Model Execution Module implementation

content objects back to an XML document. Using the process of *unmarshalling*, the framework creates runtime models based on a DSIM or PSIM descriptor file as shown in Fig. 7.15. The process of *marshalling* is used to take a snapshot of the current description of a runtime model to be saved as an XML file.

The MEM includes the *model parser and binder (MPB)* component which is generated by the JAXB 2.0 *binding compiler* based on the DSIM schema (xsd) and PSIM schema (xsd) (see Appendix E). The MPB is used to generate the *DSIMFunctional@Runtime* and *PSIMFunctional@Runtime* models based on a descriptor such as *ConvoyDSIM.xml* and *Car#1PSIM.xml*. The descriptor file must conform to the DSIM or PSIM schemas, as appropriate. Therefore, any tool that generates the descriptor file should ensure that the output conforms to the DSIM or PSIM schemas.

We use the *Drools rule language* [47] to implement *social interactions* related constraints such as *conversations* and *obligations*. From the implementation

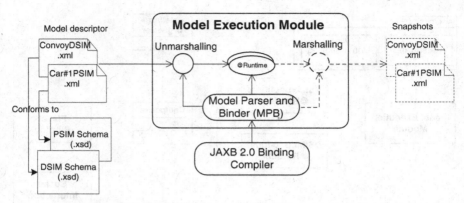

Fig. 7.15: Marshalling and unmarshalling via JAXB 2.0 bindings

point of view, there are many advantages of integrating Drools as the rule engine [8, 47]. Apart from the advantages discussed in Sect. 7.2.3, Drools allows dynamically injecting facts (Java objects) and rules (Drools rules) into its *Stateful Knowledge Session* [30]. The *Stateful Knowledge Session* is long-lived and can be iteratively modified during the runtime (in contrast to its counterpart, the *Stateless Knowledge Session*). Thus, we have used the *Stateful Knowledge Session* for executing conversation and obligation rules.

Figure 7.14 shows the classes associated with the Drools implementation. As shown, any rule base implementation to be integrated with the MEM has to implement the *RelationshipRuleBase* interface. Accordingly, the *ObligationRuleBase* and *ConversationRuleBase* implement the interface using the Drools plugin for the MEM to enforce the obligations and conversations using Drools rule. A social relationship maintains its associated *ObligationRuleBase* and *ConversationRuleBase* during the runtime. New rules can be added and existing rules can be removed from the rule base. Eventually, the rule base is deleted when no longer required, i.e., when the social relationship is removed. When a social interaction, i.e., a message, needs to be evaluated against the specified constraints, i.e., conversations and/or obligations, the corresponding conversation rules and/or obligations rules in their respective rule base are fired via the *fireRule()* method.

Drools rules are condition-action rules [47]. Therefore, a Drools rule contains two main parts, i.e., the *when* and *then* parts, which are also refereed to as the *Left Hand Side (LHS)* and *Right Hand Side (RHS)*.

- The *when* part specifies a certain condition to trigger the rule. This condition may be evaluated to true or false based on the properties of facts in the *Stateful Knowledge Session* [8]. Here, a *fact* means a Java object, such as a *message* inserted into the *Stateful Knowledge Session*.

- The *then* part specifies what needs to be done if the condition is evaluated to true. The action part is written here, which also might be subject to a further checking of a condition.

Figure 7.16 shows a sample Drools rule that interprets the obligation *o1* in the *ConvoyDSIM* (presented in Sect. 6.2.1.1). The Rule names should be unique in a rule base. Thus, we use the *id* of the obligation as the *name* of its corresponding rule, for example, here *o1* is used as the name of the rule. The obligation *o1* defines that the *notifyPositionUpdate* interaction (id="*i1*") occur in every 10 s. Thus, the *when* part of the rule first identifies the target interaction by checking its id as: *MessageReceivedEvent(id=="i1")*. The *MessageReceivedEvent* is a fact type (Java class) that interprets the arrival of a message to a social relationship. A *MessageReceivedEvent* fact, i.e., an instance of the *MessageReceivedEvent* class, is inserted into the rule base when the constraints related to that message needs to be evaluated. The *then* part of the rule evaluates the constraints. In this part, the *isObliged* function is invoked, which returns true if the obligation is satisfied, otherwise false. In the case of a false return value, an alert message is passed to the respective role/player.

```
//an instance of the obligation rule base
global ObligationRuleBase oRBIns;
//time of the last notifyPositionUpdate interaction
global long lastIntrTime = 0;
rule "o1"
    when
        //notifyPositionUpdate interaction
        $msg:MessageReceivedEvent(id=="i1")
    then
        long currentTime = System.currentTimeMillis();
        if(!oRBIns.isObliged($msg,currentTime,lastIntrTime)){
            $msg.setAlert("Obligation is violated");
        }
        lastIntrTime = currentTime;
    end
```

Fig. 7.16: A Drools rule for the obligation *o1*

## 7.4.2 *Implementing the Management Module*

The *Management Module (MM)* supports the adaptation of the runtime models instantiated by the MEM module. The main classes associated with MM are shown in Fig. 7.17. The MM comprises four main classes:

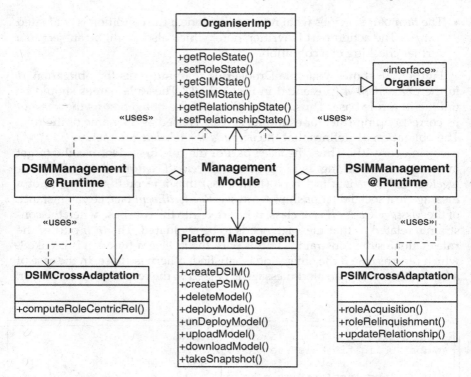

Fig. 7.17: Class Diagram: Management Module implementation

*Platform Management, OrganiserImp, DSIMCrossAdaptation, PSIMCrossAdaptation, DSIMManagement@Runtime* and *PSIMManagement@Runtime*.

The *Platform Management* class implements the platform level management operations listed in Table 7.6. The *OrganiserImp* class implements the *Organiser role interface* including *state*, *structure* and *parameter* related management operations, described in Sect. 6.2.2.3. The *DSIMCrossAdaptation* and *PSIMCrossAdaptation* classes implement cross adaptation related operations. In particular, the *DSIMCrossAdaptation* implements *computeRoleCentricRel* while the *PSIMCrossAdaptation* implements *roleAcquisition, roleRelinquishment* and *updateRelationship*. Both of the *DSIMManagement@Runtime* and *PSIMManagement@Runtime* uses *OrganiserImp* to support *state management*, *behaviour* and *parametric* adaptation in their respective *functional* model. In addition, the *DSIMManagement@Runtime* and *PSIMManagement@Runtime* use the *DSIMCrossAdaptation* and *PSIMCrossAdaptation*, respectively, to support adaptation *across* functional models.

### 7.4.3 *The Deployment Layer*

The current implementation of the SIM supports the Web service based deployment. We exploit ROAD4WS [118] for the Web service based deployment. It uses the Apache Axis2 [2] as the Web service engine (e.g., Apache Tomcat web server [3]). The issues of transport layer protocols, message processing and security are handled by the Axis2 engine. This ensures that the implementation conforms to the existing Web services standards such as SOAP [20] and WSDL [21].

Once ROAD4WS is installed a new directory called *road_composites* is created under AXIS2_HOME. In order to deploy a DSIM or PSIM model, the XML descriptor such as *ConvoyDSIM.xml* or *Car#1PSIM.xml* is placed inside this *road_composites* directory. This can be done *before* or *while* the server (Tomcat) is running. Once the model descriptor is deployed, the XML file is automatically picked up by ROAD4WS and uses the MEM and MM to instantiate both the *functional* (*DSIMFunctional@Runtime* or *PSIMFunctional@Runtime*) and *management* (*DSIMManagement@Runtime* or *PSIMManagement@Runtime*) part of the model. ROAD4WS creates the *service interfaces* (both the *functional* and *management* interface) for each and every *role* based on the *functional* and *management* part of the instantiated model. This service interfaces are exposed according to the WSDL 2.0 standard [21]. The service name is created by combining the model and social role name, following the pattern *modelname_socialrolename*. Each and every *message signature* of the *social interactions* is exposed as a WSDL operation. For example, all the interactions directed from the *Leading Car* social role in the *ConvoyDSIM*, i.e., *positionUpdate*, *routeUpdate* and *notifyMechIssue*, are exposed as operations of the *convoydsim_leadingcar* service, as shown in Fig. 7.18. Similarly, all the state, behaviour and parameter related management operations are exposed as WSDL operations. Figure 7.19 shows the partial management operations exposed as operation of the *convoydsim_organizer* service. These interfaces allow any WSDL 2.0 compatible client to invoke the operations.

### 7.4.4 *Composing Runtime Social Interaction Models Using* SIMbuilder

As part of the *SocioPlatform*, we have implemented a *web-based tool*, called *SIMbuilder*, for the software engineer to build DSIM and PSIM models from the *social interaction information* stored in the *SCOnto* knowledge base. Figure 7.20 shows the basic steps for composing such models using *SIMbuilder* tool (Fig. 7.21).

*SIMbuilder* retrieves interaction-centric relationships and corresponding social roles from the *SCOnto* knowledge base in SCIM, and presents to the

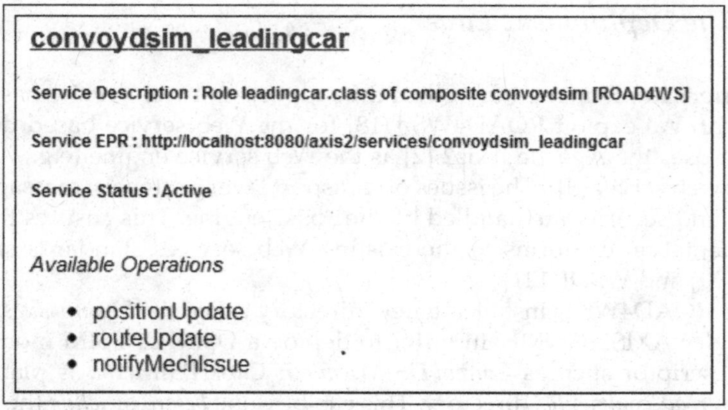

## convoydsim_leadingcar

**Service Description : Role leadingcar.class of composite convoydsim [ROAD4WS]**

**Service EPR : http://localhost:8080/axis2/services/convoydsim_leadingcar**

**Service Status : Active**

*Available Operations*

- positionUpdate
- routeUpdate
- notifyMechIssue

Fig. 7.18: *LeadingCar* social role (in *ConvoyDSIM*) related interactions are exposed as web service operations

## convoydsim_organizer

**Service Description : This is the organizer service of composite ConvoyDSIM. Purpose of the composite : Description**

**Service EPR : http://localhost:8080/axis2/services/convoydsim_organizer**

**Service Status : Active**

*Available Operations*

- deleteConversation
- getPlayerURL
- getConversationList
- takeSnapshot
- getAllInteractionsInARel
- addRelationship
- unbindRolePlayer
- deleteRelationship
- getObligationList
- getRelationshipList
⋮

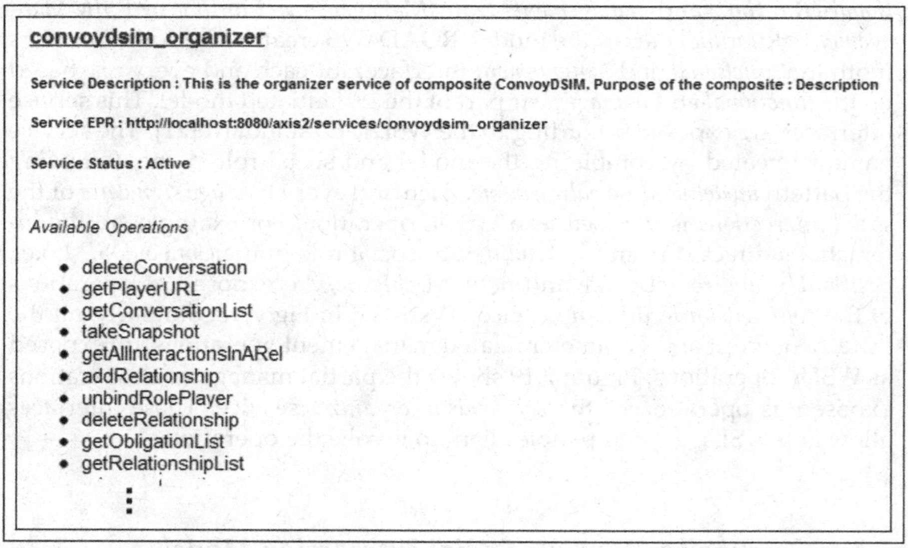

Fig. 7.19: Organiser (management) role (in *ConvoyDSIM*) operations are exposed as web service operations

user (e.g., a software engineer). The tool allows user to create a DSIM by explicitly selecting a set of *social roles* or *social relationships* for that model. For the case of *social role* based model creation, when a social role is selected for a model, all the social roles and relationships (including their interactions, conversations and obligations) those are connected with the *selected* social role are automatically added to the DSIM. For the case of *social relationship* based model creation, when a social relationship is selected for the model, just that relationship and its related social roles are added to the

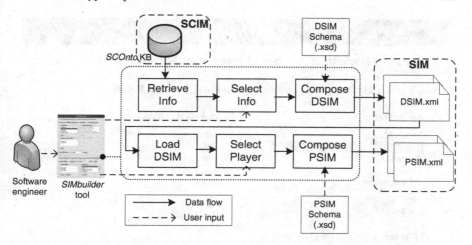

Fig. 7.20: Steps for composing DSIMs and PSIMs

model. Once the selection is done, tool automatically composes the DSIM and creates an XML descriptor, which is compliant with the DSIM schema (see Appendix E.1).

To compose a PSIM, SIMbuilder allows its user to load one or more source DSIMs and to select a role-player from whose perspective the PSIM needs to be created. Once the selection is done, tool automatically composes the PSIM and creates an XML descriptor, which is compliant with the PSIM schema (see Appendix E.2). SIM uses these DSIM and PSIM XML descriptors to generate runtime environment for mediating runtime social interactions.

### 7.4.5 Generating and Providing Interaction Events

SIM instantiates runtime social interaction models (i.e., DSIMs and PSIMs) of a collaborative application to mediate social interactions among collaborative actors/users. Users of the collaborative application interact with each other using their application through these runtime models. To allow the reasoning module of the SCIM to infer situations applications use, SIM generates an interaction event for each social interaction and sends it to the reasoning module, as shown in Fig. 7.22.

An interaction event is formatted based on the *IntEO* ontology presented in Sect. 5.4.1. Let us consider that during convoy the following car driver, i.e., Car#2, sends the *convoyBreak("food")* message to the leading car driver at 1:10 pm, and after a while, say 1:13 pm, Car#2 driver receives the *positiveResponse("food")* message from the leading car driver, i.e., Car#1. As a result, SIM generates two interaction events *ie1* and *ie2* as follows:

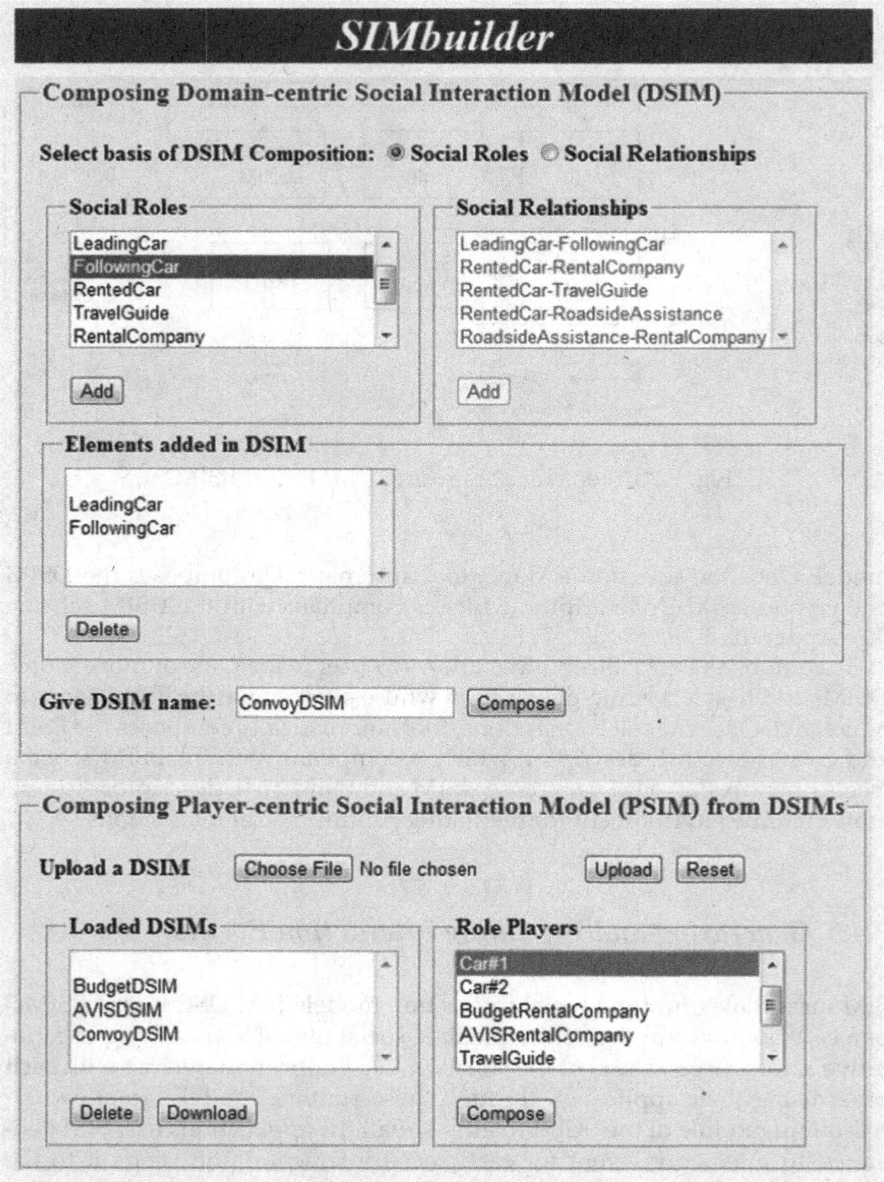

Fig. 7.21: *SIMbuilder* tool for composing DSIMs and PSIMs

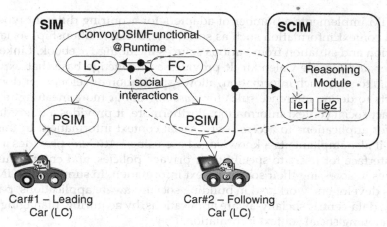

Fig. 7.22: Interaction events flow from SIM to SCIM

```
ie1:InteractionEvent(platform="CooperativeConvoy",
fromRole="FollowingCar",toRole="LeadingCar",
from="Car#2",to="Car#1",hasType="Proposing",
about="Food",atTime=TemporalEntity(start=1:10PM,
duration=0ms))

ie2:InteractionEvent(platform="CooperativeConvoy",
fromRole="LeadingCar",toRole="FollowingCar",
from="Car#1",to="Car#2",hasType="Agreeing",
about="Food",atTime=TemporalEntity(start=1:13PM,
duration=0ms))
```

Reasoning module matches these interaction events against the event patterns in situation rule to identify situations. An example is given in Sect. 8.3.6.1.

## 7.5 Summary

In this chapter, we have presented the implementation of the *SocioPlatform*. This platform assists the developers in building socially-aware applications by acquiring, storing, managing and provisioning social context information, providing a runtime environment for mediating social interactions, and managing their runtime adaptation. The *SocioPlatform* comprises two parts: *social context information management (SCIM)* and *social interaction management (SIM)*.

SCIM implements a number of adapters for acquiring different types of social context information such as social role, social relationship, social interaction and situation from various sources including Facebook, LinkedIn, Twitter and Google Calendar. It provides a knowledge base that exploits *SCOnto* to store such information, allows application developers or domain experts to define inference rules for *reasoning* about more meaningful and abstract social context information. Furthermore, it provides a query interface for applications to access users' social context information. In this regard, it also implements a knowledge base using *SACOnto*, provides a policy interface for users to specify their privacy policies, and enforces users' policies in accessing their social context information. In summary, SCIM reduces developers' workload in building socially-aware applications, particularly, data-centric socially-aware applications, by acquiring, managing and provisioning social context information.

SIM provides a runtime environment with adaptation support for developing interaction-centric socially-aware applications. It supports *adaptation* and *mediates* social interactions among users of an interaction-centric socially-aware applications. It allows the application developers to externalise inter-user relationships from the applications and model them explicitly. SIM aids the application development by providing a *runtime environment* to execute the social interaction models, and *managing runtime adaptation* of these models to cope with the changes in user requirements and environments.

# Chapter 8
# Case Studies: Social Context-Aware Mobile Applications

This chapter describes two case studies involving the development of two prototypical *social context-aware* mobile applications, in short *socially-aware* mobile applications, using our novel approach to *modelling, reasoning about* and *managing* social context information (SCI), and the associated *SocioPlatform*, introduced in the preceding four chapters. These case studies revolve around the application scenarios that have been discussed in Chap. 2 and have been used as running examples throughout this book. The goal of these case studies is to demonstrate the use and applicability of our proposed framework in developing two different types of socially-aware mobile applications. At the same time, these case studies highlight the benefits and strengths of the framework, and also validate the functionalities of the *SocioPlatform*.

The *first* case study presents the design and implementation process of developing a *data-centric* socially-aware mobile application. This case study uses the phone call interruptions scenario (discussed in Sect. 2.1.1) as an example for demonstrating how our proposed framework assists software engineers in designing and implementing such an application, called *socially-aware phone call (SPCall)*, by *acquiring, modelling, reasoning about, managing* and *provisioning* users' diverse *social context information* from various *sources*. In particular, this case study highlights the *functionalities* provided by the *Social Context Information Management (SCIM)* component of the *SocioPlatform* and demonstrates the use of these functionalities in addressing the challenges and requirements of developing *SPCall* (as identified in Sect. 2.1.2).

The *second* case study presents the design and implementation process of developing an *interaction-centric* socially-aware mobile application. This case study uses the cooperative convoy application scenario (discussed in Sect. 2.2.1) as an example for demonstrating how our proposed framework assists software engineers in designing and implementing such an application, called *socially-aware telematics (SocioTelematics)*, by modelling and managing interaction relationships and their runtime adaptation, to cope with

© Springer International Publishing Switzerland 2016
M.A. Kabir et al., *Pervasive Social Computing*,
DOI 10.1007/978-3-319-29951-8_8

the changes in requirements and environments. In particular, this case study highlights the *functionalities* provided by the *Social Interaction Management (SCM)* component of the *SocioPlatform* and demonstrates the use of these functionalities in addressing the challenges and requirements of developing *SocioTelematics* (as identified in Sect. 2.2.2).

The principal contributions of this chapter are twofold. *First*, the *challenges* and *process* associated with the design and implementation of two different types of socially-aware applications are illustrated by examples. *Second*, the principal research *contributions* of this work (*i.e.*, the aforementioned approach to *modelling*, *reasoning about* and *managing* social context information including *runtime adaptation* support, and the functionalities of the *SocioPlatform*) are validated.

The discussions of this chapter repeat the various fragments of case studies that have been used throughout the discussion in previous chapters. This chapter, however, aims to present the case studies in a *comprehensive* manner to demonstrate how the social context information modelling, reasoning and management approach can be systematically applied to developing two different types of socially-aware applications.

The structure of the chapter is as follows. Section 8.1 presents a design and implementation process of developing socially-aware applications using our proposed framework and the associated *SocioPlatform*. A case study of developing and using a data-centric socially-aware mobile application, namely *SPCall*, is presented in Sect. 8.2, while Sect. 8.3 presents a case study of developing and using an interaction-centric socially-aware mobile application, namely *SocioTelematics*.

## 8.1 Design and Implementation Process

Figure 8.1 shows the design and implementation process for socially-aware applications. Steps ①–⑤ belong to the design process while the step ⑥ belongs to the implementation process.

In the *design process*, steps ①–④ are applicable for both the *data-centric* and *interaction-centric* socially-aware applications, while step ⑤ is mainly used for the *interaction-centric* socially-aware applications. During design process, in step ①, social context information of application's interest is identified through application requirements analysis. The *SCOnto*, *i.e.*, upper social context ontology, is adopted and extended based on the identified social context information. For instance, in the *SPCall* application design process, the *SCOnto* is adopted and extended by incorporating a *interaction-oriented social relationship* ontology. In step ③, description logic based reasoning rules related to *SCOnto* are modified (*e.g.*, unnecessary rules are deleted, new rules are added) and *IntEO*, *i.e.*, interaction event upper ontology, is extended (*e.g.*, application specific concepts are added).

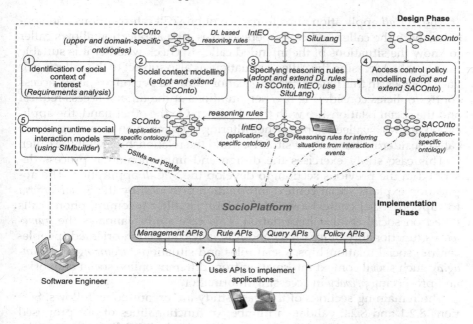

Fig. 8.1: Design and implementation process for socially-aware applications

In step ④, *SACOnto*, *i.e.*, socially-aware access control ontology, is revisited and modified based on the application requirements. As mentioned above, step ⑤ is mainly used for the *interaction-centric* socially-aware applications, to compose both the *domain-* and *player-centric social interaction models (DSIMs and PSIMs)* from the *connection-oriented social relationships* information captured in *SCOnto*. In this step, software engineers use the *SIMbuilder* tool to compose these DSIMs and PSIMs. All of these generated artifacts in the design process, *i.e.*, ontologies, rules and models, are used by the *SocioPlatform* to provide runtime support to the applications.

In the *implementation process*, *i.e.*, in step ⑥, software engineers or application developers use APIs provided by the *SocioPlatform* to implement socially-aware applications. Section 8.2.4 presents the implementation of the *SPCall* application, while Sect. 8.3.5 presents the implementation of the *SocioTelematics* application.

## 8.2 Case Study #1: The *SPCall* Application

The *SPCall* application is a *data-centric* socially-aware application, where the data, *i.e.*, social context information such as *social relationships* and *situations*, is the basis of the application's behaviour.

The *SPCall* application aims to reduce phone call interruptions and considers both the caller and callee perspectives. The application allows caller to know the situations of the intended callee to check whether it is suitable time to call. Accessing the callee's situations is also subject to the callee's privacy policies. In this regard, the application allows a person to specify access control policies considering his/her situations at the time of access request and the social relationship with the requester. On the other hand, the application allows a callee to specify her filtering preference on incoming phone calls considering her current situations and the relationships with the caller.

This case study exercises the design and implementation process described in the previous section, to develop the *SPCall* application. The application exploits social context information provided by the *SocioPlatform* to support social context-aware behaviour, *i.e.,* filter incoming phone calls based on social context information. This case study validates the *framework's* functionality of *modelling* and *reasoning* connection-oriented (people-centric) social relationships, social roles and situations, *acquiring* and *managing* such social context information from different online social networks, and preserving *privacy* in accessing information.

The remaining sections of this case study are organised as follows. Sections 8.2.1 and 8.2.2 validate a number of functionalities of our proposed framework by utilising these functionalities in the *SPCall* application development to achieve its design features. In this regard, Sect. 8.2.1 presents *design goals* and *constraints* related to the development of *SPCall* application. The *design features* to address the *design goals* and *constraints*, and how our proposed *framework* supports these design features are described in Sect. 8.2.2. By following the guidelines presented in Sect. 8.1, Sect. 8.2.3 presents the *design process* of the *SPCall* application, while Sect. 8.2.4 describes a prototype *implementation* of the *SPCall* client for Android. The artifacts, *i.e.,* ontology models and reasoning rules, that are generated in the design process are used by the *SocioPlatform*. At runtime, *SocioPlatform acquires* social context information from online social networks and *reason about* social context information. These are presented in Sects. 8.2.5 and 8.2.6, respectively. Finally, Sect. 8.2.7 illustrates the *use* of *SPCall* client together with the social context information provided by the *SocioPlatform* for two use case scenarios.

## 8.2.1 Design Goals and Constraint

As discussed in Sect. 2.1.2, the requirements analysis of the *SPCall* application identifies two main *design goals*: (1) minimizing mobile phone interruptions by automatically filtering/handling incoming phone calls based on user preferences that consider user's social context information such as social relationships and situations, and (2) improving situation awareness by supplying callers with situation information of the intended callee that will lead to a suitable decision on making phone calls. However, supplying a callee's situation information to a caller raises a serious concern regarding *privacy*.

## 8.2.2 Design Features

The above two *design goals* and a *design constraint* can be addressed by three *design features*. Below we describe these design features and how our proposed *framework* supports these features.

*Provisioning social context information*   To address the first design goal, the *SPCall* application needs to be provisioned with its user's social context information. However, users' social context information is distributed all over the web, emerging from and fragmented across may different proprietary applications such as Facebook, LinkedIn, and Twitter. Thus, it is a challenge for application developers as they must collect information from different sources and wade through a lot of irrelevant information to obtain the social context information of interest to the targeted functionality. Our proposed framework addresses this challenge by providing an approach to modelling, representing and reasoning about different types of social context information, and platform support for acquiring, storing and accessing such social context information (see, for example, Sects. 4.3, 5.2 and 7.1). It has already been recognised that separating the process of acquiring contextual information from actual applications is key to facilitating application development and maintenance [68, 99]. In our framework, the *SocioPlatform* separates the process of acquiring social context information from the actual applications and provides the design feature of provisioning social context information, which subsequently enhances the application development process.

*Allowing a person to access others' situation information*   To address the second design goal, the *SPCall* application needs to allow its user to access others' situation information so that the user can decide whether it is an appropriate situation to make a phone call. Therefore, it is not a good design decision to manage a user's social context information locally in his/her mobile device as technically it is hardly possible for other users to access that information. In our proposed framework, the *SocioPlatform* supports this design feature (*i.e.*, allows a person to access others' situation information) as the platform separates the acquisition and management of users' social context information from the actual applications and can be deployed as a Web service in a cloud. As a result, the *SPCall* application can collect others' situation information from the *SocioPlatform*. Therefore, a person can access other persons' situation information using the *SPCall* application running in a mobile device having internet connectivity.

*Allowing owners to control their information access*    The users' social context information is inherently sensitive. But for the *SPCall* application, a user needs to share his/her situation information with other users. This information sharing raises serious concerns regarding the privacy and access control over users' situation information. Thus, the application should allow its users to retain control over who has access to her situation information under which conditions. In our framework, as discussed in Sect. 6.1, we propose a way to preserve the information owner's privacy by allowing the owners to fine-tune the granularity of information access and to specify access control policies. Therefore, our framework addresses this *constraint* by *allowing* information owners to *specify* their privacy preferences, *i.e.*, who can access what information (here user situation) under which conditions. The *SocioPlatform* implements the proposed privacy preserving technique and *enforces* users' privacy preferences when disclosing their situation information to others (see Sect. 7.2.4). Therefore, the *SPCall* application can meet this *constraint* through the *SocioPlatform*.

## 8.2.3 Design Process

By following the design process described in Sect. 8.1, we build artifacts, *i.e.*, ontologies and rules, for the *SPCall* application. In Sect. 2.1.2, the requirements of the *SPCall* application are analysed (step ①), where we have pointed out that the *people-centric social relationships* (*e.g.*, father-child, mother-child, husband-wife, etc.) and *situations* (*e.g.*, meeting, seminar, watching game in a stadium, etc.) are the key social context information for the *SPCall* application. Thus, in step ②, we adopt and extend the *upper SCOnto* (see Sect. 4.2) by incorporating a *people-centric social relationship ontology* (described in Sect. 4.3.2.1) and a *situation ontology* (described in Sect. 4.3.4). The *people-centric social relationship ontology* includes family, friend and work related social relationships such as father-son, graduate school friend and student-supervisor, while the *situation ontology* includes business and non-business related situations such as meeting, seminar, lecture and watching game in a stadium. Figure 8.2 shows an excerpt of the extended *SCOnto* for the *SPCall* application.

In step ③, we further enrich *SCOnto* by incorporating description logic based *reasoning rules* for deriving social relationships and situations. These reasoning rules have described in Sects. 5.2 and 5.3.1. A complete list of these reasoning rules are given in Appendix A. To infer situations (*e.g.*, user is watching game in a stadium) from user's interaction events information on Facebook, we adopt and extend *IntEO* (see Sect. 5.4.1) by

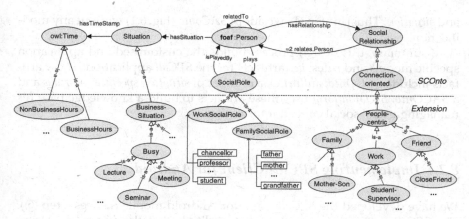

Fig. 8.2: A excerpt of the extended *SCOnto* for *SPCall* application

incorporating a *domain-specific interaction event ontology* for Facebook (see Sect. 5.4.3). Figure 8.3 shows an excerpt of the extended *IntEO* for the *SPCall* application.

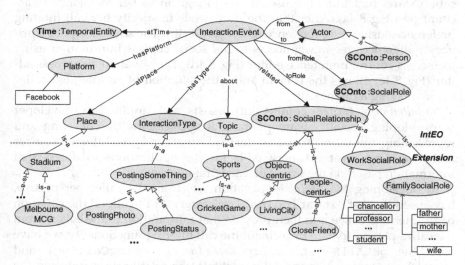

Fig. 8.3: A excerpt of the extended *IntEO* for *SPCall* application

Using *SituLang* (see Sect. 5.4.5), we specify a situation inference rule to detect the 'watching game in a stadium' situation (see Sect. 5.4.7). The *SPCall* application requires *people-centric social relationship* and *situation* based access control, as discussed in Sect. 2.1.2. Our access control policy model, *socially-aware access control ontology (SAConto)*, considers both the *social relationship* and *situation*. Thus, in step ④, we adopt *SAConto* (Fig. 6.1) without any modification.

In summary, this design process builds the customised and application specific models and rules, *i.e.*, artifacts for the *SPCall* application. These artifacts include a *SCOnto*, an *IntEO*, a number of *situation specification rules* and a *SACOnto*. *SocioPlatform* uses these artifacts to build a knowledge base for managing users' social context information.

### 8.2.4  Implementing SPCall Client for Android

We have developed the *SPCall* client for Android mobile devices (step ⑥). The *SPCall* application provides functionality both caller and callee. Using the application a caller can obtain the situation of an intended callee to check whether it is a suitable time to call. On the other hand, to reduce interruptions, a callee can specify her preferences on incoming calls such as ring, vibrate, reject, or reject and send situation, based on her current situation and the relationship with the caller.

Figure 8.4 shows some screenshots of the application. When the application starts first time, the user needs to sign in to her *SocioPlatform* account (see Fig. 8.4a). After that the user needs to specify her call filtering preferences using the preference editor (Fig. 8.4b). The user can specify privacy preferences regarding access to her social context information using the access control preference editor (Fig. 8.4d). The situation awareness editor (Fig. 8.4c) allows the user to know the situation of an intended callee before making a phone call.

*SocioPlatform* (*SCIM* component) assists the application developer in developing socially-aware phone call applications by collecting and representing the users' social context information from different sources and providing a set of query APIs for the applications to access that information based on the users' privacy preferences.

In developing the *SPCall* application we, from the caller perspective, have used the `getSituation(callee)` query API to obtain the situation of an intended callee and then provide that information to the caller. From the callee perspective, to implement the call filtering functionality, we have used the `getAllRelationshipsName(me,inComingCallNum)` and `getSituation(me)` query APIs to obtain the relationships between the caller and callee, and the current situation of the callee. Then, based on the specified filtering preferences in the application, it decides whether to ring, vibrate, reject, or reject and send situation information at a specific granularity. In the case of a "send situation at a specific granularity" decision, the application invokes the `getSituAtGranularity(me,gLevel)` query API to obtain the situation information of the callee at the specified granularity level and then sends it to the caller.

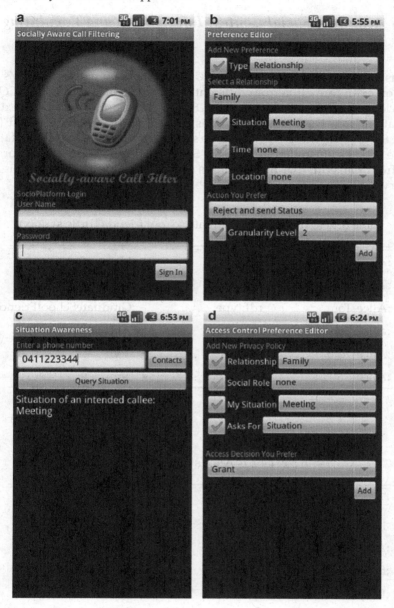

Fig. 8.4: Screen shots of the *SPCall* client application for Android. (**a**) Sign in screen. (**b**) Editor for specifying call filtering preferences. (**c**) Editor for querying situation of an intended callee. (**d**) Editor for specifying information access preferences

### 8.2.5 *Acquiring Social Context Information and Populating Knowledge Base*

Let us consider that *SocioPlatform* (*SCIM* component) acquires Alice's social context information from different OSNs and stores it into her *SCOnto* knowledge base. As illustrated in Fig. 8.5a, SCIM acquires social context information from Facebook that Tom is Alice's graduate school friend (see Table 8.1 for specification in the Turtle syntax [87]), and Jack is Alice's father (Table 8.2). As illustrated in Fig. 8.5b, SCIM collects social context information from LinkedIn that Bob is Alice's colleague (Table 8.3) and John is her supervisor (Table 8.4).

Table 8.1: Tom is Alice's graduate school friend (Turtle syntax)

| :Alice | rdf:type | :Me |
|--------|----------|-----|
| :Tom | rdf:type | :Person |
| :Alice-Tom | rdf:type | :GraduateSchoolFriend |
| :Alice-Tom | :relates | :Alice |
| :Alice-Tom | :relates | :Tom |
| :Alice | :relatedTo | :Tom |

Table 8.2: Jack is Alice's father (Turtle syntax)

| :Alice | rdf:type | :Me |
|--------|----------|-----|
| :Jack | rdf:type | :Person |
| :Alice-Jack | rdf:type | :SocialRelationship |
| :father | rdf:type | :FamilySocialRole |
| :Jack | :plays | :father |
| :Alice | :gender | female |

**a**

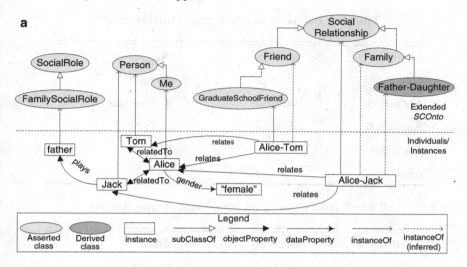

**b**

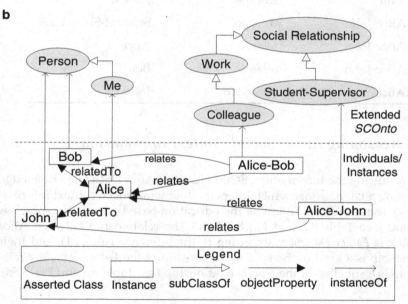

Fig. 8.5: *SocioPlatform* acquires social context information from OSNs. (**a**) Alice's social context information acquired from Facebook. (**b**) Alice's social context information acquired from LinkedIn

Table 8.3: Bob is Alice's colleague (Turtle syntax)

| :Alice | rdf:type | :Me |
|--------|----------|-----|
| :Bob | rdf:type | :Person |
| :Alice-Bob | rdf:type | :Colleague |
| :Alice-Bob | :relates | :Alice |
| :Alice-Bob | :relates | :Bob |
| :Alice | :relatedTo | :Bob |

Table 8.4: John is Alice's supervisor (Turtle syntax)

| :Alice | rdf:type | :Me |
|--------|----------|-----|
| :John | rdf:type | :Person |
| :Alice-John | rdf:type | :Student-Supervisor |
| :Alice-John | :relates | :Alice |
| :Alice-John | :relates | :Bob |
| :Alice | :relatedTo | :John |

## 8.2.6  Reasoning About Social Context Information

After acquiring the information, SCIM classifies Alice's *SCOnto* knowledge base using a DL reasoner which infers the following social context information: (1) Tom is Alice's friend as the education-based friend is a sub-class of friend (see Table 8.5 and Fig. 8.5a); (2) The relationship between Alice and Jack is *Father-Daughter* according to the inference rule (5.1), and their relationship is a kind of the *Family* relationship as the *Father-Daughter* relationship is a subclass of the *Family* relationship (see Table 8.6 and Fig. 8.5a).

Table 8.5: Tom is Alice's friend as the education-based friend is a sub-class of friend (Turtle syntax)

| :EducationBasedFriend | rdf:subClassOf | :Friend |
|-----------------------|----------------|---------|
| :Alice-Tom | rdf:type | :Friend |

Table 8.6: The relationship between Jack and Alice is father-daughter which is a kind of family relationship (Turtle syntax)

| :Alice-Jack | rdf:type | :Father-Daughter |
|---|---|---|
| :Father-Daughter | rdf:subClassOf | :Family |
| :Alice-Jack | rdf:type | :Family |

### 8.2.7  SPCall Use Scenarios

Let us consider that Alice, an university graduate student, uses the *SPCall* application to filter her incoming phone calls. She specifies her call filtering preferences in the *SPCall* as:

i. If my situation is *meeting* or *seminar*, and a call comes from *friend*, the action is to reject;

ii. If my situation is *meeting* or *seminar*, and a call comes from *family*, the action is to reject and forward my status at granularity level 2 (Busy);

iii. If my situation is *meeting* or *seminar*, and a call comes from *colleague*, the action is to reject and forward status at granularity level 3 (*i.e.,* meeting or seminar);

iv. If my situation is *meeting* or *seminar*, and a call comes from the *supervisor*, the action is to vibrate;

v. If my situation is a type of non-business situation, the action is ring.

We further assume that Alice specifies the following Policy#1 and Policy#2 (described in Sect. 6.1.2) as her privacy preferences regarding access to her status information which are stored in Alice's *SACOnto* knowledge base.

Policy#1:

$$Granted \equiv Access \sqcap$$
$$\exists\ decision(Requester \sqcap \exists asksFor.\textbf{Situation} \sqcap$$
$$\exists\ hasRelationship.\textbf{Colleague} \sqcap$$
$$\exists\ relatedTo.(Owner \sqcap \exists hasSituation.\textbf{Meeting}))$$

Policy#2:

$$GrantedInGL5 \equiv Access \sqcap$$
$$\exists\ decision(Requester \sqcap \exists asksFor.\textbf{Situation} \sqcap$$
$$\exists\ hasRelationship.\textbf{Student-Supervisor} \sqcap$$
$$\exists\ relatedTo.(Owner \sqcap \exists hasSituation.\textbf{Chatting}))$$

Based on the above settings we can analyse several scenarios:

*Scene#1:*   Once on a Monday 2:30 pm, Alice is in a meeting with her supervisor. One of her colleagues, Bob, wants to talk with Alice. Using the *SPCall*, Bob requests for Alice's situation. When the request comes to SCIMS, it first deduces Alice's situation using time instant, as described in Sect. 5.3.1, and finds that Alice is now supposed to be in a meeting. SCIMS updates Alice's *SCOnto* knowledge base with her situation being 'Meeting'. After that SCIMS checks Alice's privacy preferences (stored in the *SACOnto* KB) regarding Bob's request by following the steps specified in Sect. 6.1.3, and finds that Policy#1 gives permission to send her situation to Bob. Thus, Bob gets the reply about Alice's situation being 'Meeting' and decides not to make a phone call.

*Scene#2:*   During the same period of time, Alice receives a phone call from her father Jack. Alice's *SPCall* application sends requests to SCIMS to ask for Alice's situation and her relationships with the caller. As in scene#1, SCIMS identifies that Alice is in meeting. SCIMS executes the query against Alice's *SCOnto* knowledge base to identify her relationships with the caller and finds that the relationship is 'Father-Daughter' which is a type of 'Family' relationship. Upon receiving the situation and relationship information from SCIMS, Alice's *SPCall* application checks with the Alice's filtering preferences and decides to reject the call and send Alice's situation at granularity level 2 according to the preference number (ii). The application then requests from SCIMS the situation at granularity level 2 and gets 'Busy' as the reply. Finally, the application sends the situation, 'Busy', as a message to Jack.

## 8.3 Case Study #2: The *SocioTelematics* Application

The *SocioTelematics* application is an interaction-centric socially-aware application, where *agreements* and *constraints*, about social interactions among collaborative actors, are the basis of the application.

The *SocioTelematics* application aims to allow two or more vehicle drivers to form a cooperative convoy by supporting their social interactions. Such social interactions are based on predefined *agreements* and *constraints* that characterise the interaction relationships between the players, such as drivers. In complex and changing environments, such *agreements* and *constraints*, and thus *interaction relationships* are subject to change. Thus, the behaviour of the application needs to be adapted to cope with the changes.

This case study exercises the design and implementation process described in Sect. 8.1 to develop the *SocioTelematics* application. The application uses the *runtime environment* and *adaptation management* functionalities of *SocioPlatform* to facilitate interactions and to cope with changes in requirements and environments. This case study validates our proposed approach to *modelling* runtime social interactions and *managing* their runtime adaptation.

The remaining sections of this case study are organised as follows. Section 8.3.1 presents design goals and constraints of developing the *SocioTelematics* application. A set of design features (provided by our proposed framework) to address these design constraints is presented in Sect. 8.3.2. Section 8.3.3 presents the design process of developing the *SocioTelematics* application. Section 8.3.4 describes how the *SocioPlatform* creates a runtime environment for the *SocioTelematics* to use by using the artifacts that are generated in design process. Section 8.3.5 describes an implementation of the *SocioTelematics* client application for Android. Finally, a number of use case scenarios of the *SocioTelematics* application are described in Sect. 8.3.6.

## 8.3.1 Design Goals and Design Constraints

The requirements analysis of the *SocioTelematics* application (described in Sect. 2.2.2) identifies three main *design goals*: (1) the application should support social interactions and enforce users' agreements in such interactions, (2) the application should provide a coordinated view of the different interactions and allows its users to perform coordination in an automated manner, and (3) the application needs to support adaptation in interaction relationships at runtime. There exists a *constraint* related to the third design goal—perform adaptation in a safe manner without affecting the interactions.

## 8.3.2 Design Features

The above three design goals and the design constraint can be addressed by four design features. Below we describe how our proposed framework supports these design features.

*Modelling runtime social interactions from a domain perspective*   To   address the *first* design goal, it is required to model and represent users' agreements related to their social interactions. This model should have a runtime representation to enforce constraints and agreements while social interactions are happening. Our proposed framework provides a role based approach to model and represent users' agreements related to their social interactions, namely the *domain-centric social interaction model (DSIM)* (see Sect. 6.2.1.1). Our *SocioPlatform* provides a runtime environment to instantiate the DSIM and to facilitate social interactions complying with the model specification (see Sect. 7.3.1).

*Modelling runtime social interaction from a player perspective* To address the second design goal, it is required to model and represent social interactions from a player (user) perspective, to allow the player to specify his/her coordination preferences, and to support execution of these preferences. Our proposed framework provides an approach to model social interaction from a player perspective that represents a player's coordinated view of all his/her social interactions, namely the *player-centric social interaction model (PSIM)* (see Sect. 6.2.1.2). Like for a DSIM, the *SocioPlatform* also provides a runtime environment for instantiating a PSIM (see Sect. 7.3.1).

*Supporting runtime adaptation* To address the third design goal, *i.e.,* allow one to modify runtime social interaction models, it is required to support runtime adaptation in social interaction models. However, social interaction models are interrelated with each other. For instance, one or more player-centric social interaction models might be associated with a domain-centric social interaction model. Thus, a change in a domain-centric social interaction model needs to be propagated to the associated player-centric social interaction model(s). Our framework provides a mechanism for adaptation in a social interaction model (see Sect. 6.2.2.2) and adaptation propagation across social interaction models (see Sect. 6.2.3). The *SocioPlatform* implements this mechanism and provides the adaptation management functionality for applications to use (see Sect. 7.4.2).

*Runtime model states and safe change* To address the design constraint, *i.e.,* performing adaptation without affecting social interactions, it requires the safe change. Our framework defines *safe change* based on the *state* of each entity, *i.e.,* social role, social relationship and interaction model as a whole. An entity can be adapted safely only when the entity is in the *IDLE* state (see Sect. 6.2.2.4). The *SocioPlatform* manages the states of the runtime models and their entities, ensures safe adaptation to the runtime models without affecting social interactions.

It has already been recognised that the model based development approach is key to facilitating the application development process and managing runtime adaptation [84, 155, 175]. In our approach, inter-actor relationships in an application are (externalised from the application implementation and) modelled explicitly using DSIMs and PSIMs, their runtime (execution) environment is generated, and adaptation is managed by the *SocioPlatform*.

## 8.3.3 Design Process

By following the design process described in Sect. 8.1, we build artifacts, *i.e.,* DSIMs and PSIMs, for the *SocioTelematics* application. Section 8.3.3.1

presents step ② of the design process that extends *SCOnto* to model and represent social context information related to this case study. Section 8.3.3.2 presents step ③ of the design process that extends *IntEO* and specifies a rule to infer a situation from drivers' social interactions at runtime. As step ⑤ of the design process, Sect. 8.3.3.3 shows how to compose domain- and player-centric social interaction models from the extended *SCOnto* using *SIMbuilder*.

### 8.3.3.1  Extending *SCOnto* and Specifying Social Interactions

In Sect. 2.2.2, the requirements of the *SocioTelematics* application are analysed (step ①), where we have identified that the *interaction-oriented* social relationships are the basis for the *SocioTelematics* application. To model and represent such social context information of interest, in step ②, we adopt and extend the *upper SCOnto* (see Sect. 4.2) by incorporating the cooperative convoy related *social role ontology* (presented in Sect. 4.3.1), *interaction-oriented social relationship ontology* (presented in Sect. 4.3.3) and *driving-in-convoy ontology* (described in Sect. 4.3.4). Figure 8.6 shows an excerpt of the extended *SCOnto*.

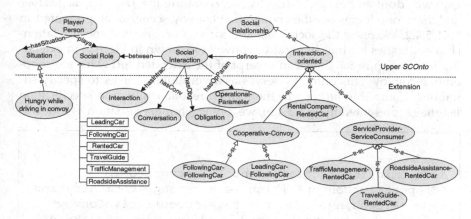

Fig. 8.6: An excerpt of the extended *SCOnto* for *SocioTelematics* case study

We specify the social interactions and their related conversations, obligations and operational parameters based on the agreements among the collaborative actors in the cooperative convoy scenario, as discussed in Sect. 4.3.3. Each social interaction is represented as an instance of the *SCOnto:SocialInteraction*. For example, Table 8.7 presents a social interaction (written in Turtle syntax [40]) which represents the agreement—*"upon receiving a route request from a driver of a rented car, a travel guide service should send a route notification in 15 seconds"*. This social interaction (*si1*) consists of two basic interactions (*i7* and *i8*), a conversation (*c1*), an obligation (*o3*) and an operational Parameter (*p3*). The *i7* interaction represents the route request from the rented car social role to the travel guide social role, while the *i8* interaction captures the route notification from the travel guide to the rented car. The *c1* conversation specifies a sequence between *i7* and *i8*, i.e., *i7 leadsTo i8*, which states that after the *i7* interaction there will eventually be an *i8* interaction. The *c1* conversation is also subject to obligation *o3*. This obligation constrains the time duration between *i7* and *i8* which is maximum 15 s, as represented by the *p3* operational parameter.

Similarly, we specify all other *interactions, conversations, obligations* and *operational parameters* based on the actors' agreements in the cooperative convoy (see Appendix B). At the end of this step ② of the design process, a *SCOnto* knowledge base is developed that contains the *interaction-oriented* relationships information among the collaborative actors in a cooperative convoy scenario.

### 8.3.3.2 Extending *IntEO* and Specifying Situation Reasoning Rules

In step ③ of the design process, to infer situations (*e.g.*, drivers are hungry) we adopt and extend *IntEO* by incorporating the *Time, InteractionType* and *Topic* ontologies for the cooperative convoy scenario, as presented in Sect. 5.4.2. We reuse the social role and interaction-oriented social relationship ontologies for the cooperative convoy (as shown in Fig. 8.6) in extending *IntEO*. Figure 8.7 shows an excerpt of the extended *IntEO* for the cooperative convoy. This ontology serves as a vocabulary for us to specify situations. Using this *IntEO* and the human readable situation specification language (presented in Sect. 5.4.5), we define a hungry situation as follows:

```
when
An atomic interaction event IE1 occurred in
"CooperativeConvoy" which is a message communication,
type "Proposing" and from role "CooperativeConvoy"
and discussing about "Food" and (at time "Breakfast"
or at time "Lunch" or at time "Dinner")

A complex interaction event CIE1 observed between IE1
and IE2, where interaction event IE2 is a message
communication, type "Agreeing" and from
role "CooperativeConvoy" and discussing about "Food",
has occurred "after" IE1
```

Table 8.7: A social interaction (si1) that consists of two basic interactions (i7 and i8), a conversation (c1), a obligation (o3) and an operational parameter (p3)

| | | |
|---|---|---|
| :si1 | rdf:type | :SocialInteraction |
| :si1 | :hasIntrac | :i7 |
| :si1 | :hasIntrac | :i8 |
| :si1 | :hasConv | :c1 |
| :si1 | :hasObg | :o3 |
| :si1 | :hasOpParam | :p3 |
| :i7 | rdf:type | :Interaction |
| :i7 | :msgSignature | "routeRequest" |
| :i7 | :fromRole | :RentedCar |
| :i7 | :toRole | :TravelGuide |
| :i8 | rdf:type | :Interaction |
| :i8 | :msgSignature | "routeNotification" |
| :i8 | :fromRole | :TravelGuide |
| :i8 | :toRole | :RentedCar |
| :p3 | rdf:type | :OperationalParameter |
| :p3 | :paramName | "maxTimeDelay" |
| :p3 | :value | 15 |
| :p3 | :timeUnit | SEC |
| :o3 | rdf:type | :Obligation |
| :o3 | :timer | :duration |
| :o3 | :relatedOP | :p3 |
| :c1 | rdf:type | :Conversation |
| :c1 | :intrac1 | :i7 |
| :c1 | :intrac2 | :i8 |
| :c1 | :hasSequence | :leadsTo |
| :c1 | :relatedObg | :o3 |

The social interaction can be read as—*upon receiving a route request from a driver of a rented car, a travel guide service should send a route notification in 15 seconds*

```
then
Notify "Hungry"
```

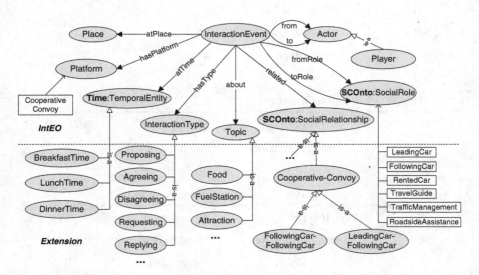

Fig. 8.7: An excerpt of the extended *IntEO* for the cooperative convoy

In summary, in this step, a cooperative convoy application specific *IntEO* is build and a *rule* to recognise the hungry situation is specified.

### 8.3.3.3 Composing Domain- and Player-Centric Social Interaction Models

In step ⑤ of the design process, we use *SCOnto* that has developed in Sect. 8.3.3.1 and the *SIMbuilder* tool, to compose both the *domain-centric social interaction models (DSIMs)* and *player-centric social interaction models (PSIMs)*. In Sect. 7.4.4, we have described steps for composing such DSIMs and PSIMs using the *SIMbuilder* tool. We use social roles as the basis to compose the DSIMs. We compose three DSIMs: *ConvoyDSIM*, *BudgetDSIM* and *AVISD-SIM*. The *ConvoyDSIM* consists of the *LeadingCar* and *FollowingCar* social roles. Thus, all the *interactions, conversations, obligations* and *operational parameters* related to these social roles, as captured in the *SCOnto*, are automatically added to the *ConvoyDSIM* by the *SIMbuilder*. See Appendix C.1.1 for the complete specification of the *ConvoyDSIM*. Similarly, we compose the *BudgetDSIM* and *AVISDSIM*. The *BudgetDSIM* consists of the *Rented-Car*, *RentalCompany*, *TravelGuide* and *RoadsideAssitance* social roles, while the *AVISDSIM* consists of the *RentedCar*, *RentalCompany*, *TrafficManagement* and *RoadsideAssistance* social roles. The complete specifications of the *BudgetD-SIM* and *AVISDSIM* are presented in Appendices C.1.2 and C.1.3, respectively.

We use the *SIMbuilder* to further compose *PSIMs* from the Car#1 and Car#2 perspectives, namely *Car#1PSIM* and *Car#2PSIM*. *SIMbuilder* takes the *ConvoyDSIM*, *BudgetDSIM* and *AVISDSIM* as inputs and automatically generates these two PSIMs. Appendices C.2.1 and C.2.2 present the complete specification of *Car#1PSIM* and *Car#2PSIM*, respectively. At the end of this step ⑤, five social interaction models—*ConvoyDSIM*, *BudgetDSIM*, *AVISDSIM*, *Car#1PSIM*, and *Car#2PSIM*—have been built, which we will use to generate the runtime execution environment for *SocioTelematics*.

### 8.3.4 Instantiating Models and Creating Runtime Environment

Section 8.3.3 has described steps ①–⑤ of the design process that build artifacts such as *SCOnto*, *IntEO*, a *situation inference rule*, *ConvoyDSIM*, *BudgetDSIM*, *AVISDSIM*, *Car#1PSIM* and *Car#2PSIM* for developing the *SocioTelematics* application. The *SocioPlatform* uses these artifacts, *i.e.*, models and rules, to create a runtime environment for the application to use. In particular, SIM instantiates DSIMs and PSIMs, and creates a runtime environment, *i.e.*, *DSIMFunctional@Runtime*, *DSIMManagement@Runtime PSIMFunctional@Runtime*, and *PSIMManagement@Runtme*, for mediating social interactions (see Sect. 7.3.1). SIM also generates a Web service interface for the *SocioTelematics* application to invoke. On the other hand, SCIM uses *SCOnto*, *IntEO* and the situation inference rule to create a knowledge base and semantic event processing environment for inferring users' situations from interaction events. SCIM exploits the rule translation script (*RuleTrans.dsl*) (provided in Appendix D) to convert the situation inference rule, specified in Sect. 8.3.3.2, to the Drools executable format.

### 8.3.5 Implementing SocioTelematics Client for Android

We have implemented the *SocioTelematics* application for Android mobile devices and Tablets (step ⑥). To support map, we use Google Map APIs for Android. To interact with the *SocioPlatform* and process SOAP messages, we use ksoap2 [12]—a lightweight SOAP library for the Android platform. The application executes a number of tasks running as background services:

- *Location sharing service*—Listen to the location update from specified location provider (*e.g.*, GPS, Network) and send the position to the other cars as *positionUpdate* interaction messages.
- *Message fetching service*—Pull the received messages from the queue in a proxy running on the server.
- *Message processing service*—Extract information from the fetched message, evaluate and fire coordination rules, and update the interaction history accordingly.
- *Map viewer service*—Periodically update the cars' (both leading and following) positions on the map viewer so that drivers can see each other's positions.
- *Text to speech conversion service*—To reduce driver distraction, this service provides voice notification (message name and contents) when a message comes

The application has four fundamental panels such as *settings*, *convoy*, *interaction* and *adaptation* (see Fig. 8.8). When the application starts, the driver needs to configure the application using the *settings panel* (see Fig. 8.8a) by providing a user ID (to recognise the car) and password. Using the user's credential, the application invokes the *getRoleList* organiser role function at the server side, fetches all social roles associated to its user and populates those roles in the main screen. Also based on each social role in the role list, the application invokes the *getInteractionList* function and accumulates associated interaction definitions for each social role. This means that the application is not tightly coupled with the social roles played by the car in a cooperative convoy and also the company from which the car has been rented. Thus, it serves the purpose of multi-modal use, *i.e.*, without any internal logic change this application can be used in a car from any rental company as well as by a driver playing either the leading car or following car social role.

During driving, for the driver to perform the additional tasks in the cooperative convoy (*e.g.*, forwarding information) as agreed may cause distraction. To facilitate such collaboration but with less distraction, the application allows the driver to specify coordination rules for, say, forwarding information. In the *settings panel*, a driver can select an *incoming* interaction message and its corresponding *outgoing* message(s) as his/her coordination preferences. For example, the following car driver specifies a coordination preference as: "when a road block notification is received from the roadside assistance service (as the *roadBlockNotification* interaction), forward it to the leading car (as the *notifyRoadBlock* interaction)". Figure 8.9 shows this coordination rule specified in the *SocioTelematics* application. Thus, when the application receives a message that matches with an incoming message in the coordination preferences, the application (as a coordinator player) sends the corresponding outgoing message(s) immediately on behalf of the driver. Also, the application provides voice notification (message name and contents) when a message comes.

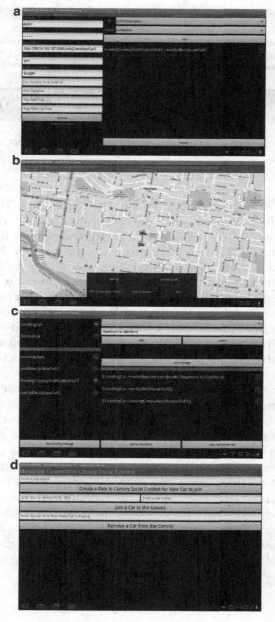

Fig. 8.8: Some screenshots of the *SocioTelematics* application for Android.
(**a**) Settings panel. (**b**) Convoy panel. (**c**) Interaction panel. (**d**) Adaptation
panel

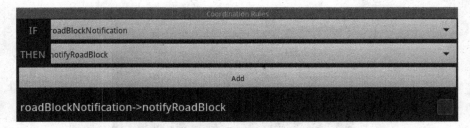

Fig. 8.9: A screen-shot of a coordination rule specified in *SocioTelematics* application

Figure 8.8b shows the *convoy panel* of the application. The map of the screen shows the cars' positions in the cooperative convoy. The application uses GPS to show its car position on the map and notifies that position to others (as the *notifyPosition* interaction) using the location sharing service. The application gets the other car's position once it receives a *notifyPosition* message from the other car. Also it shows a warning message as pop-up, for example, if the distance between the two cars violates their agreed distance.

The *interaction panel* (see Fig. 8.8d) of the application allows a driver to perform interactions and displays: the role list—associated with the driver of the car, the interactions list—list of interactions corresponding to the selected role in the role list, and the interaction log—interactions so far occurred. Section 8.3.6.1 presents some interaction examples.

The *adaptation panel* (see Fig. 8.8d) allows the leading car driver to perform adaptation on the *ConvoyDSIM*. The current version of the application provides an interface for the organiser player, *e.g.*, the driver of the leading car, to perform/trigger three structural adaptation: create a new position (*i.e.*, social role) for a new car to join in the convoy, join a car to the convoy and remove a car from the convoy. As required, options to trigger other types of structural adaptation can easily be incorporated to the interface. A number of parametric adaptation can be performed through the *settings panel*. The current version provides options to set the position update frequency and maximum desired distance. Here, it is worth noting that using the application interface the organiser player only triggers or requests adaptation, while the actual adaptation is performed on the server side. Section 8.3.6.2 illustrates a number of adaptation scenarios.

### 8.3.6 SocioTelematics *Use Scenarios*

This section describes a number of use cases for the *SocioTelematics* application. Section 8.3.6.1 presents use cases where drivers in the cooperative convoy use the application to perform social interactions. Section 8.3.6.2

describes use cases where drivers use the *SocioTelematics* application to perform runtime adaptation.

### 8.3.6.1  Performing Social Interactions

At runtime, the drivers of the cooperative convoy use the *SocioTelematics* application to perform social interactions adhering with their agreements and constraints. Through these interactions, drivers perform tasks and achieve their goals.

For instance, during convoy, if any driver needs to stop for some reason, *e.g.*, food, fuel, etc., he/she can propose it to other drivers using the *convoyBreak(reason)* social interaction. Other drivers can reply with a *positiveResponse* or *negativeResponse* social interaction. These interactions are mediated by the SIM of the SocioPlatform. SIM generates an *interaction event* for each social interaction and insert that interaction event to the reasoning module of the SCIM. The complex event processing engine of the reasoning module incrementally matches the inserted interaction events with the event patterns in the situation inference rule. When a rule is matched, the situation is identified and inserted to the *SCOnto* knowledge base.

Assume that the following car driver sends the *convoyBreak("food")* message to the leading car driver and after a while receives the *positiveResponse("food")* message. As a result, SIM generates two interaction events *ie*1 and *ie*2 as follows:

```
ie1:InteractionEvent(platform="CooperativeConvoy",
fromRole="FollowingCar",hasType="Proposing",
about="Food",atTime=TemporalEntity(start=1:10PM,
duration=0ms))

ie2:InteractionEvent(platform="CooperativeConvoy",
toRole="LeadingCar",hasType="Agreeing",about="Food",
atTime=TemporalEntity(start=1:13PM,duration=0ms))
```

Also assume that the inference rule to identify the hungry situation, as described in Sect. 8.3.3.2, is running in the reasoning module. Therefore, the hungry situation is identified by the above two interaction events, and is stored into the *SCOnto* knowledge base. As a result of this situation, the *SocioTelematics* application of the leading car sends a nearby restaurant address request as a *addressRequest("restaurant")* interaction to the travel guide service. Once it receives the restaurant addresses as a *responseAddress* interaction, the convoy panel highlights those addresses on the map. The driver can choose any of the restaurant and drive to there for food.

### 8.3.6.2  Performing Runtime Adaptation

In this section, we consider a number of use cases that require adaptation in the *ConvoyDSIM* and the associated PSIMs. The organiser player of the *ConvoyDSIM*, here the driver of the leading car, triggers the adaptation by using the *SocioTelematics* application, while the adaptation request is executed and managed by the *SocioPlatform*. Figure 8.10 illustrates the modifications of the runtime DSIM and PSIMs as adaptation is carried out.

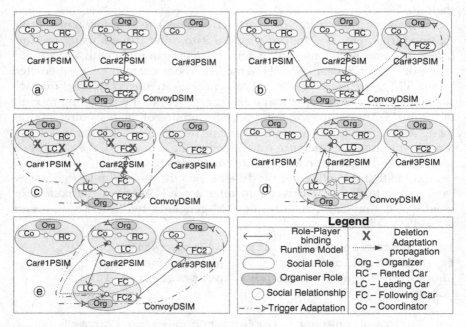

Fig. 8.10: An illustration of the runtime adaptation in the *ConvoyDSIM* and associated *PSIMs* to cope with changes in user requirements and environments

- To *add* a new car, say Car#3, as a following car in the convoy, the leading car driver (the *ConvoyDSIM* organiser player) presses the respective button in the *adaptation panel* (Fig. 8.8d) of the *SocioTelematics* application that invokes the following management methods (see Fig. 8.10ⓐ): (1) *addSocialRole ("FC2")*—to add another following car role, namely FC2, to the *ConvoyDSIM*, (2) *addSRelationship("LC", "FC2", relName)*—to add a relationship between the LC and FC2 social roles, (3) *addInteraction, addConversation, addObligation and addOperationalParam*—to add functional and non-functional information to the relationship as required, and finally (4) *bindRolePlayer*—to bind the third vehicle to the FC2 role. Because the

*bindRolePlayer* is invoked, the *ConvoyDSIM* (as part of the cross adaptation process) computes the role-centric relationship of the FC2 (say
Rr5) using Algorithm 1 (see Sect. 6.2.3) and invokes the *triggerRoleAcquisition* method in *Car#3PSIM* with *FC2* and *Rr5* as parameters. As a result, the *Car#3PSIM* updates its structure by adding the FC2 role and the
*Rr5* role-centric relationship between the FC2 and Coordinator roles (see
Fig. 8.10(b)). As a result of these sequence of adaptations, *Car#3PSIM* is
linked with the *ConvoyDSIM*, and thus using the *SocioTelematics* application driver of Car#3 can perform interactions with other car drivers of the
convoy through the *Car#3PSIM*.

- If the leading car (Car#1) breaks-down, the *ConvoyDSIM* organizer
  player (the leading car driver) presses the respective button in the
  adaptation panel of the *SocioTelematics* application that invokes the
  *unbindRolePlayer* method to unbind *Car#1PSIM* from the LC. As a
  consequence, the *ConvoyDSIM* (as part of the cross adaptation process)
  invokes the *triggerRoleRelinquishment("LC")* method in *Car#1PSIM*.
  As a result, the *Car#1PSIM* updates its structure by deleting the LC
  role and the relationship between the LC and Coordinator roles (see
  Fig. 8.10(c)). Furthermore, to assign a following car (say Car#2) to
  play the leading car role, the leading car driver presses the respective
  button that invokes *unbindRolePlayer("FC", urlCar#2PSIM)* followed by
  *bindRolePlayer("LC",urlCar#2PSIM)* to first unbind *Car#2PSIM* from the
  following car role and then bind it to the leading car role. As a result,
  the *ConvoyDSIM* (as part of the cross adaptation process) invokes the
  *triggerRoleRelinquishment* and *triggerRoleAcquisition* methods respectively
  which ultimately updates the *Car#2PSIM* by removing the FC role
  and its associated relationship (see Fig. 8.10(c)) followed by adding the
  LC role and its associated relationship (see Fig. 8.10(d)). As a result of
  these sequence of adaptations, the *Car#1PSIM* has detached from the
  *ConvoyDSIM*, and thus using the *SocioTelematics* application, the driver
  of Car#1 will no longer be able to perform interactions with other car
  drivers.
- The heavy raining situation can be detected by Car#2's (LC) wet-sensor
  and an adaptation rule (defined in Sect. 6.2.2.3) embedded in the leading
  car's *SocioTelematics* application can trigger adaptation automatically or
  the driver of the leading car can trigger adaptation manually by pressing
  a button in the application. This adaptation request invokes the *update-
  OperationalParam(r1,maxDesiredDistance,600m)* method in *ConvoyDSIM* to
  change the *maxDesiredDistance* parameter value from 1 km to 600 m. Both
  the *Car#2PSIM* and *Car#3PSIM* are related to the R4 relationship. Thus,
  the *ConvoyDSIM* (as part of the cross adaptation process) invokes the *triggerUpdateRelationship* method in *Car#2PSIM* and *Car#3PSIM* to update the
  *maxDesiredDistance* value in both of these PSIMs (see Fig. 8.10(e)).

## 8.4 Summary

In this chapter, we have presented two case studies of developing and using social context-aware applications. In this regard, we have presented a *design* and *implementation* process of developing such applications. We have also described a number of *use case* scenarios to illustrate the *usefulness* of these applications. The first case study is a *data-centric* socially-aware phone call application, namely *SPCall*, while the second case study is an *interaction-centric* socially-aware application, namely *SocioTelematics*.

On one hand, these two case studies have highlighted various challenges in terms of *design goals* and *constraints*, for developing two different types of socially-aware applications. The *design features* provided by our *framework* and the *SocioPlatform* to address those challenges are also illustrated.

On the other hand, these case studies have exercised our approach to *designing* and *implementing* socially-aware applications. Subsequently, they have *validated* the principal contributions of this work, *i.e.*, an approach to *modelling*, *reasoning* about and *managing* social context information including *runtime adaptation* support.

# Chapter 9
# Experimental Evaluations

In this chapter, we evaluate the *SocioPlatform* presented in Chap. 7, and the two socially-aware applications (*SPCall* and *SocioTelematics*) developed in Chap. 8.

As discussed in Chap. 7, the *SocioPlatform* provides high-level support for developing socially-aware applications by *acquiring, reasoning* and *provisioning* different types of social context information and *managing* runtime adaptation. It comprises two main components, *social context information management (SCIM)* and *social interaction management (SIM)*, which provide different functionalities or services to the applications. The *SCIM* provides social context information *acquisition, reasoning* and *query processing* functionalities, while the *SIM* provides a *runtime environment* for mediating social interactions (*i.e.*, checking interaction constraints and routing interaction messages) based on the *runtime social interaction models*, and supports their *runtime adaptation*.

In order to evaluate the *SocioPlatform*, we setup an experimental environment (Sect. 9.1). We evaluate the performance of each of the aforementioned core *functionalities* provided by the *SCIM* and *SIM*. We evaluate the *information acquisition, reasoning* and *query processing* performance of *SCIM* using real data from Facebook, LinkedIn, Twitter and Google Calendar (Sect. 9.2). We quantify the *adaptation overhead* of SIM, and evaluate the *performance and resource consumption* of *SIM* related to mediating social interactions (Sect. 9.3).

Furthermore, to demonstrate the real-world *applicability* and *feasibility* of the *SPCall* and *SocioTelematics* applications that have been developed using our *framework* and the *SocioPlatform*, we evaluate the applications' *performance* and *resource consumption* using real-life experiments. Section 9.4 evaluates the *SocioTelematics* application, while Sect. 9.5 presents the evaluation of the *SPCall* application.

© Springer International Publishing Switzerland 2016
M.A. Kabir et al., *Pervasive Social Computing*,
DOI 10.1007/978-3-319-29951-8_9

## 9.1 Experimental Setup

The *SocioPlatform* is deployed and evaluated on a machine with a Core 2 Duo E8400 3 GHz processor, 3 GB RAM, Windows XP professional edition SP3. We used Java 1.6, Drools 2 [9], Tomcat 7.0.21 [3] and Axis2 1.6.1 [2] in this experiment.

To evaluate the *SPCall* and *SocioTelematics* applications in real-life experiment, it is required to deploy the *SocioPlatform* on a machine with a real IP-address so that the applications running on a mobile device can communicate with the *SocioPlatform* over the Internet. Thus, for the experiments to evaluating applications (Sects. 9.5 and 9.4), we have deployed the *Socio-Platform* on a standard windows based Apache Tomcat Web server in the Amazon Elastic Compute Cloud (Amazon EC2).[1]

## 9.2 Evaluating *SCIM*

SCIM is a knowledge management component of the *SocioPlatform*, providing information acquisition, reasoning and query processing functionalities. The reasoning functionality includes both the *description logic* based social context information (SCI) reasoning and *real time complex interaction event stream processing* based situation reasoning. Sections 9.2.1–9.2.3 present the performance evaluation of SCI acquisition, description logic based SCI reasoning and query processing over SCI, respectively. In these experiments, we consider *eight* social media users who have accounts in Facebook, LinkedIn, Twitter, and also a user of Google Calendar. These users are chosen in such a way that they have increasing numbers of friends in Facebook, including a user with 5000 friends which is the highest number Facebook allows. Note that these users gave us permission to collect their social data. The *SCOnto* and its related *reasoning rules*, as discussed in Sect. 7.2.1, have been used in these experiments.

To evaluate the performance of real time *interaction event stream processing* based situation reasoning (Sect. 9.2.4), the data set, *i.e.*, situation rules and interaction event streams, should fulfill some criteria. For instance, a specific number of *interaction events* in an *interaction event stream* should be matched with a specific number of *situation reasoning rules*. It is very difficult to collect interaction event streams from social media with such criteria. Thus, to evaluate the performance of complex event processing based situation reasoning, we have used simulated data that comply with the desired criteria but actually represent interaction events in social media.

---

[1] http://aws.amazon.com/ec2/.

## 9.2.1  *Performance Evaluation for Information Acquisition*

To assess the performance of the *information acquisition* functionality of SCIM, we evaluate the time cost of acquiring information using two metrics: (1) time required to fetch raw data from a source—to quantify the network overhead; (2) Preprocessing and storing time—time required to extract the information of interest from fetched data, transform it to the suitable format, and insert it into the *SCOnto* knowledge base (KB)—to quantify the performance of inserting information into the *SCOnto* KB of *SCIMS*.

For each Facebook account of the eight experimental subjects, we ran the experiment 50 times. Figure 9.1a, b show the result where error bars depict standard deviation. For the highest number of friends (*i.e.*, 5000), the average time to fetch information from Facebook was 12 s (see Fig. 9.1a) and the average time for preprocessing and inserting information into knowledge base was around 700 ms (see Fig. 9.1b), which is an acceptable result, since this information acquisition is usually performed off-line and might not be required to be updated very frequently. In general, the results in Fig. 9.1a, b show that time requires to acquire social context information increases with increasing size of information.

Table 9.1 reports the summary of the social context information that we have collected from these users' Facebook accounts, including the users' total connections (a connection is a link between two users), the number of connections in different categories of relationships and the number of relationship types in each category (reported in parentheses). It is worth noting that a connection could be a member of multiple relationship types. For example, a connection between two users could be a college friend, graduate school friend and also they might live in same city. The connections of *User3* are categorized into 18 types of relationships while the connections are categorized into four types for *User4*. Thus, the information fetching (Fig. 9.1a) and inserting (Fig. 9.1b) time for *User3* have taken longer than *User4* even though *User3's* number of connections is less than *User4's* number of connections.

Similarly, using SCIM, we have also collected these users' other type of social context information such as *research-topic based relationship*, *following-follower relationship*, and *situations*, from LinkedIn, Twitter and Google Calendar. At the end of this information acquisition experiment, SCIM has built eight knowledge bases for the eight users. Table 9.2 reports the details of these knowledge bases, including the number of inserted axioms[2] and the size (in kilobyte) of each knowledge base. In the table, we can see that the number of axioms in *User3's* KB is more than the number of axioms in *User4's* KB as *User3* has more classified relationships than *User4*.

---

[2] OWL uses statements to represent knowledge, which are called axioms.

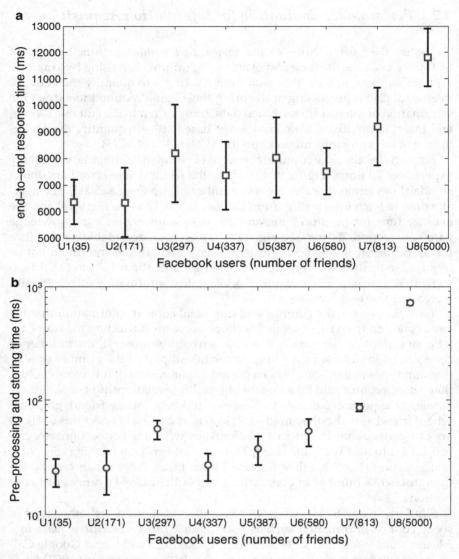

Fig. 9.1: Time taken by the *Information acquisition* module in SCIMS to acquire social context information from Facebook. (**a**) Fetching information from Facebook. (**b**) Inserting information into knowledge base

Table 9.1: Social context information collected from users' Facebook accounts

| Subjects | Connections | People-centric | | | | Object-centric | Total |
|---|---|---|---|---|---|---|---|
| | | Family | Friend | Work | User define | living address | |
| User1 | 35 | 5(3) | 37(5) | 2(1) | 0(0) | 16(3) | 60(12) |
| User2 | 171 | 0(0) | 152(3) | 0(0) | 51(2) | 44(1) | 247(4) |
| User3 | 297 | 12(3) | 202(3) | 32(2) | 120(3) | 185(7) | 551(18) |
| User4 | 338 | 1(1) | 326(1) | 12(1) | 0(0) | 55(1) | 394(4) |
| User5 | 387 | 5(4) | 143(2) | 18(1) | 331(4) | 25(1) | 522(12) |
| User6 | 580 | 1(1) | 502(3) | 54(1) | 3(1) | 91(1) | 651(7) |
| User7 | 813 | 3(2) | 809(4) | 33(1) | 63(4) | 45(1) | 953(12) |
| User8 | 5000 | 0(0) | 3126(2) | 21(1) | 3(2) | 1920(1) | 5070(6) |

The number reported in parentheses is relationship types in each category

Table 9.2: Knowledge bases (KBs) have built for experimental subjects

| KB No. | Experimental subjects | Before classification and reasoning | | After classification and reasoning | |
|---|---|---|---|---|---|
| | | Asserted axioms count (after inserting SCI into KB) | KB size in kilobyte | Inferred axioms count | Overall KB size in kilobyte |
| 1 | User1 | 657 | 90 | 528 | 116 |
| 2 | User2 | 1513 | 234 | 1401 | 267 |
| 3 | User3 | 2167 | 358 | 2576 | 430 |
| 4 | User4 | 1822 | 287 | 2557 | 400 |
| 5 | User5 | 2489 | 410 | 2907 | 493 |
| 6 | User6 | 3389 | 616 | 4756 | 772 |
| 7 | User7 | 4583 | 829 | 5422 | 1011 |
| 8 | User8 | 24,245 | 4499 | 32,381 | 5318 |

### 9.2.2 *Performance Evaluation for Description Logic Based Reasoning*

To measure the SCIM's performance on classifying and reasoning, we have used the eight knowledge bases that have been built in the above experiments. Figure 9.2 shows the results of knowledge base initialisation and classification time using five different reasoners. In general, the initialisation and classification time increases with increasing sizes of the knowledge base. The results show that TrOWL performs very well for a small sized KB, but as the KB size increases the computation cost increases dramatically. However, Fact++ outperforms consistently from small to large sized KBs. Table 9.2 reports the number of inferred axioms newly created after classifying each KB and the overall size of the KB.

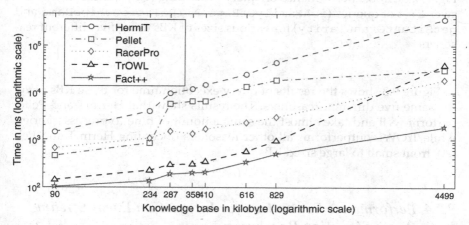

Fig. 9.2: Reasoning time for various sizes of KBs using five different reasoners

### 9.2.3 *Performance Evaluation for Query Processing*

To measure the SCIM's performance on *query processing*, we measure the time to answer a set of queries—isAFamilyOfB, getAllRelationshipsName and getSituAtGranularity. The eight knowledge bases (see Table 9.2) that have been built in previous experiments using users' social context information acquired from Facebook, LinkedIn, Twitter and Google calendar, are used for performance evaluation.

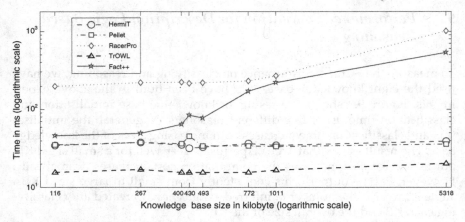

Fig. 9.3: SCIMS's performance on query processing (QP)—time taken to answer a set of queries (`isAFamilyOfB`, `getAllRelationshipsName` and `getSituAtGranularity`) for various sizes of KBs using five different reasoners

Figure 9.3 shows the results of query execution time for these KBs using the same five different reasoners. The results show that HermiT and Pellet perform well and take almost the same amount of time to process queries, while TrOWL outperforms all other reasoners (including HermiT and Pellet), from small to large sized KBs.

### 9.2.4  Performance Evaluation for Interaction Event Stream Based Situation Reasoning

To evaluate the performance of the *Interaction Event Stream based Situation Reasoning*, we have conducted a series of experiments. The goal of these experiments was to *quantify* the platform performance in processing interaction event streams (IESs), executing situation specification rule (SSR) sets and detecting situations. In these experiments, we have used the TrOWL reasoner in semantic matching, as the experimental results presented in Sect. 9.2.3 showed that the TrOWL reasoner outperforms, *i.e.,*, takes comparatively less time to perform matching, over the RacerPro, Fact++, HermiT and Pellet reasoners.

We have measured the *situation reasoning time* with increasing sizes of SSR sets where each rule in the rule sets consists of six simple interaction event patterns (IEPs) and three to five complex interaction event patterns (CIEPs). Each IEP uses two to eight ontological properties. We have created three interaction event streams (IESs) where each IES comprised 1000 interaction events (IEs). These three IESs match all rules in the SSR sets exactly one, fifty and hundred times respectively. This means that for a SSR set with 500 rules, an IES that matches each rule 50 times will detect 25,000 situations (i.e., 500 × 50). For each of the three IESs, we execute each set of SSRs 1000 times. The results in Fig. 9.4 show that for a given number (1, 50 or 100) in which each rule is fired, the total time to fire a set of SSRs increases approximate linearly with the size of the SSR set. For a particular size of SSR set, the time taken to fire the rule set increases as the number times each rule is fired increases. Moreover, the results also show that for a particular number of detected situations, an SSR set of smaller size takes less time compared to an SSR set of larger size. For instance, as illustrated in Fig. 9.4, both the case where each of 500 SSRs fire 100 times and the case where each of 1000 SSRs fire 50 times, detect 50,000 situations. However, the former case takes less time than the latter, in detecting the same number of situations.

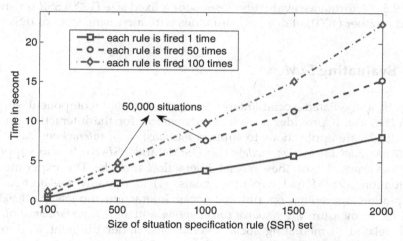

Fig. 9.4: Performance evaluation results for a fixed size (1000) of interaction event stream (IES) with increasing situation specification rule (SSR) set sizes and event firing occurrences

We have also measured the *situation reasoning time* for 1000 SSRs with increasing sizes of IESs (or the volumes of the interaction events). We have created a set of IESs where each IES matches each rule of the 1000 SSRs exactly once, *i.e.*, regardless the size of the IES, each experimental IES will detect 1000 situations. The error bars in Fig. 9.5 show that for 1000 SSRs and 1000 detected situations, the execution time does not vary much with the sizes of the IESs and lies between 3.94 and 3.97 s (on average). That is, for a fixed size of SSR set and a fixed number of detected situations, the size of the inserted IES does not have much impact on the platform performance in terms of computation time.

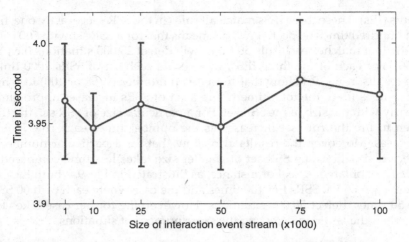

Fig. 9.5: Performance evaluation results for a fixed size (1000) SSR set and a fixed number (1000) of detected situations with increasing sizes of IESs

## 9.3 Evaluating *SIM*

*SIM* is a mediated social interactions management component of the *SocioPlatform*. It provides a *runtime environment* for the interaction-centric socially-aware applications to support *mediated social interactions* based on runtime *social interaction models* (*i.e., DSIMs* and *PSIMs*). It also supports *runtime adaptation* of these social interaction models. The experimental evaluation of SIM had two main goals: (1) to measure the *overhead* of adaptation operations on runtime social interaction models (Sect. 9.3.1), and (2) to measure the *resource consumption* and *system performance* of the SIM, related to mediating social interactions, under different workloads (Sect. 9.3.2).

### 9.3.1 *Quantifying Adaptation Overhead*

To *quantify* the adaptation overhead, we deployed 100 domain-centric social interaction models (DSIMs) where each DSIM consists of ten social roles connected in a ring topology using ten social relationships. Each relationship is comprised of six interactions, six conversations and six obligations. Using *SIMbuilder*, we created ten PSIMs for ten players where each player plays a role in each of the 100 DSIMs. Thus, each PSIM contained 100 social roles and 100 role-centric relationships. We executed each of the *structural* and *parametric* adaptation operations 1000 times over the 100 DSIMs. We measured the time from the moment the adaptation was requested, to the moment Axis2 updated the services. The box plots in Figs. 9.6 and 9.7 show the summary of the results where the horizontal line inside each of the boxes represents the median. The results show that the deletion operations (*e.g., delSocialRole, delSRelationship,* and *unbindRP*) take less time compared to the addition operations (*i.e., addSocialRole, addSRelationship,* and *bindRP*).

Figure 9.6a, b present the time required to perform different *structural* and *parametric* adaptation in a *social interaction model* at *runtime*. The results show that the *structural* adaptation takes more time than the parametric adaptation. Among the structural adaptation operations, adding a social relationship (*addSRelationship*) in the model takes the longest time, around 68 ms (on average), as it needs to update the configuration of two social roles,

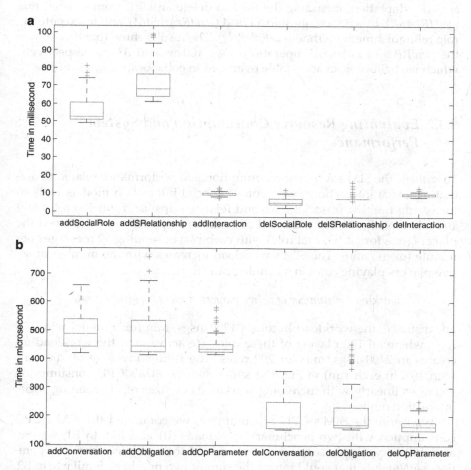

Fig. 9.6: Adaptation in a runtime social interaction model. (**a**) Structural adaptation. (**b**) Parametric adaptation

whereas deleting a social role (*delSocialRole*) takes the least time, around 5 ms. For different *parametric* adaptation operations, the required time is related to rule injections and deletions in the Drools engine and lies between 162 and 486 µs.

The box plots in Fig. 9.7 illustrate the *adaptation overhead* results across a DSIM and a PSIM. Figure 9.7a shows the total time required for the *bindRP* (bind role-player) and *unbindRP* (unbind role-player) structural adaptation. Figure 9.7b shows the time required for each step in the *bindRP* adaptation, including the time to add a URL to a social role (*addURLtoSR*), to compute a role centric relationship (*compRoleCenRel*) using Algorithm 1, to send a request to a PSIM (*sendReqToPSIM*), and to execute the role acquisition method (*exeRoleAcq*). Figure 9.7c shows the time required for each step in the *unbindRP* adaptation, including the time to delete an URL from a social role (*delURL4SR*), to send a request to a PSIM (*sendReqToSIM*), and to execute the role relinquishment method (*exeRoleRelq*). The results show that on average the *bindRP* and *unbindRP* operations take 100 ms and 33 ms, respectively, which we believe is an acceptable overhead in collaborative applications.

## 9.3.2 Evaluating Resource Consumption and System Performance

To *evaluate* the SIM's resource consumption and performance related to mediating social interactions, we deployed social interaction models with an increasing number of social roles and relationships, *i.e.*, from 100 roles and 100 relationships to 500 roles and 500 relationships. We also deployed the players (one for each social role) with each player sending 12 messages per minute (msgs/min). The SIM's workload increases with the number of active players playing roles in a running model, *i.e.*,

$$workload = number\ of\ active\ players \times message\ sending\ rate$$

For instance, the workload becomes 1200 msgs/min for a model with 100 roles where all 100 players of these roles are active, and the workload increases to 2400 msgs/min for 200 roles. The results (average of 100 runs with 10 min each run) in Fig. 9.8a show that the SIM's CPU consumption increases linearly with increasing workloads or sizes of the running social interaction model.

To *quantify* the SIM's CPU consumption, we compared the SIM's CPU consumption with two benchmark workloads (B1 and B2). In B1, we created 100 very simple services where each of these services had an operation *addNumbers* that could return the sum of two numbers. Similarly in B2, we created 100 services where each of them had an operation *sendMessage* that could receive a message from a client and pass it on to another client.

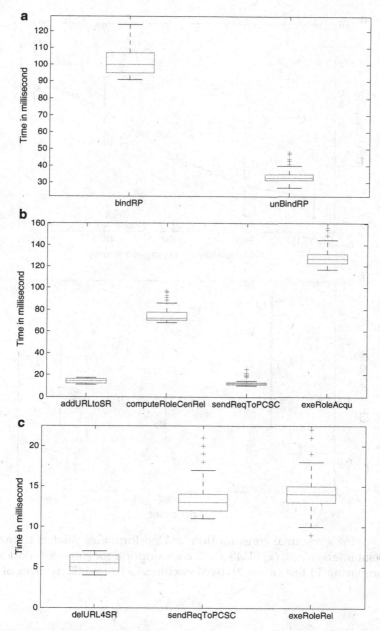

Fig. 9.7: Adaptation across social interaction models caused by binding and unbinding role player structural adaptation. (**a**) Binding and unbinding role player structural adaptation. (**b**) Steps in binding role player adaptation. (**c**) Steps in unbinding role player adaptation

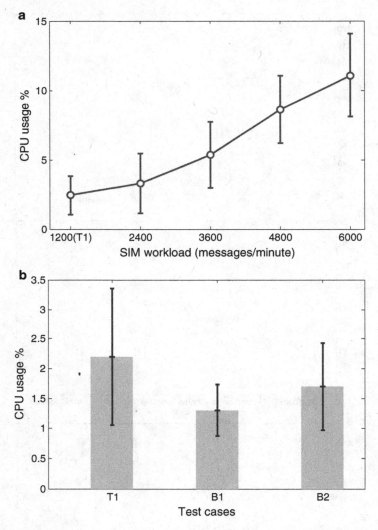

Fig. 9.8: SIM's resource consumption and performance related to mediating social interactions. (**a**) SIM's CPU consumption for different workloads. (**b**) Comparing T1 test case with two benchmarks B1 and B2 in terms of CPU usage

The service in B2 is very similar to the SIM as it also routes messages. However, SIM performs some additional tasks, *i.e.*, checks the messages against *constraints* defined in the relationships. We also deployed a client for each of the 100 services of these benchmarks, where a client invokes the corresponding service at a rate of 12 requests/min. We deployed B1 and B2 separately in the Axis2 web service engine and ran the experiment 100 times (10 min each time). For both B1 and B2, the server workload was 1200 requests/min, *i.e.*, the same as the T1 test case of SIM (see Fig. 9.8a). Figure 9.8b shows that on average the SIM's CPU consumption is a little higher than B1 and B2 due to the additional constraints evaluation.

To measure the *performance*, we computed the time taken by the SIM to process an incoming message and route it from one (source) role to another (destination) role. The box plots in Fig. 9.9 (right) (zoom in view of Fig. 9.9 (left) between 20 and 80 ms processing time) shows that on average SIM takes 32 ms to process and route a message regardless of the SIM workload. However, the most extreme value of the processing time [see Fig. 9.9 (left)] increases with increasing SIM workload.

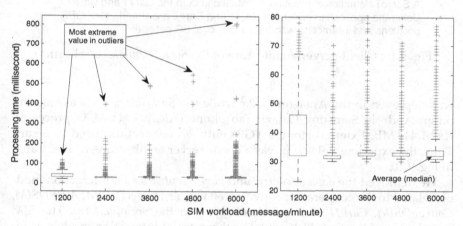

Fig. 9.9: SIM's performance results are illustrated using the box plots—the *left figure* depicts the most extreme value in outliers, the *right figure* (zoom in view of the *left figure*) highlights the average processing time

## 9.4 Evaluating the *SocioTelematics* Application

In this section, we present the experimental results that demonstrate the *feasibility* and *applicability* of the *SocioTelematics* application with respect to the *resource consumption* and *performance*. In this experiment, the *SocioPlatform*

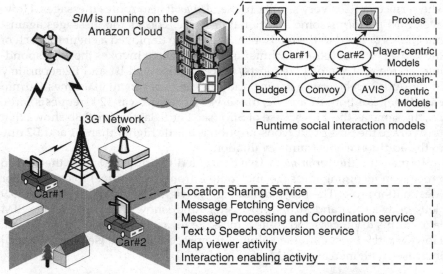

* A SocioTelematics application is installed in both the Car#1 and Car#2
* Using the application drivers' of Car#1 and Car#2 are sharing their GPS
  positions and interacting with each other over 3G network

Fig. 9.10: Client-server architecture of the *SocioTelematics* application

was deployed in the Amazon EC2,[3] while the *SocioTelematics* was running
on an Android Samsung Galaxy Tab phone (ARMv7 800 MHz processor,
RAM 444 MB, External storage 4 GB) with 3G connection (used in a car).
Thus, the experimental setup was a client-server architecture, as illustrated
in Fig. 9.10.

We deployed the *domain-centric* and *player-centric* social interaction models related to the cooperative convoy scenario, *i.e., BudgetDSIM, AVISDSIM,
ConvoyDSIM, Car#1PSIM* and *Car#2PSIM*, to the *SocioPlatform*. The *SIM*
component of the *SocioPlatform* takes these social interaction models as input and dynamically generates Web services with each *social role* being exposed as a *service* and each *interaction term* exposed as an *operation* in the
service (as discussed in Sect. 7.4.3). *SIM* manages and mediates social interactions by routing the messages, coming from the *SocioTelematics client application* (*i.e.,* player) running in a car, to the destination endpoint. For each
of the player a proxy service is maintained at the server to store all the incoming messages directed to that player. Given the devices' limited computation power and battery life—the proxy service allows the player (client
application running in a device) to communicate asynchronously with the
server (social interaction models) via SOAP interfaces.

---

[3] http://aws.amazon.com/ec2/.

Section 9.4.1 benchmarks the *resource consumption* of the *SocioTelematics* application on an Android Samsung Galaxy Tab phone. The results demonstrate that the application can be deployed on an off-the-shelf smart phone or Tablet with limited resource and computation power. Section 9.4.2 quantifies the *performance* of both the functional and management operations of the *SocioTelematics* application with respect to the communication latency between applications via the server. The results show that the application's performance is acceptable in a cooperative convoy.

## 9.4.1 Evaluating Resource Consumption

We have profiled the *resource consumption* of the *SocioTelematics* prototype application on an Android Samsung Galaxy Tab, for *CPU, memory (RAM),* and *storage.* Figure 9.11a, b show the application's CPU and memory consumptions, respectively, over 5 min while the application was fetching messages from the SIM in every 3 s, updating Google maps view in every 5 s, and sending messages (*i.e.,* performing interactions) once in every second.

Table 9.3 presents a comparison (average over a 5 min run) of *SocioTelematics* with two widely used similar (in terms of service used) Android Applications—*Gmail* and *Google Maps. Gmail* is an application that has a background service to interact with a web server for fetching and sending emails while the *Google Maps* uses a location service to show position on the map view. This comparison is performed using the built-in task manager application of Samsung Galaxy Tab. The results in Table 9.3 show that *SocioTelematics* consumes reasonable resources and is competitive with existing applications in terms of resource efficiency.

## 9.4.2 Quantifying Performance

We have examined both the *functional* and *adaptation* performance of the *SocioTelematics* using two cars in a cooperative convoy in 50 km of driving.

To *quantify* the *functional* performance, we have evaluated the communication latency between applications. Figure 9.12b shows that the application takes an average 1100 ms to fetch a message from the server over 3G network. Figure 9.12c shows that the server takes an average 250 ms to route a message from a proxy to another proxy via Car#1PSIM, ConvoyDSIM and Car#2PSIM, on the server. It is worth noting that the communication latency is highly variable and generally depends on the network traffic and the server working load. In our testbed, we have also found that to pass a message from one client application to another client application takes

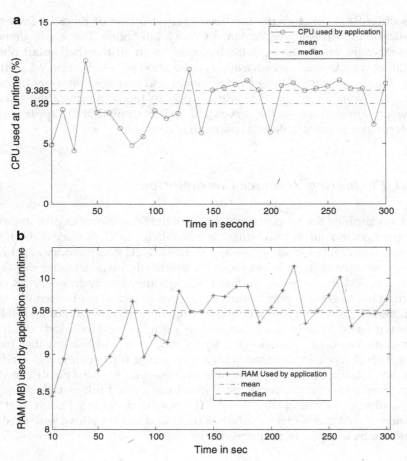

Fig. 9.11: Resource consumption of the *SocioTelematics* while it was fetching messages from the SIM in every 3 s, updating Google maps view in every 5 s, and sending messages (*i.e.*, performing interactions) once in every second. (**a**) Application's CPU consumption over 5 min. (**b**) Application's memory (RAM) usage over 5 min

around 1.6 s (given the fetching message interval is one second). This means that the application running in a car can display the other car's position every 1.6 s which we believe is an acceptable time in a cooperative convoy scenario.

Table 9.3: *SocioTelematics* vs. benchmark applications—CPU, memory and storage usage

| | Applications | CPU | Memory | Storage |
|---|---|---|---|---|
| · | SocioTelematics | 9.3 % | 9.6 MB | 520 KB |
| Benchmark | Gmail | 13 % | 15.27 MB | 1050 KB |
| | Google Maps | 21 % | 25.8 MB | 2560 KB |

To *quantify* the application's *adaptation* overhead, we have performed a number of adaptation operations, including *add* a car to the convoy and *remove* a car from the convoy. The results in Table 9.4 show that given the 1.12 s communication latency between the application and the server, on average the time to *add* and *remove* a car to and from the convoy at runtime takes 1.33 s (*i.e.*, 1.121 + 0.209 s) and 1.167 s (*i.e.*, 1.121 + 0.046 s), respectively. It takes around 0.42 ms to modify the *maxDesiredDistance* operational parameter. We believe these adaptation times are acceptable in a cooperative convoy.

## 9.5 Evaluating the *SPCall* Application

In this section, we present experimental results that demonstrate the *feasibility* and *applicability* of the *SPCall* application with respect to the *resource consumption* and *performance*. Like the client-server experimental setup for evaluating *SocioTelematics*, in this experiment, the *SocioPlatform* was deployed in the Amazon EC2, while the *SPCall* was running on the same Android Samsung Galaxy Tab phone with 3G internet connection.

Section 9.5.1 benchmarks the resource consumption of the *SPCall* application on an Android Samsung Galaxy Tab phone. The results demonstrate that the application can be deployed on an off-the-shelf smart phone and Tablet. Section 9.5.2 quantifies the performance of the *SPCall* application with respect to the communication latency between the application and the server. We observe that the application is able to acquire information from *SocioPlatform* and make decision in time before the call is forwarded to the voice-mail of the callee.

## 9.5.1 *Evaluating Resource Consumption*

In this experiment, we compare the *SPCall* application with an Android default dialler application and three highly downloaded (more than 10,000

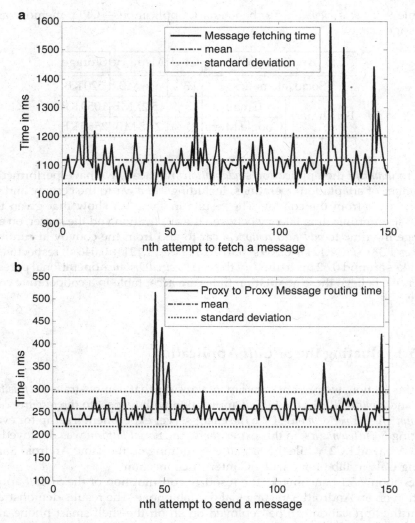

Fig. 9.12: Communication latency. (a) Time taken by the SocioTelematics client application (running on the Samsung Galaxy Tab) to fetch a message from the SIM (running on the Amazon cloud). (b) Time taken by the SIM (running on the Amazon cloud) to route a message between Car#1 proxy and Car#2 proxy services through the appropriate running social interaction models

Table 9.4: Time required to perform adaptation operations

| Operations | Time |
|---|---|
| Send an adaptation request from the *SocioTelematics* application to the Amazon server over a 3G network | 1.121 s |
| Add a new car to the *ConvoyDSIM* at runtime, *i.e., addSocialRole, addSRelationship* and *bindRP* | 0.209 s |
| Remove a car from the *ConvoyDSIM* at runtime, *i.e., unbindRP, delSRelationship* and *delSocialRole* | 0.046 s |
| Modify the *maxDesiredDistance* operational parameter in *ConvoyDSIM* | 0.422 ms |

times) and ratted (greater than 4 out of 5) Android applications that also aim to filter incoming calls. The *dialer* (some Android version named *Phone*) is a default Android application comes with every Android phone. It allows a person to make a phone call and manages phone call logs, *i.e.,* incoming and outgoing calls. However, it does not provide automatic call filtering functionality. The other three proprietary Android applications (*i.e., CallFilter,*[4] *Call Control*[5] and *Call Blocker*[6]) provide different features to its users. One common feature is filtering incoming phone calls based on user specified call filtering preferences. These applications only allow users to consider *time* in day and *phone number* for defining call filtering preferences. However, unlike *SPCall*, none of these applications able to recognise *social relationships* with the caller and allow users to consider such relationships for defining their call filtering preferences. Moreover, none of these applications have considered the *caller perspective* like the *SPCall*. That is, among all the applications mentioned above, only the *SPCall* allows a caller to know the *situation* of the intended callee to decide suitable time to call.

We have measured the resource consumption of these applications on an Android Samsung Galaxy Tab, for *CPU*, *memory (RAM)*, and *storage*. Table 9.5 presents a comparison (average of 100 phone calls receiving attempts). The results show that *SPCall* consumes reasonable resources and is competitive with existing applications in terms of resource efficiency.

---

[4] https://market.android.com/details?id=jp.co.telemarks.CallFilter2.

[5] https://market.android.com/details?id=com.flexaspect.android.everycallcontrol.

[6] https://play.google.com/store/apps/details?id=com.netqin.mm.

Table 9.5: *SPcall* vs. benchmark applications—CPU, Memory and Storage usage

| Applications | | CPU | Memory | Storage |
|---|---|---|---|---|
| SPCall | | 7.8 % | 4.6 MB | 527 KB |
| Benchmark | Android dialler | 11.2 % | 38.73 MB | 748 KB |
| | Call filter | 7.1 % | 3.6 MB | 1023 KB |
| | Call control | 17.7 % | 12 MB | 2365 KB |
| | Call blocker | 21 % | 23 MB | 6307 KB |

### 9.5.2 *Quantifying Performance*

In this experiment, we have used the *SCOnto* knowledge base that has been built in previous experiment for the *user3*. The knowledge base contains a reasonable number of different types of social context information such as 12 instances of *family* relationships, 202 instances of *friend* relationships, 32 instances of *work* relationships and 187 instances of *living address* based relationships (see Table 9.1). When a phone call comes, the *SPCall* application communicates with the *SCIM* of the *SocioPlatform* to collect users' social context information such as social relationships and situations, and behaves according to the specified filtering preferences. In this experiment, we have defined 100 call filtering preferences including the five preferences that are described in the use case scenarios (see Sect. 8.2.7).

Table 9.6 presents the details performance result (an average of 100 runs) of the call filtering process. Major portion of the total time is taken for communication between the *SPCall* client and the *SocioPlatform* server, which was around 1106 ms. It is worth noting that the communication time mainly depends on the internet speed of the mobile and the network traffic at the time of communication, and nothing related to the implementation of the *SPCall* client and the *SocioPlatform*. In the server side (running on the Amazon EC2), it took 13.64 ms to process queries which are basically for answering the social relationships between the caller and callee, and answering the current situation of the callee. Once the *SPCall* client application, running on the mobile, receives the social relationship and situation information, it starts to check call filtering preferences. In our case, it took 7.4 ms to check 100 filtering preferences. In total, it took around 1127 ms to take a decision whether to ring or vibrate or reject or forward to the voice-mail. For the call filtering application, this time is very critical as if it takes longer to take a decision the call is automatically forwarded to the voice mail. In our experiment, in 7 out of 100 test runs, application could not successfully take decision on time. There are two possible options to overcome this limitation. *First*, using high speed mobile internet. *Second*, increasing the time limit to forwarding a call to voice mail.

Table 9.6: Call filtering performance of the *SPCall* application

| Task | Time |
|------|------|
| SPCall client to SocioPlatform (server) communication latency | 1106 ms |
| Time required to process queries (server side) | 13.64 ms |
| Time required to check call filtering preferences (SPCall client) | 7.4 ms |
| Total | 1127.04 ms |

## 9.6 Summary

In this chapter, we have evaluated the *SocioPlatform* for developing social context-aware applications, using a series of experiments at two different fronts.

*Firstly*, we have quantified the *performance* of the core *functions* provided by the *SocioPlatform*. As appropriate, in some cases, we have also measured the *resource consumption*. To evaluate the *performance* of some functions such as social context information acquisition, DL based reasoning and query processing, we have used real data from online social networks to evaluate these functions in a real world context. To evaluate the *performance* of other functions such as real time interaction events based situation reasoning, mediating social interactions and supporting runtime adaptation, we have used simulated data and application scenario based models, as appropriate. We have also quantified *resource consumption* and *compared* with two benchmark workloads related to mediating social interactions. The overall results of the experiment have shown that the performance and resource consumption of the *SocioPlatform* is acceptable with respect to the data volume size and platform workload.

*Secondly*, we have quantified *performance* and measured *resource consumption* of two socially-aware applications using real-life experiment. These socially-aware applications, *i.e., SocioTelematics* and *SPCall*, have been developed using our proposed *framework* and the *SocioPlatform*. We have also *compared* the resource consumption of these applications with other existing similar applications. The results of this experiment show that the *performance* of these applications is *acceptable* in real-world scenario and the *resource usage* of these applications is *reasonable*.

In *summary*, the results of these experiments demonstrate the real-world *applicability* and *feasibility* of developing socially-aware applications using our framework.

# Chapter 10
# Conclusion

We have presented, in this book, a *framework* for social context-aware applications, which includes an approach for *modelling, reasoning about* and *managing* social context information and a *platform*, namely *SocioPlatform*, for assisting the development of such applications. The motivation of this research stems from the need to address the *limitations* of existing approaches as well as the new *challenges* faced by the design and implementation of socially-aware applications in terms of *social context information* provisioning and adaptability. The outcome of this study is a novel *framework* for the social context-aware applications.

In this chapter, we first highlight the important *contributions* this work to the field of *pervasive social computing*, and then discuss some related topics for *future* investigation.

## 10.1 Contributions

In general, the aim of this work was to address the challenges associated with the engineering of social context-aware applications, by developing a framework consisting of both sound conceptual foundations and a supporting software platform. The framework differs significantly from the previously proposed solutions described in Chap. 3, such as Prometheus [121], as it is founded on a set of well-integrated approaches to *modelling, reasoning about* and *managing* social context that allows context to be described at varying levels of abstraction with its semantics, deducing more meaningful and interesting social context information, and managing its acquisition, provisioning and runtime adaptation. The framework makes a number of important research contributions, which are summarised in the remainder of this section.

© Springer International Publishing Switzerland 2016
M.A. Kabir et al., *Pervasive Social Computing*,
DOI 10.1007/978-3-319-29951-8_10

I. **An ontology based** *social context model* **that includes ontologies for social role, social relationship, social interaction and situation**. In order to capture both the *general* and *domain-specific* concepts, we have provided both an *upper* and *domain-specific* ontologies. The *upper ontology* captures the basic concepts abstracted from the analysis of socially-aware applications and different sources of social context information. This upper ontology can be shared, reused and adapted to various applications. This can be customised to represent concepts in different forms for different users. It is also extensible to allow for the incorporation of new concepts and the specialisation of concepts and constraints for a particular application or domain, which we refer to as *application-* or *domain-specific* ontologies. As examples, domain-specific ontologies for family, educational organisation and cooperative convoy have been presented. One of the key characteristics of our modelling approach is that we model social context information, e.g. social relationship, as *first-class* entities rather than representing them as a generic *link* between people (as in existing approaches such as [178], discussed in Chap. 3). This way of modelling allows us to benefit from description logic (DL) in *classifying* and *reasoning* about social context information at different levels of *abstraction* based on the *properties* of social context.

II. **An ontology based approach to** *reasoning* **about social context information**. Socially-aware applications may require some social context information that cannot be acquired directly from the possible sources, but can be inferred from the acquired basic information. For example, an exact social relationship between an individual and a person can be *derived* from the individual's gender information and the social role of the person who is related with the individual, acquired from Facebook. Moreover, new social relationships (e.g. best friend) and situations (e.g. busy), as required by applications can be *deduced* and *abstracted* from the existing concepts. We have adopted an ontology based approach to *deriving, deducing* and *abstracting* social context information considering their *structural/parametric, time-stamp* and *abstraction* aspects. To date, OWL2-DL has been the most practical choice for most ontological applications as it supports maximum *expressiveness* while retaining computational completeness and decidability [150]. As such, we have used the OWL2-DL *class constructors, semantics* and *property characteristics* to represent and specify reasoning rules. The main advantage of their use is that a description logic reasoner can be used for *automatically* reasoning about social context information in the knowledge base.

III. **A novel approach to** *inferring* **users' situations from their** *interaction events*. The novelties of this approach lie in considering users' *interaction events* in inferring situations and combining *semantic matching* and *temporal* aspects of interaction events in *specifying* and *deducing* situations. In doing so, an *interaction event ontology* is proposed to capture users' interaction activities in different social interaction platforms.

To capture both the *general* and *domain-specific* concepts, the ontology includes an *upper* interaction ontology, namely *IntEO*, which can be customised and specialised to form *domain-specific* ontologies. As examples, domain-specific ontologies for Facebook and Cooperative Convoy have been presented. To allow domain experts to specify situations based on interaction event patterns and their correlations, a *situation specification language*, both for the technical and non-technical persons, is proposed that integrates the *IntEO* with *temporal relations*, where *IntEO* serves as a vocabulary for domain experts to specify the attribute values in an interaction event pattern. The key features of this approach are that (1) the proposed situation language is expressive enough to cover the temporal aspects of situation specification and reasoning as the language incorporates all possible types of temporal correlations, and (2) it simplifies the situation rules by incorporating an interaction event ontology in the situation specification language.

IV. **An ontology based *privacy policy model* and a *language* to specify privacy preferences.** Users' social context information is inherently sensitive. In pervasive social computing environments, users might need to allow others to *access* their social context information for greater benefits but this may also compromise their privacy. Thus, users should be able to *retain control* over *who* has access to their personal information under *which* conditions. Our proposed policy model provides intuitive support by considering *social role*, *social relationship* and *situation* information when defining privacy preferences, and allowing owners to fine-tune the *granularity* of accessed information. In this regard, we have also provided a mechanism to check *inconsistency* in policy specification and to *enforce* users' policies while accessing their social context information. The main advantages of our approach are that a description logic reasoner can be used for *detecting* automatically inconsistencies in the specification of policies, and *executing* policies.

V. **An approach to *modelling runtime social interactions*.** We have taken a role based approach to modelling runtime social interactions as it has been evaluated as being very useful in modelling entities, their relationships, functionality and interactions [51]. Our approach utilises the notion of roles for functional abstractions. Among the many different approaches to role modelling, one common way to develop role based models is to use organisational concepts [60]. We adopt the view of an organisation being a composition structure of dynamic social roles in order to model social interactions at runtime. The essences of our approach are the *externalisation* of the interaction relationships from the applications and the *explicit* modelling of such relationships from *domain-* and *player-perspectives*. The *domain-centric model* captures a *collaborative* view of the interaction relationships among the users/actors whereas the *player-centric model* captures an individual's *coordinated* view of all its interactions (across different domains). The player-centric model allows a user to specify his/her *coordination preferences* and perform coordination in an *automated* manner. These runtime models are realised through a platform, and are used to *mediate social interactions* between users in interaction-centric socially-aware applications.

VI. **An approach to *managing runtime adaptation* in social interaction models**. Runtime social interaction models capture predefined agreements and constraints, i.e. interaction relationships, among collaborative users in interaction-centric socially-aware applications. In complex and changing environments, such interaction relationships, and thus social interaction models, need to be *adapted* because of the *changes* in users' requirements and environments. To manage such adaptation: (1) we have identified different *types of changes* (i.e. user requirements and environments) and the various *adaptations* (i.e. parametric and structural) to deal with such changes; (2) we have proposed *adaptation* and *management operations*, and presented possible ways (i.e. manually and rule-based) to perform adaptations using those operations; (3) we have introduced social interaction *states* to support adaptation in a *safe* manner; and (4) finally, we have considered inherent *dependencies* among player- and domain-centric social interaction models, and proposed a *protocol* with associated *algorithms* for *cross-model* adaptation (i.e. adaptation propagation). The essence of our adaptation approach is the *separation* of functional and management operations, which facilitates the management of dynamic relationships between collaborative users, and supports their adaptation to cope with the continuous changes in their requirements and environments.

VII. *Finally,* **a *platform*, namely *SocioPlatform*, to provide high-level support for developing socially-aware applications**. The *SocioPlatform* integrates the aforementioned theoretical contributions into a system architecture and subsequently a platform by incorporating such capabilities as the *acquisition, management* and *querying* of social context information, providing an *environment* for executing social interaction models and *managing* their runtime adaptation, and presenting a set of APIs to developers to build socially-aware applications.

Overall, our *framework* for social context-aware applications addresses the key challenges of designing and implementing novel socially-aware applications, i.e. *social context modelling, reasoning* and *management*. In this book, we have presented how these key challenges can be addressed by our novel *framework* that includes *techniques* for modelling, reasoning about and managing different types of social context information, and *platform* for better supporting the development of socially-aware applications.

## 10.2  Future Work

Much work can be done, in *pervasive social computing* area, and more specifically, to further enhance the *framework*. The following are two possible research directions for further investigation.

*Quality of Social Context*    An essential topic for future research is that of quality of social context. The quality of context (QoC) plays an important role in improving context-based adaptation and in ensuring the correct behaviour of context-aware applications and services. The usefulness problem arising in context-aware software as a result of imperfect context information is well recognised. A number of research efforts (e.g. [78, 98, 131]) have attempted to present QoC parameters and QoC measuring methods for context of a physical nature such as location and time. Parameters to define QoC from different perspectives have been proposed. To characterise imperfect context information, Henricksen et al. [98] proposed four QoC parameters: *unknown, ambiguous, imprecise* and *erroneous*. Manzoor et al. [131] defined *up-to-dateness, trustworthiness, completeness, consistency* and *precision* as generic QoC parameters, and proposed techniques to evaluate these parameters. All of the above work identified that errors in context information mainly arise as a result of sensing. The work presented in this book addressed the issue of *up-to-dateness* in acquiring users' situation information from social media. However, many other aspects related to the *quality of social context* such as imprecise and trust-worthiness yet need to be addressed.

*Social Signal Processing and Behaviour Awareness*    One of the goal of pervasive social computing is to provide services to the human by detecting human social context and recognising human social intentions. As such, behaviour awareness is identified as an important research direction in *pervasive social computing* [192]. Vinciarelli et al. [179] argue that next generation computing needs to include the essence of social intelligence—the ability to recognise human social signals and social behaviours like politeness and disagreement, in order to become more effective and efficient in dealing with user needs. For example, an audio player in a mobile phone can choose music to play based on its user's current behaviour pattern and mood. Behaviour awareness aims to analyse various kinds of behavioural cues and social signals, in order to identify their features and meanings. One of the research issues in this direction would be how ontology-based approach can be exploited in modelling behavioural cues into computer systems, so that social signals can be effectively analysed by machines in order to recognise human social intentions.

# Appendix A
# Description Logic-Based Reasoning Rules and Constraints

## A.1 Classification and Reasoning Rules

$$
\begin{aligned}
\textit{Father-Son} \equiv\ &(\ \exists relates(Person \sqcap plays \cdot \{father\}) \sqcap \\
&\quad \exists relates(Me \sqcap gender \cdot \{male\})) \\
&)\ \sqcup\ ( \\
&\quad \exists relates(Person \sqcap plays \cdot \{son\}) \sqcap \\
&\quad \exists relates(Me \sqcap gender \cdot \{male\}) \\
&)
\end{aligned}
\tag{A.1}
$$

$$
\begin{aligned}
\textit{Mother-Son} \equiv\ &(\ \exists relates(Person \sqcap plays \cdot \{mother\}) \sqcap \\
&\quad \exists relates(Me \sqcap gender \cdot \{male\})) \\
&)\ \sqcup\ ( \\
&\quad \exists relates(Person \sqcap plays \cdot \{son\}) \sqcap \\
&\quad \exists relates(Me \sqcap gender \cdot \{female\}) \\
&)
\end{aligned}
$$

$$
\begin{aligned}
\textit{Mother-Daughter} \equiv\ &(\ \exists relates(Person \sqcap plays \cdot \{mother\}) \sqcap \\
&\quad \exists relates(Me \sqcap gender \cdot \{female\})) \\
&)\ \sqcup\ ( \\
&\quad \exists relates(Person \sqcap plays \cdot \{daughter\}) \sqcap \\
&\quad \exists relates(Me \sqcap gender \cdot \{female\}) \\
&)
\end{aligned}
$$

© Springer International Publishing Switzerland 2016
M.A. Kabir et al., *Pervasive Social Computing*,
DOI 10.1007/978-3-319-29951-8

$$GrandFather\text{-}GrandSon \equiv (\ \exists relates(Person \sqcap plays \cdot \{grandfather\}) \sqcap$$
$$\exists relates(Me \sqcap gender \cdot \{male\}))$$
$$)\ \sqcup\ ($$
$$\exists relates(Person \sqcap plays \cdot \{grandson\}) \sqcap$$
$$\exists relates(Me \sqcap gender \cdot \{male\})$$
$$)$$

$$GrandFather\text{-}GrandDaughter \equiv (\ \exists relates(Person \sqcap plays \cdot \{grandfather\}) \sqcap$$
$$\exists relates(Me \sqcap gender \cdot \{female\}))$$
$$)\ \sqcup\ ($$
$$\exists relates(Person \sqcap plays \cdot \{granddaughter\}) \sqcap$$
$$\exists relates(Me \sqcap gender \cdot \{male\})$$
$$)$$

$$Mother\text{-}Son \equiv (\ \exists relates(Person \sqcap plays \cdot \{grandmother\}) \sqcap$$
$$\exists relates(Me \sqcap gender \cdot \{male\}))$$
$$)\ \sqcup\ ($$
$$\exists relates(Person \sqcap plays \cdot \{grandson\}) \sqcap$$
$$\exists relates(Me \sqcap gender \cdot \{female\})$$
$$)$$

$$Mother\text{-}Daughter \equiv (\ \exists relates(Person \sqcap plays \cdot \{grandmother\}) \sqcap$$
$$\exists relates(Me \sqcap gender \cdot \{female\}))$$
$$)\ \sqcup\ ($$
$$\exists relates(Person \sqcap plays \cdot \{granddaughter\}) \sqcap$$
$$\exists relates(Me \sqcap gender \cdot \{female\})$$
$$)$$

$$Uncle\text{-}Niece \equiv (\ \exists relates(Person \sqcap plays \cdot \{uncle\}) \sqcap$$
$$\exists relates(Me \sqcap gender \cdot \{male\}))$$
$$)\ \sqcup\ ($$
$$\exists relates(Person \sqcap plays \cdot \{niece\}) \sqcap$$
$$\exists relates(Me \sqcap gender \cdot \{male\})$$
$$)$$

$$
\begin{aligned}
\textit{Aunt-Nephew} \equiv (\ &\exists relates(Person \sqcap plays \cdot \{aunt\}) \sqcap \\
&\exists relates(Me \sqcap gender \cdot \{female\})) \\
)\ \sqcup\ (\ & \\
&\exists relates(Person \sqcap plays \cdot \{nephew\}) \sqcap \\
&\exists relates(Me \sqcap gender \cdot \{female\}) \\
)
\end{aligned}
$$

$$
\begin{aligned}
\textit{Aunt-Niece} \equiv (\ &\exists relates(Person \sqcap plays \cdot \{aunt\}) \sqcap \\
&\exists relates(Me \sqcap gender \cdot \{male\})) \\
)\ \sqcup\ (\ & \\
&\exists relates(Person \sqcap plays \cdot \{niece\}) \sqcap \\
&\exists relates(Me \sqcap gender \cdot \{female\}) \\
)
\end{aligned}
$$

$$
\begin{aligned}
\textit{Father\_in\_law-Son\_in\_law} \equiv (\ &\exists relates(Person \sqcap plays \cdot \{father\_in\_law\}) \sqcap \\
&\exists relates(Me \sqcap gender \cdot \{male\})) \\
)\ \sqcup\ (\ & \\
&\exists relates(Person \sqcap plays \cdot \{son\_in\_law\}) \sqcap \\
&\exists relates(Me \sqcap gender \cdot \{male\}) \\
)
\end{aligned}
$$

$$
\begin{aligned}
\textit{Father\_in\_law-Daughter\_in\_law} \equiv (\ &\exists relates(Person \sqcap plays \cdot \{father\_in\_law\}) \sqcap \\
&\exists relates(Me \sqcap gender \cdot \{female\})) \\
)\ \sqcup\ (\ & \\
&\exists relates(Person \sqcap plays \cdot \{daughter\_in\_law\}) \sqcap \\
&\exists relates(Me \sqcap gender \cdot \{male\}) \\
)
\end{aligned}
$$

$$
\begin{aligned}
\textit{Mother\_in\_law-Son\_in\_law} \equiv (\ &\exists relates(Person \sqcap plays \cdot \{mother\_in\_law\}) \sqcap \\
&\exists relates(Me \sqcap gender \cdot \{male\})) \\
)\ \sqcup\ (\ & \\
&\exists relates(Person \sqcap plays \cdot \{son\_in\_law\}) \sqcap \\
&\exists relates(Me \sqcap gender \cdot \{female\}) \\
)
\end{aligned}
$$

$$Mother\_in\_law\text{-}Daughter\_in\_law \equiv (\ \exists relates(Person \sqcap plays \cdot \{mother\_in\_law\}) \sqcap$$
$$\exists relates(Me \sqcap gender \cdot \{female\}))$$
$$)\sqcup ($$
$$\exists relates(Person \sqcap plays \cdot \{daughter\_in\_law\}) \sqcap$$
$$\exists relates(Me \sqcap gender \cdot \{female\})$$
$$)$$

$$Brother\text{-}Brother \equiv (\ \exists relates(Person \sqcap plays \cdot \{brother\}) \sqcap$$
$$\exists relates(Me \sqcap gender \cdot \{male\}))$$
$$)$$

$$Sister\text{-}Sister \equiv (\ \exists relates(Person \sqcap plays \cdot \{sister\}) \sqcap$$
$$\exists relates(Me \sqcap gender \cdot \{female\}))$$
$$)$$

$$Brother\text{-}Sister \equiv (\ \exists relates(Person \sqcap plays \cdot \{brother\}) \sqcap$$
$$\exists relates(Me \sqcap gender \cdot \{female\}))$$
$$)\sqcup ($$
$$\exists relates(Person \sqcap plays \cdot \{sister\}) \sqcap$$
$$\exists relates(Me \sqcap gender \cdot \{male\})$$
$$)$$

$$Weekends \equiv \exists inDateTime(DateTimeDescription \sqcap$$
$$(dayOfWeek \cdot \{Saturday\} \sqcup dayOfWeek \cdot \{Sunday\}))$$

$$Weekdays \equiv \exists inDateTime(DateTimeDescription \sqcap$$
$$(dayOfWeek \cdot \{Monday\} \sqcup dayOfWeek \cdot \{Tuesday\}$$
$$\sqcup dayOfWeek \cdot \{Wednesday\} \sqcup dayOfWeek \cdot \{Thursday\}$$
$$\sqcup dayOfWeek \cdot \{Friday\}))$$

$$Holidays \equiv NewYearDay \sqcup ChristmasDay \sqcup BoxingDay$$
$$\sqcup GoodFriday \sqcup LabourDay \sqcup AustraliaDay$$
$$\sqcup QueenBrithDay \sqcup ANZACDay \sqcup EsaterMonday$$
$$\sqcup MelbourneCupDay \sqcup SaturdayBeforeEasterSunday$$

$$NewYearDay \equiv \exists inDateTime(DateTimeDescription \sqcap$$
$$(year \cdot \{2013\} \sqcap month \cdot \{--01\} \sqcap day \cdot \{---01\}))$$

$$ChristmasDay \equiv \exists inDateTime(DateTimeDescription \sqcap$$
$$(year \cdot \{2013\} \sqcap month \cdot \{--12\} \sqcap day \cdot \{---25\}))$$

$$EasterMonday \equiv \exists inDateTime(DateTimeDescription \sqcap$$
$$(year \cdot \{2013\} \sqcap month \cdot \{--04\} \sqcap day \cdot \{---01\}))$$

$$BoxingDay \equiv \exists inDateTime(DateTimeDescription \sqcap$$
$$(year \cdot \{2013\} \sqcap month \cdot \{--12\} \sqcap day \cdot \{---26\}))$$

$$GoodFriday \equiv \exists inDateTime(DateTimeDescription \sqcap$$
$$(year \cdot \{2013\} \sqcap month \cdot \{--03\} \sqcap day \cdot \{---29\}))$$

$$LabourDay \equiv \exists inDateTime(DateTimeDescription \sqcap$$
$$(year \cdot \{2013\} \sqcap month \cdot \{--03\} \sqcap day \cdot \{---11\}))$$

$$AustraliaDay \equiv \exists inDateTime(DateTimeDescription \sqcap$$
$$(year \cdot \{2013\} \sqcap month \cdot \{--01\} \sqcap day \cdot \{---28\}))$$

$$QueenBrithDay \equiv \exists inDateTime(DateTimeDescription \sqcap$$
$$(year \cdot \{2013\} \sqcap month \cdot \{--06\} \sqcap day \cdot \{---10\}))$$

$$ANZACDay \equiv \exists inDateTime(DateTimeDescription \sqcap$$
$$(year \cdot \{2013\} \sqcap month \cdot \{--04\} \sqcap day \cdot \{---25\}))$$

$$MelbourneCupDay \equiv \exists inDateTime(DateTimeDescription \sqcap$$
$$(year \cdot \{2013\} \sqcap month \cdot \{--11\} \sqcap day \cdot \{---05\}))$$

$$SaturdayBeforeEasterSunday \equiv \exists inDateTime(DateTimeDescription \sqcap$$
$$(year \cdot \{2013\} \sqcap month \cdot \{--03\} \sqcap$$
$$day \cdot \{---30\}))$$

$$BusinessHours \equiv Weekdays \sqcap (\neg Holidays) \sqcap$$
$$\exists inDateTime(DateTimeDescription \sqcap (hour \geq \{9\}$$
$$\sqcap hour \leq \{16\}))$$
$$LunchHours \equiv inDateTime(DateTimeDescription \sqcap hour \cdot \{12\})$$
$$WorkingHours \equiv BusinessHours \sqcap (\neg LunchHours)$$
$$NonBusinessHours \equiv \neg BusinessHours$$

## A.2 Constraints

$$Father\_in\_law\text{-}Son\_in\_law \sqcap Father\_in\_law\text{-}Daughter\_in\_law = \bot$$
$$Mother\_in\_law\text{-}Son\_in\_law \sqcap Mother\_in\_law\text{-}Daughter\_in\_law = \bot$$
$$Father\_in\_law\text{-}Child\_in\_law \sqcap Mother\_in\_law\text{-}Child\_in\_law = \bot$$
$$Mother\text{-}Son \sqcap Mother\text{-}Daughter = \bot$$
$$Father\text{-}Child \sqcap Mother\text{-}Child = \bot$$
$$Grandfather\text{-}Grandson \sqcap Grandfather\text{-}Granddaughter = \bot$$
$$Grandmother\text{-}Grandson \sqcap Grandmother\text{-}Granddaughter = \bot$$
$$Grandfather\text{-}Grandchild \sqcap Grandmother\text{-}Grandchild = \bot$$
$$Brother\text{-}Brother \sqcap Brother\text{-}Sister = \bot$$
$$Brother\text{-}Brother \sqcap Sister\text{-}Sister = \bot$$
$$Brother\text{-}Sister \sqcap Sister\text{-}Sister = \bot$$
$$Father\text{-}Daughter \sqsubseteq relates \leq 1(Person \sqcap plays \cdot father)$$
$$Mother\text{-}Son \sqsubseteq relates \leq 1(Person \sqcap plays \cdot mother)$$
$$Mother\text{-}Daughter \sqsubseteq relates \leq 1(Person \sqcap plays \cdot mother)$$
$$Father\_in\_law\text{-}Daughter\_in\_law \sqsubseteq relates \leq 1(Person \sqcap plays \cdot father\_in\_law)$$
$$Mother\_in\_law\text{-}Daughter\_in\_law \sqsubseteq relates \leq 1(Person \sqcap plays \cdot mother\_in\_law)$$

## A.2.1 Constraints Defined in SACOnto

$$Policy \sqsubseteq \; = 1 \, policyStatement$$
$$Granted \sqcap Denied \sqsubseteq \perp$$
$$Granted \sqcap GrantedInGL1 \sqsubseteq \perp$$
$$Granted \sqcap GrantedInGL2 \sqsubseteq \perp$$
$$Granted \sqcap GrantedInGL3 \sqsubseteq \perp$$
$$Granted \sqcap GrantedInGL4 \sqsubseteq \perp$$
$$Denied \sqcap GrantedInGL1 \sqsubseteq \perp$$
$$Denied \sqcap GrantedInGL2 \sqsubseteq \perp$$
$$Denied \sqcap GrantedInGL3 \sqsubseteq \perp$$
$$Denied \sqcap GrantedInGL4 \sqsubseteq \perp$$
$$GrantedInGL1 \sqcap GrantedInGL2 \sqsubseteq \perp$$
$$GrantedInGL1 \sqcap GrantedInGL3 \sqsubseteq \perp$$
$$GrantedInGL1 \sqcap GrantedInGL4 \sqsubseteq \perp$$
$$GrantedInGL2 \sqcap GrantedInGL3 \sqsubseteq \perp$$
$$GrantedInGL2 \sqcap GrantedInGL4 \sqsubseteq \perp$$
$$GrantedInGL3 \sqcap GrantedInGL4 \sqsubseteq \perp$$

# Appendix B
# Social Interactions in a Cooperative Convoy

See Tables B.1, B.2, B.3, B.4, B.5, B.6, B.7, B.8, B.9, B.10, B.11, B.12, B.13, B.14, B.15, B.16, B.17, B.18, B.19, B.20, B.21, B.22, B.23, B.24, B.25.

Table B.1: Interaction (i1): leading car notifies its position to the following car

| :i1 | rdf:type | :Interaction |
|-----|----------|--------------|
| :i1 | :msgSignature | "notifyPosition" |
| :i1 | :fromRole | :LeadingCar |
| :i1 | :toRole | :FollowingCar |

Table B.2: Interaction (i2): following car notifies its position to the leading car

| :i2 | rdf:type | :Interaction |
|-----|----------|--------------|
| :i2 | :msgSignature | "notifyPosition" |
| :i2 | :fromRole | :FollowingCar |
| :i2 | :toRole | :LeadingCar |

© Springer International Publishing Switzerland 2016
M.A. Kabir et al., *Pervasive Social Computing*,
DOI 10.1007/978-3-319-29951-8

Table B.3: Obligation (o1) and related Operational parameter (p1): both the leading and following cars notify each other of their positions every 10 s

| :p1 | rdf:type | OperationalParameter |
|---|---|---|
| :p1 | :paramName | "posUpdateFreq" |
| :p1 | :value | 10 |
| :p1 | :timeUnit | "SEC" |
| :o1 | rdf:type | :Obligation |
| :o1 | :time | "duration" |
| :o1 | :relatedOP | :p1 |
| :i1 | :hasObg | :o1 |
| :i2 | :hasObg | :o1 |

Table B.4: Obligation (o2) and related Operational parameter (p2): maximum desired distance between the leading car and following car is 1 km

| :p2 | rdf:type | OperationalParameter |
|---|---|---|
| :p2 | :paramName | "maxDesiredDistance" |
| :p2 | :value | 1 |
| :p2 | :distanceUnit | "KM" |
| :o2 | rdf:type | :Obligation |
| :o2 | :time | "duration" |
| :o2 | :relatedOP | :p1 |
| :i1 | :hasObg | :o2 |
| :i2 | :hasObg | :o2 |

Table B.5: Interaction (i3): following car sends ahead road block information to the leading car

| :i3 | rdf:type | :Interaction |
|---|---|---|
| :i3 | :msgSignature | "notifyRoadBlock" |
| :i3 | :fromRole | :FollowingCar |
| :i3 | :toRole | :LeadingCar |

Table B.6: Interaction (i4): leading car updates the route information to the following car

| :i4 | rdf:type | :Interaction |
|---|---|---|
| :i4 | :msgSignature | "routeUpdate" |
| :i4 | :fromRole | :LeadingCar |
| :i4 | :toRole | :FollowingCar |

Table B.7: Interaction (i5): leading car notifies its mechanical issue to the following car

| :i5 | rdf:type | :Interaction |
|---|---|---|
| :i5 | :msgSignature | "notifyMechanicalIssue" |
| :i5 | :fromRole | :LeadingCar |
| :i5 | :toRole | :FollowingCar |

Table B.8: Interaction (i6): following car notifies its mechanical issue to the leading car

| :i6 | rdf:type | :Interaction |
|---|---|---|
| :i6 | :msgSignature | "notifyMechanicalIssue" |
| :i6 | :fromRole | :FollowingCar |
| :i6 | :toRole | :LeadingCar |

Table B.9: Interaction (i7): a rented car sends a route request to a travel guide

| :i7 | rdf:type | :Interaction |
|---|---|---|
| :i7 | :msgSignature | "routeRequest" |
| :i7 | :fromRole | :RentedCar |
| :i7 | :toRole | :TravelGuide |

Table B.10: Interaction (i8): a travel guide sends a route notification to a rented car

| :i8 | rdf:type | :Interaction |
|-----|----------|--------------|
| :i8 | :msgSignature | "routeNotification" |
| :i8 | :fromRole | :TravelGuide |
| :i8 | :toRole | :RentedCar |

Table B.11: Conversation (c1), and related Obligation (o3) and Operational Parameter (p3): upon receiving a route request, travel guide should send a route notification by 15 s

| :p3 | rdf:type | :OperationalParameter |
|-----|----------|------------------------|
| :p3 | :paramName | "maxTimeDelay" |
| :p3 | :value | 15 |
| :p3 | :timeUnit | SEC |
| :o3 | rdf:type | :Obligation |
| :o3 | :timer | :duration |
| :o3 | :relatedOP | :p3 |
| :c1 | rdf:type | :Conversation |
| :c1 | :intrac1 | :i7 |
| :c1 | :intrac2 | :i8 |
| :c1 | :hasSequence | :leadsTo |
| :c1 | :relatedObg | :o3 |

Table B.12: Interaction (i9): driver of the rented car notifies a mechanical issue to the rental company

| :i9 | rdf:type | :Interaction |
|-----|----------|--------------|
| :i9 | :msgSignature | "notifyMechanicalIssue" |
| :i9 | :fromRole | :RentedCar |
| :i9 | :toRole | :RentalCompany |

Table B.13: Interaction (i10): driver of the rented car requests for a mechanical assistance to the roadside assistance service

| :i10 | rdf:type | :Interaction |
|------|----------|--------------|
| :i10 | :msgSignature | "mechanicalAssistanceRequest" |
| :i10 | :fromRole | :RentedCar |
| :i10 | :toRole | :RoadsideAssistance |

Table B.14: Interaction (i11): a roadside assistance service responses on an assistance request

| :i11 | rdf:type | :Interaction |
|------|----------|--------------|
| :i11 | :msgSignature | "assistanceResponse" |
| :i11 | :fromRole | :RoadsideAssistance |
| :i11 | :toRole | :RentedCar |

Table B.15: Conversation (c2), and related Obligation (o4) and Operational Parameter (p4): upon receiving a mechanical assistance request, roadside assistance service should send an assistance response by 5 min

| :p4 | rdf:type | :OperationalParameter |
|-----|----------|-----------------------|
| :p4 | :paramName | "maxTimeDelay" |
| :p4 | :value | 5 |
| :p4 | :timeUnit | MIN |
| :o4 | rdf:type | :Obligation |
| :o4 | :timer | :duration |
| :o4 | :relatedOP | :p4 |
| :c2 | rdf:type | :Conversation |
| :c2 | :intrac1 | :i10 |
| :c2 | :intrac2 | :i11 |
| :c2 | :hasSequence | :leadsTo |
| :c2 | :relatedObg | :o4 |

Table B.16: Interaction (i12): roadside assistance service verifies car id with the rental company

| :i12 | rdf:type | :Interaction |
|------|----------|--------------|
| :i12 | :msgSignature | "carIDVerificationRequest" |
| :i12 | :fromRole | :RoadsideAssistance |
| :i12 | :toRole | :RentalCompany |

Table B.17: Interaction (i13): rental company sends car id verification result to the roadside assistance

| :i13 | rdf:type | :Interaction |
|------|----------|--------------|
| :i13 | :msgSignature | "carIDVerificationResult" |
| :i13 | :fromRole | :RentalCompany |
| :i13 | :toRole | :RoadsideAssistance |

Table B.18: Conversation (c3): upon receiving a car id verification request from a roadside assistance, the car rental company verifies the car id and sends the result back to the roadside assistance service

| :c3 | rdf:type | :Conversation |
|-----|----------|---------------|
| :c3 | :intrac1 | :i12 |
| :c3 | :intrac2 | :i13 |
| :c3 | :hasSequence | :leadsTo |

Table B.19: Interaction (i14): a driver of the rented car requests to a traffic management service to check whether a road is blocked to a destination

| :i14 | rdf:type | :Interaction |
|------|----------|--------------|
| :i14 | :msgSignature | "roadBlockCheckingRequest" |
| :i14 | :fromRole | :RentedCar |
| :i14 | :toRole | :TrafficManagement |

Table B.20: Interaction (i15): a traffic management service responses on a road block checking request

| :i15 | rdf:type | :Interaction |
|------|----------|--------------|
| :i15 | :msgSignature | "roadBlockCheckingResult" |
| :i15 | :fromRole | :TrafficManagement |
| :i15 | :toRole | :RentedCar |

Table B.21: Conversation (c4), and related Obligation (o6) and Operational Parameter (p6): upon receiving a road block checking request, traffic management service should send the checking result by 10 s

| :p6 | rdf:type | :OperationalParameter |
|-----|----------|-----------------------|
| :p6 | :paramName | "maxTimeDelay" |
| :p6 | :value | 10 |
| :p6 | :timeUnit | SEC |
| :o6 | rdf:type | :Obligation |
| :o6 | :timer | :duration |
| :o6 | :relatedOP | :p6 |
| :c4 | rdf:type | :Conversation |
| :c4 | :intrac1 | :i14 |
| :c4 | :intrac2 | :i15 |
| :c4 | :hasSequence | :leadsTo |
| :c4 | :relatedObg | :o6 |

Table B.22: Interaction (i16): following car proposes a convoy break to the leading car

| :i16 | rdf:type | :Interaction |
|------|----------|--------------|
| :i16 | :msgSignature | "convoyBreak" |
| :i16 | :fromRole | :FollowingCar |
| :i16 | :toRole | :LeadingCar |

Table B.23: Interaction (i17): leading car agrees to the convoy break request

| :i17 | rdf:type      | :Interaction       |
|------|---------------|--------------------|
| :i17 | :msgSignature | "positiveResponse" |
| :i17 | :fromRole     | :LeadingCar        |
| :i17 | :toRole       | :FollowingCar      |

Table B.24: Interaction (i18): address request from a rented car to a travel guide service

| :i18 | rdf:type      | :Interaction    |
|------|---------------|-----------------|
| :i18 | :msgSignature | "addressRequest"|
| :i18 | :fromRole     | :RentedCar      |
| :i18 | :toRole       | :TravelGuide    |

Table B.25: Interaction (i19): travel guide service sends address(es), as requested, to a rented car

| :i19 | rdf:type      | :Interaction      |
|------|---------------|-------------------|
| :i19 | :msgSignature | "responseAddress" |
| :i19 | :fromRole     | :TravelGuide      |
| :i19 | :toRole       | :RentedCar        |

# Appendix C
# Social Interaction Models

## C.1 Domain-Centric Social Interaction Models (DSIMs)

### C.1.1 ConvoyDSIM

```
DSIM ConvoyDSIM{
    SocialRole LeadingCar, FollowingCar;
    OrganiserRole Organiser;

    RolePlayerBinding org{
        RoleName Organiser;
        Player Car#1.SocioTelematics;
    };
    RolePlayerBinding b1{
        RoleName LeadingCar;
        Player Car#1PSIM;
    };
    RolePlayerBinding b2{
        RoleName FollowingCar;
        Player Car#2PSIM;
    };
```

© Springer International Publishing Switzerland 2016
M.A. Kabir et al., *Pervasive Social Computing*,
DOI 10.1007/978-3-319-29951-8

```
SocialRelationship R1{
  RelationshipName LeadingCar-FollowingCar;
  RoleA LeadingCar;
  RoleB FollowingCar;
  SocialInteraction i1{
    MsgSignature notifyPosition(float:latitude,float:longitude);
    Direction RoleBToRoleA;
    RelatedObligation o1, o2;
  };
  SocialInteraction i2{
    MsgSignature notifyPosition(float:latitude,float:longitude);
    Direction RoleAToRoleB;
    RelatedObligation o1, o2;
  };
  SocialInteraction i3{
    MsgSignature notifyRoadBlock(String roadAddress);
    Direction RoleBToRoleA;
  };
  SocialInteraction i4{
    MsgSignature routeUpdate(String route);
    Direction RoleAToRoleB;
  };
  SocialInteraction i5{
    MsgSignature notifyMechanicalIssue(String issueDescription);
    Direction RoleAToRoleB;
  };
  SocialInteraction i6{
    MsgSignature notifyMechanicalIssue(String issueDescription);
    Direction RoleBToRoleA;
  };
  Obligation o1{
    Timer PERIOD;
    RelatedOperationalParam p1;
  };
  Obligation o2{
    RelatedOperationalParam p2;
  };
  OperationalParam p1{
    OPParamName posUpdateFreq;
    OPParamValue 10;
    TimeUnit SEC;
  };
```

```
        OperationalParam p2{
           OPParamName maxDesiredDistance;
           OPParamValue 1;
           DistanceUnit KM;
        };
        SocialInteraction i16{
           MsgSignature convoyBreak(String cause);
           Direction RoleBToRoleA;
        };
        SocialInteraction i17{
           MsgSignature positiveResponse(String cause);
           Direction RoleAToRoleB;
        };
};
```

## C.1.2 BudgetDSIM

```
DSIM BudgetDSIM{
     SocialRole RentedCar, RoadsideAssistance;
     SocialRole RentalCompany, TravelGuide;
     OrganiserRole Organiser;

     RolePlayerBinding org{
        RoleName Organiser;
        Player Budget;
     };
     RolePlayerBinding b3{
        RoleName RentedCar;
        Player Car#1PSIM;
     };
     RolePlayerBinding b4{
        RoleName RoadsideAssistance;
        Player RACV;
     };
     RolePlayerBinding b5{
        RoleName RentalCompany;
        Player Budget;
     };
     RolePlayerBinding b6{
        RoleName TravelGuide;
        Player TravelGuide.org;
     };
```

```
RolePlayerBinding b3{
   RoleName OrganiserRole;
   Player Budget;
};

SocialRelationship R2{
   RelationshipName RentedCar-TravelGuide;
   RoleA RentedCar;
   RoleB TravelGuide;
   SocialInteraction i7{
      MsgSignature routeRequest(String sourceAddr, String destAddr,
                                    String preference);
      Direction RoleAToRoleB;
   };
   SocialInteraction i8{
      MsgSignature routeNotification(String route);
      Direction RoleBToRoleA;
   };
   SocialInteraction i18{
      MsgSignature addressRequest(String placeType);
      Direction RoleAToRoleB;
   };
   SocialInteraction i9{
      MsgSignature responseAddress(String addresses);
      Direction RoleBToRoleA;
   };
   Conversation c1{
      SocialInteractionX i7;
      SocialInteractionX i8;
      Sequence leadsTo; // i7 leadsTo i8
      RelatedObligation o3;
   };
   Obligation o3{
      Timer DURATION;
      RelatedOperationalParam p3;
   };
   OperationalParam p3{
      OPParamName maxTimeDelay;
      OPParamValue 15;
      TimeUnit SEC;
   };
};
```

```
    SocialRelationship R3{
      RelationshipName RentedCar-RentalCompany;
      RoleA RentedCar;
      RoleB RentalCompany;
      SocialInteraction i9{
        MsgSignature notifyMechanicalIssue(String issueDescription);
        Direction RoleAToRoleB;
      };
    };

  SocialRelationship R4{
    RelationshipName RentedCar-RoadsideAssistance;
    RoleA RentedCar;
    RoleB RoadsideAssistance;
    SocialInteraction i10{
      MsgSignature mechanicalAssistanceRequest(String issueDescription);
        Direction RoleAToRoleB;
    };
    SocialInteraction i11{
        MsgSignature assistanceResponse(String description);
        Direction RoleBToRoleA;
    };
    Conversation c2{
        SocialInteractionX i10;
        SocialInteractionX i11;
        Sequence leadsTo; // i10 leadsTo i11
        RelatedObligation o4;
    };
    Obligation o4{
        Timer DURATION;
        RelatedOperationalParam p4;
    };
    OperationalParam p4{
        OPParamName maxTimeDelay;
        OPParamValue 5;
        TimeUnit MIN;
    };
  };

SocialRelationship R5{
    RelationshipName RoadsideAssistance-RentalCompany;
    RoleA RoadsideAssistance;
    RoleB RentalCompany;
    SocialInteraction i12{
        MsgSignature carIDVerificationRequest(String carID);
```

```
        Direction RoleAToRoleB;
    };
    SocialInteraction i13{
        MsgSignature carIDVerificationResult(Boolean result);
        Direction RoleBToRoleA;
    };
    Conversation c3{
        SocialInteractionX i12;
        SocialInteractionX i13;
        Sequence leadsTo; // i12 leadsTo i13
    };
};
```

## C.1.3  AVISDSIM

```
DSIM AVISDSIM{
    SocialRole RentedCar, RoadsideAssistance;
    SocialRole RentalCompany, TrafficManagement;
    OrganiserRole Organiser;

    RolePlayerBinding org{
        RoleName Organiser;
        Player AVIS;
    };
    RolePlayerBinding b7{
        RoleName RentedCar;
        Player Car#2PSIM;
    };
    RolePlayerBinding b8{
        RoleName RoadsideAssistance;
        Player RACV;
    };
    RolePlayerBinding b9{
        RoleName RentalCompany;
        Player AVIS;
    };
    RolePlayerBinding b10{
        RoleName TrafficManagement;
        Player VicRoad.org;
    };
```

```
SocialRelationship R6{
   RelationshipName RentedCar-TrafficManagement;
   RoleA RentedCar;
   RoleB TrafficManagement;
   SocialInteraction i14{
      MsgSignature roadBlockCheckingRequest(String sourceAddr,
                   String destAddr);
      Direction RoleAToRoleB;
   };
   SocialInteraction i15{
      MsgSignature roadBlockCheckingResult(String address);
      Direction RoleBToRoleA;
   };
   Conversation c4{
      SocialInteractionX i14;
      SocialInteractionX i15;
      Sequence leadsTo;
      RelatedObligation o6;
   };
   Obligation o6{
      Timer DURATION;
      RelatedOperationalParam p6;
   };
   OperationalParam p6{
      OPParamName maxTimeDelay;
      OPParamValue 10;
      TimeUnit SEC;
   };
};


SocialRelationship R7{
   RelationshipName RentedCar-RentalCompany;
   RoleA RentedCar;
   RoleB RentalCompany;
   SocialInteraction i16{
      MsgSignature notifyMechanicalIssue(String issueDescription);
      Direction RoleAToRoleB;
   };
};


SocialRelationship R8{
   RelationshipName RentedCar-RoadsideAssistance;
   RoleA RentedCar;
   RoleB RoadsideAssistance;
   SocialInteraction i17{
```

```
    MsgSignature mechanicalAssistanceRequest(String issueDescription);
      Direction RoleAToRoleB;
   };
   SocialInteraction i18{
      MsgSignature assistanceResponse(String description);
      Direction RoleBToRoleÁ;
   };
   Conversation c5{
      SocialInteractionX i17;
      SocialInteractionX i18;
      Sequence leadsTo; // i17 leadsTo i18
      RelatedObligation o7;
   };
   Obligation o7{
      Timer DURATION;
      RelatedOperationalParam p7;
   };
   OperationalParam p7{
      OPParamName maxTimeDelay;
      OPParamValue 8;
      TimeUnit MIN;
   };
};


SocialRelationship R9{
   RelationshipName RoadsideAssistance-RentalCompany;
   RoleA RoadsideAssistance;
   RoleB RentalCompany;
   SocialInteraction i19{
      MsgSignature carIDVerificationRequest(String carID);
      Direction RoleAToRoleB;
   };
   SocialInteraction i20{
      MsgSignature carIDVerificationResult(Boolean result);
      Direction RoleBToRoleA;
   };
};
```

## C.2 Player-Centric Social Interaction Models (PSIMs)

### C.2.1  Car#1PSIM

```
PSIM Car#1PSIM{
   SocialRole LeadingCar, RentedCar;
   CoordinatorRole Coordinator;
   OrganiserRole Organiser;

   RolePlayerBinding org{
      RoleName Organiser;
      Player Car#1.SocioTelematics;
   };
   RolePlayerBinding b1{
      RoleName LeadingCar;
      Player Car#1.SocioTelematics;
   };
   RolePlayerBinding b7{
      RoleName RentedCar;
      Player Car#1.SocioTelematics;
   };
   RolePlayerBinding b7{
      RoleName Coordinator;
      Player Car#1.CoordinationRules;
   };

   RoleCentricSocialRelationship Rr1{
      RelationshipName LeadingCar-Coordinator;
      RoleA LeadingCar;
      RoleB Coordinator;
      SocialInteraction i1{
         MsgSignature notifyPosition(float:latitude,float:longitude);
         Direction RoleBToRoleA;
         RelatedObligation o1, o2;
      };
      SocialInteraction i2{
         MsgSignature notifyPosition(float:latitude,float:longitude);
         Direction RoleAToRoleB;
         RelatedObligation o1;
      };
      SocialInteraction i3{
         MsgSignature notifyRoadBlock(String address);
         Direction RoleBToRoleA;
      };
```

```
SocialInteraction i4{
   MsgSignature routeUpdate(String route);
   Direction RoleAToRoleB;
};
SocialInteraction i5{
   MsgSignature notifyMechanicalIssue(String issueDescription);
   Direction RoleAToRoleB;
};
SocialInteraction i6{
   MsgSignature notifyMechanicalIssue(String issueDescription);
   Direction RoleBToRoleA;
};
SocialInteraction i16{
   MsgSignature convoyBreak(String cause);
   Direction RoleBToRoleA;
};
SocialInteraction i17{
   MsgSignature positiveResponse(String cause);
   Direction RoleAToRoleB;
};
Obligation o1{
   Timer PERIOD;
   RelatedOperationalParam p1;
};
Obligation o2{
       RelatedOperationalParam p2;
};
OperationalParam p1{
   OPParamName posUpdateFreq;
   OPParamValue 10;
   TimeUnit SEC;
};
OperationalParam p2{
   OPParamName maxDesiredDistance;
   OPParamValue 1;
   DistanceUnit KM;
};
};

RoleCentricSocialRelationship Rr2{
RelationshipName RentedCar-Coordinator;
RoleA RentedCar;
RoleB Coordinator;

SocialInteraction i7{
```

```
        MsgSignature routeRequest(String sourceAddr, String destAddr,
                                    String preference);
        Direction RoleAToRoleB;
    };
    SocialInteraction i8{
        MsgSignature routeNotification(String route);
        Direction RoleBToRoleA;
    };
    SocialInteraction i9{
        MsgSignature notifyMechanicalIssue(String issueDescription);
        Direction RoleAToRoleB;
    };
    SocialInteraction i10{
      MsgSignature mechanicalAssistanceRequest(String issueDescription);
        Direction RoleAToRoleB;
    };
    SocialInteraction i11{
        MsgSignature assistanceResponse(String description);
        Direction RoleBToRoleA;
    };
    SocialInteraction i18{
        MsgSignature addressRequest(String placeType);
        Direction RoleAToRoleB;
    };
    SocialInteraction i9{
        MsgSignature responseAddress(String addresses);
        Direction RoleBToRoleA;
    };
    Conversation c1{
        SocialInteractionX i7;
        SocialInteractionX i8;
        Sequence leadsTo; // i7 leadsTo i8
        RelatedObligation o3;
    };
    Obligation o3{
        Timer DURATION;
        RelatedOperationalParam p3;
    };
    OperationalParam p3{
        OPParamName maxTimeDelay;
        OPParamValue 15;
        TimeUnit SEC;
    };
```

```
    Conversation c2{
       SocialInteractionX i10;
       SocialInteractionX i11;
       Sequence leadsTo; // i10 leadsTo i11
       RelatedObligation o4;
    };
    Obligation o4{
       Timer DURATION;
       RelatedOperationalParam p4;
    };
    OperationalParam p4{
       OPParamName maxTimeDelay;
       OPParamValue 5;
       TimeUnit MIN;
    };
    Conversation c3{
       SocialInteractionX i12;
       SocialInteractionX i13;
       Sequence leadsTo; // i12 leadsTo i13
    };
  };
};
```

## C.2.2  Car#2PSIM

```
PSIM Car#2PSIM{
  SocialRole FollowingCar, RentedCar;
  CoordinatorRole Coordinator;
  OrganiserRole Organiser;

  RolePlayerBinding org{
    RoleName Organiser;
    Player Car#2.SocioTelematics;
  };
  RolePlayerBinding b1{
    RoleName FollowingCar;
    Player Car#2.SocioTelematics;
  };
  RolePlayerBinding b2{
    RoleName RentedCar;
    Player Car#2.SocioTelematics;
  };
```

```
RolePlayerBinding b3{
   RoleName Coordinator;
   Player Car#2.CoordinationRules;
};


RoleCentricSocialRelationship Rr3{
   RelationshipName FollowingCar-Coordinator;
   RoleA Coordinator;
   RoleB FollowingCar;
   SocialInteraction i1{
      MsgSignature notifyPosition(float:latitude,float:longitude);
      Direction RoleBToRoleA;
      RelatedObligation o1, o2;
   };
   SocialInteraction i2{
      MsgSignature notifyPosition(float:latitude,float:longitude);
      Direction RoleAToRoleB;
      RelatedObligation o1;
   };
   SocialInteraction i3{
      MsgSignature notifyRoadBlock(String roadAddress);
      Direction RoleBToRoleA;
   };
   SocialInteraction i4{
      MsgSignature routeUpdate(String route);
      Direction RoleAToRoleB;
   };
   SocialInteraction i5{
      MsgSignature notifyMechanicalIssue(String issueDescription);
      Direction RoleAToRoleB;
   };
   SocialInteraction i16{
      MsgSignature convoyBreak(String cause);
      Direction RoleBToRoleA;
   };
   SocialInteraction i17{
      MsgSignature positiveResponse(String cause);
      Direction RoleAToRoleB;
   };
   Obligation o1{
      Timer PERIOD;
      RelatedOperationalParam p1;
   };
```

```
     Obligation o2{
        RelatedOperationalParam p2;
     };
     OperationalParam p1{
        OPParamName posUpdateFreq;
        OPParamValue 10;
        TimeUnit SEC;
     };
     OperationalParam p2{
        OPParamName maxDesiredDistance;
        OPParamValue 1;
        DistanceUnit KM;
     };
  };


  RoleCentricSocialRelationship Rr4{
     RelationshipName RentedCar-Coordinator;
     RoleA RentedCar;
     RoleB Coordinator;
     SocialInteraction i14{
        MsgSignature roadBlockCheckingRequest(String sourceAddr,
                                              String destAddr);
        Direction RoleAToRoleB;
     };
     SocialInteraction i15{
        MsgSignature roadBlockCheckingResult(String address);
        Direction RoleBToRoleA;
     };
     SocialInteraction i16{
        MsgSignature notifyMechanicalIssue(String issueDescription);
        Direction RoleAToRoleB;
     };
     SocialInteraction i17{
      MsgSignature mechanicalAssistanceRequest(String issueDescription);
        Direction RoleAToRoleB;
     };
     SocialInteraction i18{
        MsgSignature assistanceResponse(String description);
        Direction RoleBToRoleA;
     };
     Conversation c4{
        SocialInteractionX i14;
        SocialInteractionX i15;
        Sequence leadsTo;
        RelatedObligation o6;
     };
```

```
    Obligation o6{
        Timer DURATION;
        RelatedOperationalParam p6;
    };
    OperationalParam p6{
        OPParamName maxTimeDelay;
        OPParamValue 10;
        TimeUnit SEC;
    };
    Conversation c5{
        SocialInteractionX i17;
        SocialInteractionX i18;
        Sequence leadsTo; // i17 leadsTo i18
        RelatedObligation o7;
    };
    Obligation o7{
        Timer DURATION;
        RelatedOperationalParam p7;
    };
    OperationalParam p7{
        OPParamName maxTimeDelay;
        OPParamValue 8;
        TimeUnit MIN;
    };
  };
};
```

# Appendix D
# Rule Translation Script (*RuleTrans.dsl*)

This *RuleTrans.dsl* is used by the Drools engine to automatically translate situation rules written in human readable format to the Drools executable format.

```
[when][] an atomic interaction event {atomic_event_name
  } occurred in "{source}" which is a message
  communication, {constraints} = ${atomic_event_name}:
  InteractionEvent({constraints})from entry−point "{
  source}"

[when][] an atomic interaction event {atomic_event_name
  } occurred which is a message communication,{
  constraints} = ${atomic_event_name}:InteractionEvent
  ({constraints})

[when][] a complex interaction event {
  complex_event_name} observed between {event1} and {
  event2} where event {event2} occurred in "{source}"
  is a message communication, {constraints} = ${
  complex_event_name}:InteractionEvent({constraints})
  from entry−point"{source}"

[when][] a complex interaction event {
  complex_event_name} observed between {event1} and {
  event2} where event {event2} is a message
  communication, {constraints} = ${complex_event_name}
  :InteractionEvent({constraints})
```

[when][] an atomic interaction event {atomic_event_name
} occurred in "{source}" = ${atomic_event_name}:
InteractionEvent()from entry−point "{source}"

[when][] an atomic interaction event {atomic_event_name
} occurred = ${atomic_event_name}:InteractionEvent()

[when][] is less than or equal to=<=

[when][] is less than=<

[when][] is greater than or equal to=>=

[when][] is greater than=>

[when][] is equal to===

[when][] equals===

[when][] from actor "{value}" = eval(kbIns.
semanticMatching("fromActor",fromActor,"{value}"))

[when][] to actor "{value}" = eval(kbIns.
semanticMatching("toActor",toActor,"{value}"))

[when][] from role "{value}" = eval(kbIns.
semanticMatching("fromRole",fromRole,"{value}"))

[when][] to role "{value}" = eval(kbIns.semanticMatching
("toRole",toRole,"{value}"))

[when][] related with "{value}" relationship = eval(
kbIns.semanticMatching("related",related,"{value}"))

[when][] discussing about "{value}" = eval(kbIns.
semanticMatching("about",about,"{value}"))

[when][] has occurred "before" ${event2}$ by '{value}' =
this before[1ms,{value}] ${event2}

[when][] has occurred "before" ${event2}$ between '{
value1}' and '{value2}' = this before[{value1},{
value2}] ${event2}

[when][] has occurred "after" ${event2}$ by '{value}' = this before[1ms,{value}] ${event2}

[when][] has occurred "after" ${event2}$ between '{value1}' and '{value2}' = this after[{value1},{value2}]${event2}

[when][] has occurred "coincides" ${event2}$ by '{value}' = this coincides[{value}] ${event2}

[when][] has occurred "coincides" ${event2}$ by '{value1}' and '{value2}' = this coincides[{value1},{value2}] ${event2}

[when][] has occurred "during" ${event2}$ by '{value}' = this during[{value}] ${event2}

[when][] has occurred "during" ${event2}$ by '{value1}' and '{value2}' = this during[{value1},{value2}] ${event2}

[when][] has occurred "during" ${event2}$ by '{value1}','{value2}','{value3}' and '{value4}' = this during[{value1},{value2},{value3},{value4}] ${event2}

[when][] has occurred "finishes" ${event2}$ by '{value}'=this finishes[{value}] ${event2}

[when][] has occurred "finishedby" ${event2}$ by '{value}'=this finishedby[{value}] ${event2}

[when][] has occurred "includes" ${event2}$ by '{value}'=this includes[{value}] ${event2}

[when][] has occurred "includes" ${event2}$ by '{value1}' and '{value2}'=this includes[{value1},{value2}] ${event2}

[when][] has occurred "includes" ${event2}$ by '{value1}','{value2}','{value3}' and '{value4}'=this includes[{value1},{value2},{value3},{value4}] ${event2}

[when][] has occurred "meets" ${event2}$ by '{value}'=this meets[{value}] ${event2}

[when][] has occurred "metby" ${event2}$ by '{value}'=
this metby[{value}] ${event2}

[when][] has occurred "starts" ${event2}$ by '{value}'=
this starts[{value}] ${event2}

[when][] has occurred "startedby" ${event2}$ by '{value
}'=this startedby[{value}] ${event2}

[when][] has occurred "overlaps" ${event2}$ by '{value
}'=this overlaps[{value}] ${event2}

[when][] has occurred "overlaps" ${event2}$ by '{value1
}' and '{value2}'=this overlaps[{value1},{value2}]${
event2}

[when][] has occurred "overlappedby" ${event2}$ by '{
value}'=this overlappedby[{value}] ${event2}

[when][] has occurred "overlappedby" ${event2}$ by '{
value1}' and '{value2}'=this overlappedby[{value1},{
value2}] ${event2}

[when][] has occurred "{temp_op}" ${event2}$=this {
temp_op} ${event2}

[when][] and=&&

[when][] or =||

# Appendix E
# Schema Definitions

The schema definition of the deployable descriptor is given below. The schema definition is captured by the files ... These files can be visualised and navigated via suitable software tool such as Eclipse XSD Editor. [1]

## E.1 DSIM Schema

```
<?xml version="1.0" encoding="UTF-8"?>
<schema xmlns="http://www.w3.org/2001/XMLSchema" targetNamespace
   ="http://www.example.org/DSIMSchema" elementFormDefault="
   qualified" xmlns:dsim="http://www.example.org/DSIMSchema">

<element name="DSIM">
<complexType>
<sequence>
<element name="SocialRole" minOccurs="2" maxOccurs="unbounded">
<complexType>
<simpleContent>
<extension base="string">
<attribute name="id" type="string">
</attribute>
</extension>
</simpleContent>
</complexType>
</element>
<element name="SocialRelationship" minOccurs="1" maxOccurs="
   unbounded">
<complexType>
<sequence>
<element name="RoleA" type="string"
```

---

[1] http://wiki.eclipse.org/index.php/Introduction_to_the_XSD_Editor

© Springer International Publishing Switzerland 2016
M.A. Kabir et al., *Pervasive Social Computing*,
DOI 10.1007/978-3-319-29951-8

```xml
minOccurs="1" maxOccurs="1">
</element>
<element name="RoleB" type="string"
minOccurs="1" maxOccurs="1">
</element>
<element name="SocialInteraction"
minOccurs="1" maxOccurs="unbounded">
<complexType>
<sequence>
<element name="MsgName"
        type="string" minOccurs="1" maxOccurs="1">
</element>
<element name="Direction"
        type="dsim:DirectionType" minOccurs="1" maxOccurs="1">
</element>
<element name="Type"
        type="string" minOccurs="0" maxOccurs="unbounded">
</element>
</sequence>
<attribute name="id"
type="string">
</attribute>
</complexType>
</element>
<element name="OperationalParam"
minOccurs="0" maxOccurs="unbounded">
<complexType>
<sequence>
<element name="ParamName"
        type="string" minOccurs="1" maxOccurs="1">
</element>
<element name="ParamValue"
        type="string" minOccurs="1" maxOccurs="1">
</element>
<element name="TimeUnit"
        minOccurs="0" maxOccurs="1">
<simpleType>
        <restriction
                base="dsim:TimeUnitType">
                <enumeration
                        value="MS">
                </enumeration>
                <enumeration
                        value="SEC">
                </enumeration>
                <enumeration
                        value="MIN">
                </enumeration>
                <enumeration
                        value="HOUR">
                </enumeration>
                <enumeration
                        value="DAY">
                </enumeration>
```

```
                        </restriction>
        </simpleType>
        </element>
        <element name="DistanceUnit"
                minOccurs="0" maxOccurs="1">
                <simpleType>
                        <restriction
                                base="string">
                                <enumeration
                                        value="MM'>
                                </enumeration>
                                <enumeration
                                        value="CM'>
                                </enumeration>
                                <enumeration
                                        value="M'>
                                </enumeration>
                                <enumeration
                                        value="KM'>
                                </enumeration>
                        </restriction>
                </simpleType>
        </element>
        </sequence>
        <attribute name="id"
        type="string">
        </attribute>
        </complexType>
        </element>
<element name="Obligation" minOccurs="0" maxOccurs="unbounded">
<complexType>
<sequence>
<element name="Timer"
        minOccurs="1" maxOccurs="1" type="dsim:TimerType">

</element>
<element
        name="RelatedOPParameter" type="string" minOccurs="1"
        maxOccurs="1">
</element>
</sequence>
<attribute name="id"
type="string">
</attribute>
</complexType>
</element>
<element name="Conversation" minOccurs="0" maxOccurs="unbounded">
<complexType>
<sequence>
<element
        name="SocialInteractionX" type="string" minOccurs="1"
   maxOccurs="1">
</element>
<element
```

```xml
                name="SocialInteractionY" type="string" minOccurs="1"
    maxOccurs="1">
</element>
<element name="SequenceType"
            minOccurs="1" maxOccurs="1">
        <simpleType>
                <restriction
                        base="string">
                        <enumeration
                                value="leadesTo">
                        </enumeration>
                        <enumeration
                                value="precedes">
                        </enumeration>
                </restriction>
        </simpleType>
</element>
<element
        name="RelatedObligation" type="string" minOccurs="1"
    maxOccurs="1">
</element>
</sequence>
<attribute name="id"
type="string">
</attribute>
</complexType>
</element>
</sequence>
<attribute name="id" type="string"></attribute>
</complexType>
</element>

<element name="OrganiserRole" type="string"
minOccurs="1" maxOccurs="1">
</element>
<element name="RolePlayerBinding" minOccurs="1" maxOccurs="
    unbounded">
<complexType>
<sequence>
<element name="RoleName" type="string"></element>
<element name="Player" type="string"></element>
</sequence>
</complexType></element>
</sequence>
<attribute name="id" type="string"></attribute>
<attribute name="name" type="string" use="required"></attribute>
</complexType></element>

<simpleType name="DirectionType">
<restriction base="string">
<enumeration value="RoleAToRoleB"></enumeration>
<enumeration value="RoleBToRoleA"></enumeration>
</restriction>
</simpleType>
```

```xml
<simpleType name="TimeUnitType">
<restriction base="string">
<enumeration value="MS"></enumeration>
<enumeration value="SEC"></enumeration>
<enumeration value="MIN"></enumeration>
<enumeration value="HOUR"></enumeration>
<enumeration value="DAY"></enumeration>
</restriction>
</simpleType>

<simpleType name="TimerType">
<restriction base="string">
<enumeration value="DURATION"></enumeration>
<enumeration value="PERIOD"></enumeration>
</restriction>
</simpleType>

</schema>
```

## E.2  PSIM Schema

```xml
<?xml version="1.0" encoding="UTF-8"?>
<schema xmlns="http://www.w3.org/2001/XMLSchema" targetNamespace
   ="http://www.example.org/PSIMSchema" elementFormDefault="
   qualified" xmlns:dsim="http://www.example.org/PSIMSchema">

<element name="PSIM">
<complexType>
<sequence>
<element name="SocialRole" minOccurs="1" maxOccurs="unbounded">
<complexType>
<simpleContent>
<extension base="string">
<attribute name="id" type="string"></attribute>
</extension>
</simpleContent>
</complexType>
</element>
<element name="CoordinatorRole" minOccurs="1" maxOccurs="1">
<complexType>
<simpleContent>
<extension base="string">
<attribute name="id" type="string"></attribute>
</extension>
</simpleContent>
</complexType>
</element>
<element name="RoleCentricSocialRelationship" minOccurs="1"
   maxOccurs="unbounded">
<complexType>
<sequence>
```

```xml
<element name="RoleA" type="string"
minOccurs="1" maxOccurs="1">
</element>
<element name="RoleB" type="string"
minOccurs="1" maxOccurs="1">
</element>
<element name="SocialInteraction"
minOccurs="1" maxOccurs="unbounded">
<complexType>
<sequence>
<element name="MsgName"
        type="string" minOccurs="1" maxOccurs="1">
</element>
<element name="Direction"
        type="dsim:DirectionType" minOccurs="1" maxOccurs="1">
</element>
<element name="Type"
        type="string" minOccurs="0" maxOccurs="unbounded">
</element>
</sequence>
<attribute name="id"
type="string">
</attribute>
</complexType>
</element>
<element name="OperationalParam"
minOccurs="0" maxOccurs="unbounded">
<complexType>
<sequence>
<element name="ParamName"
        type="string" minOccurs="1" maxOccurs="1">
</element>
<element name="ParamValue"
        type="string" minOccurs="1" maxOccurs="1">
</element>
<element name="TimeUnit"
        minOccurs="0" maxOccurs="1">
<simpleType>
        <restriction
                base="dsim:TimeUnitType">
                <enumeration
                        value="MS">
                </enumeration>
                <enumeration
                        value="SEC">
                </enumeration>
                <enumeration
                        value="MIN">
                </enumeration>
                <enumeration
                        value="HOUR">
                </enumeration>
                <enumeration
                        value="DAY">
```

```xml
                              </enumeration>
                </restriction>
</simpleType>
</element>
<element name="DistanceUnit"
          minOccurs="0"  maxOccurs="1">
          <simpleType>
                    <restriction
                              base="string">
                              <enumeration
                                        value="MM'>
                              </enumeration>
                              <enumeration
                                        value="CM'>
                              </enumeration>
                              <enumeration
                                        value="M'>
                              </enumeration>
                              <enumeration
                                        value="KM'>
                              </enumeration>
                    </restriction>
          </simpleType>
</element>
</sequence>
<attribute name="id"
type="string">
</attribute>
</complexType>
</element>
<element name="Obligation" minOccurs="0" maxOccurs="unbounded">
<complexType>
<sequence>
<element name="Timer"
          minOccurs="1" maxOccurs="1" type="dsim:TimerType">

</element>
<element
          name="RelatedOPParameter" type="string" minOccurs="1"
          maxOccurs="1">
</element>
</sequence>
<attribute name="id"
type="string">
</attribute>
</complexType>
</element>
<element name="Conversation" minOccurs="0" maxOccurs="unbounded">
<complexType>
<sequence>
<element
          name="SocialInteractionX" type="string" minOccurs="1"
   maxOccurs="1">
</element>
```

```
<element
        name="SocialInteractionY" type="string" minOccurs="1"
  maxOccurs="1">
</element>
<element name="SequenceType"
        minOccurs="1" maxOccurs="1">
        <simpleType>
                <restriction
                        base="string">
                        <enumeration
                                value="leadesTo">
                        </enumeration>
                        <enumeration
                                value="precedes">
                        </enumeration>
                </restriction>
        </simpleType>
</element>
<element
        name="RelatedObligation" type="string" minOccurs="1"
  maxOccurs="1">
</element>
</sequence>
<attribute name="id"
type="string">
</attribute>
</complexType>
</element>
</sequence>
<attribute name="id" type="string"></attribute>
</complexType>
</element>

<element name="OrganiserRole" type="string"
minOccurs="1" maxOccurs="1">
</element>
<element name="RolePlayerBinding" minOccurs="1" maxOccurs="
  unbounded">
<complexType>
<sequence>
<element name="RoleName" type="string"></element>
<element name="Player" type="string"></element>
</sequence>
</complexType></element>
</sequence>
<attribute name="id" type="string"></attribute>
<attribute name="name" type="string" use="required"></attribute>
</complexType></element>

<simpleType name="DirectionType">
<restriction base="string">
<enumeration value="RoleAToRoleB"></enumeration>
<enumeration value="RoleBToRoleA"></enumeration>
</restriction>
```

```
</simpleType>

<simpleType name="TimeUnitType">
<restriction base="string">
<enumeration value="MS"></enumeration>
<enumeration value="SEC"></enumeration>
<enumeration value="MIN"></enumeration>
<enumeration value="HOUR"></enumeration>
<enumeration value="DAY"></enumeration>
</restriction>
</simpleType>

<simpleType name="TimerType">
<restriction base="string">
<enumeration value="DURATION"></enumeration>
<enumeration value="PERIOD"></enumeration>
</restriction>
</simpleType>
</schema>
```

# References

1. http://news.cnet.com/8301-10784_3-9824710-7.html. Accessed 30 Sept 2010
2. Apache axis2 - next generation web services. http://ws.apache.org/axis2/
3. Apache tomcat - the apache software foundation. http://tomcat.apache.org/
4. Australian government fair work ombudsman. http://www.fairwork.gov.au
5. Bureau of labor statistics. http://www.bls.gov
6. Business victoria. http://www.business.vic.gov.au
7. Design and use of the simple event model (sem). Web Semant. Sci. Serv. Agents World Wide Web 9(2), 128–136 (2011). doi:10.1016/j.websem.2011.03.003
8. Drools expert. http://www.jboss.org/drools/drools-expert.html
9. Drools fusion. http://www.jboss.org/drools/drools-fusion.html
10. Friend of a friend (foaf). http://xmlns.com/foaf/spec
11. Graph api – facebook developers. http://developers.facebook.com
12. ksoap2-android: A lightweight and efficient soap library for the android platform. https://code.google.com/p/ksoap2-android/
13. Linkedin apis. https://developer.linkedin.com/apis
14. National safety council. http://www.nsc.org/Pages/NSCestimates 16millioncrashescausedbydriversusingcellphonesandtexting.aspx
15. Owl 2 web ontology language - manchester syntax. http://www.w3.org/TR/owl2-manchester-syntax/
16. Oxford english dictionary. http://www.oed.com/
17. Relationship. http://vocab.org/relationship
18. Roadfactory. http://www.swinburne.edu.au/ict/success/research-projects-and-grants/role-oriented-adaptive-design/implementations/road-factory.html
19. Sun developer network, java architecture for xml binding (jaxb). http://jcp.org/en/jsr/summary?id=222
20. W3c, w3c soap specifications. http://www.w3.org/TR/soap/
21. W3c, web services description language (wsdl). http://www.w3.org/TR/wsdl20/
22. Wapforum, user agent profile (uaprof). http://www.wapforum.org
23. Wikitionary, a wiki based open content dictionary. http://en.wiktionary.org/wiki/
24. Xml schema. http://www.w3.org/XML/Schema
25. Aarts, E., de Ruyter, B.: New research perspectives on ambient intelligence. J. Ambient Intell. Smart Environ. 1(1), 5–14 (2009). http://dl.acm.org/citation.cfm?id=1735821.1735822

© Springer International Publishing Switzerland 2016
M.A. Kabir et al., *Pervasive Social Computing*,
DOI 10.1007/978-3-319-29951-8

26. Abowd, G., Dey, A., Brown, P., Davies, N., Smith, M., Steggles, P.: Towards a better understanding of context and context-awareness. In: Gellersen, H.W. (ed.) Handheld and Ubiquitous Computing. Lecture Notes in Computer Science, vol. 1707, pp. 304–307. Springer, Berlin, Heidelberg (1999). doi:10.1007/3-540-48157-5_29. http://dx.doi.org/10.1007/3-540-48157-5_29

27. Abowd, G., Ebling, M., Hung, G., Lei, H., Gellersen, H.W.: Context-aware computing [guest editors' intro.].    IEEE Pervasive Comput. 1(3), 22–23 (2002). doi:10.1109/MPRV.2002.1037718

28. Allen, J., Ferguson, G.: Actions and events in interval temporal logic. J. Log. Comput. 4(5), 531–579 (1994)

29. Allman, M.: An evaluation of xml-rpc. SIGMETRICS Perform. Eval. Rev. 30(4), 2–11 (2003). doi:10.1145/773056.773057. http://doi.acm.org/10.1145/773056.773057

30. Amador, L.: Drools Developer's Cookbook. Packt, Birmingham (2012)

31. Antoniou, G., Van Harmelen, F.: Web ontology language: owl. In: Handbook on Ontologies, pp. 91–110. Springer, Berlin (2009)

32. Augusto, J., Liu, J., McCullagh, P., Wang, H., Yang, J.: Management of uncertainty and spatio-temporal aspects for monitoring and diagnosis in a smart home. Int. J. Comput. Intell. Syst. 1(4), 361–378 (2008)

33. Austin, J.L.: How to Do Things with Words, vol. 88. Harvard University Press, Cambridge, MA (1975)

34. Avrahami, D., Gergle, D., Hudson, S.E., Kiesler, S.: Improving the match between callers and receivers: a study on the effect of contextual information on cell phone interruptions.    Behav. Inform. Technol. 26(3), 247–259 (2007). doi:10.1080/01449290500402338.    http://www.tandfonline.com/doi/abs/10.1080/01449290500402338

35. Baader, F., Calvanese, D., McGuinness, D., Nardi, D., Patel-Schneider, P.:    The    Description    Logic    Handbook:    Theory,    Implementation    and Applications. Cambridge University Press, Cambridge, MA (2003)

36. Bauer, M.W., Gaskell, G.: Towards a paradigm for research on social representations. J. Theory Soc. Behav. 29(2), 163–186 (1999). doi:10.1111/1468-5914.00096. http://dx.doi.org/10.1111/1468-5914.00096

37. Bauer, B., Müller, J.P., Odell, J.: Agent uml: a formalism for specifying multiagent software systems. In: First International Workshop, AOSE 2000 on Agent-Oriented Software Engineering, pp. 91–103. Springer, New York, Secaucus, NJ (2001). http://dl.acm.org/citation.cfm?id=370834.370845

38. Beach, A., Gartrell, M., Xing, X., Han, R., Lv, Q., Mishra, S., Seada, K.: Fusing mobile, sensor, and social data to fully enable context-aware computing. In: Proceedings of the Eleventh Workshop on Mobile Computing Systems & Applications, HotMobile '10, pp. 60–65. ACM, New York (2010). doi:10.1145/1734583.1734599. http://doi.acm.org/10.1145/1734583.1734599

39. Beckett, D., McBride, B.: Rdf/xml syntax specification, w3c recommendation 10 February 2004. http://www.w3.org/TR/rdf-syntax-grammar/

40. Beckett, D., Berners-Lee, T., Prud'hommeaux, E., Carothers, G., E.P., Carothers, G.: Terse rdf triple language, w3c candidate recommendation 19 February 2013. http://www.w3.org/TR/turtle/

41. Ben Mokhtar, S., Capra, L.: From pervasive to social computing: algorithms and deployments. In: Proceedings of the 2009 International Conference on Pervasive Services, ICPS '09, pp. 169–178. ACM, New York (2009). doi:10.1145/1568199.1568229. http://doi.acm.org/10.1145/1568199.1568229

42. Bettini, C., Brdiczka, O., Henricksen, K., Indulska, J., Nicklas, D., Ranganathan, A., Riboni, D.: A survey of context modelling and reasoning techniques. Pervasive Mob. Comput. **6**(2), 161–180 (2010). doi:10.1016/j.pmcj.2009.06.002. http://www.sciencedirect.com/science/article/pii/S1574119209000510

43. Biamino, G.: Modeling social contexts for pervasive computing environments. In: IEEE International Conference on Pervasive Computing and Communications Workshops (PERCOM Workshops), pp. 415–420 (2011). doi:10.1109/PERCOMW.2011.5766925

44. Blair, G., Bencomo, N., France, R.B.: Models@ run.time. Computer **42**(10), 22–27 (2009). doi:10.1109/MC.2009.326. http://dx.doi.org/10.1109/MC.2009.326

45. Bouassida Rodriguez, I., Sancho, G., Villemur, T., Tazi, S., Drira, K.: A model-driven adaptive approach for collaborative ubiquitous systems. In: Proceedings of the 3rd Workshop on Agent-Oriented Software Engineering Challenges for Ubiquitous and Pervasive Computing, AUPC 09, pp. 15–20. ACM, New York (2009). doi:10.1145/1568181.1568187. http://doi.acm.org/10.1145/1568181.1568187

46. Brickley, D., Guha, R.: Rdf vocabulary description language 1.0: Rdf schema, w3c recommendation 10 February 2004. http://www.w3.org/TR/rdf-schema/

47. Browne, P.: JBoss Drools Business Rules. Packt, Birmingham (2009)

48. Cabitza, F., Locatelli, M., Sarini, M., Simone, C.: Casmas: supporting collaboration in pervasive environments. In: Fourth Annual IEEE International Conference on Pervasive Computing and Communications, 2006. PerCom 2006, pp. 286–295 (2006). doi:10.1109/PERCOM.2006.15

49. Cabri, G., Leonardi, L., Zambonelli, F.: Brain: a framework for flexible role-based interactions in multiagent systems. In: Meersman, R., Tari, Z., Schmidt, D. (eds.) On the Move to Meaningful Internet Systems 2003: CoopIS, DOA, and ODBASE. Lecture Notes in Computer Science, vol. 2888, pp. 145–161. Springer, Berlin, Heidelberg (2003). doi:10.1007/978-3-540-39964-3_11. http://dx.doi.org/10.1007/978-3-540-39964-3_11

50. Cabri, G., Ferrari, L., Leonardi, L.: Agent role-based collaboration and coordination: a survey about existing approaches. In: 2004 IEEE International Conference on Systems, Man and Cybernetics, vol. 6, pp. 5473–5478 (2004). doi:10.1109/ICSMC.2004.1401064

51. Cabri, G., Leonardi, L., Ferrari, L., Zambonelli, F.: Role-based software agent interaction models: a survey. Knowl. Eng. Rev. **25**, 397–419 (2010). doi:10.1017/S026988891000024X. http://journals.cambridge.org/article_S026988891000024X

52. Cardellini, V., Casalicchio, E., Grassi, V., Iannucci, S., Lo Presti, F., Mirandola, R.: Moses: a framework for qos driven runtime adaptation of service-oriented systems. IEEE Trans. Softw. Eng. **38**(5), 1138–1159 (2012). doi:10.1109/TSE.2011.68. http://dx.doi.org/10.1109/TSE.2011.68

53. Carminati, B., Ferrari, E., Heatherly, R., Kantarcioglu, M., Thuraisingham, B.: A semantic web based framework for social network access control. In: Proceedings of the 14th ACM Symposium on Access Control Models and Technologies, SACMAT '09, pp. 177–186. ACM, New York (2009). doi:10.1145/1542207.1542237. http://doi.acm.org/10.1145/1542207.1542237

54. Castelli, G., Rosi, A., Zambonelli, F.: Design and implementation of a socially-enhanced pervasive middleware. In: 2012 IEEE International Conference on Pervasive Computing and Communications Workshops (PERCOM Workshops), pp. 137–142 (2012). doi:10.1109/PerComW.2012.6197465

55. Cernuzzi, L., Zambonelli, F.: Adaptive organizational changes in agent-oriented methodologies. Knowl. Eng. Rev. **26**, 175–190 (2011). doi:10.1017/S0269888911000014. http://journals.cambridge.org/article_S0269888911000014

56. Chen, L., Rashidi, P.: Situation, activity and goal awareness in ubiquitous computing. Int. J. Pervasive Comput. Commun. **8**(3), 216–224 (2012)

57. Chen, H., Finin, T., Joshi, A.: An intelligent broker for context-aware systems. In: Adjunct Proceedings of Ubicomp, vol. 3, pp. 183–184 (2003)

58. Chen, H., Finin, T., Joshi, A.: An ontology for context-aware pervasive computing environments. Knowl. Eng. Rev. **18**(3), 197–207 (2003). doi:10.1017/S0269888904000025. http://dx.doi.org/DOI:10.1017/S0269888904000025

59. Colman, A.: Role oriented adaptive design. Ph.D. thesis, Swinburne University of Technology (2006)

60. Colman, A., Han, J.: Roles, players and adaptable organizations. Appl. Ontol. **2**(2), 105–126 (2007). http://dl.acm.org/citation.cfm?id=1412401.1412404

61. Connolly, D., van Harmelen, F., Horrocks, I., McGuiness, Deborah L., Patel-Schneider, P.F., Stein, L.A.: Daml+oil (March 2001) reference description, w3c note 18 December 2001. http://www.w3.org/TR/daml+oil-reference

62. Cortés, M., Mishra, P.: Dcwpl: a programming language for describing collaborative work. In: Proceedings of the 1996 ACM Conference on Computer Supported Cooperative Work, CSCW '96, pp. 21–29. ACM, New York (1996). doi:10.1145/240080.240176. http://doi.acm.org/10.1145/240080.240176

63. Daft, R.L.: Organization Theory and Design. South-Western Publishing, Nashville, TN (2009)

64. De Guzman, E.S., Sharmin, M., Bailey, B.P.: Should i call now? Understanding what context is considered when deciding whether to initiate remote communication via mobile devices. In: Proceedings of Graphics Interface 2007, GI '07, pp. 143–150. ACM, New York (2007). doi:10.1145/1268517.1268542. http://doi.acm.org/10.1145/1268517.1268542

65. Dearle, A., Kirby, G.N.C., Morrison, R., McCarthy, A., Mullen, K., Yang, Y., Connor, R.C.H., Welen, P., Wilson, A.: Architectural support for global smart spaces. In: Proceedings of the 4th International Conference on Mobile Data Management, MDM '03, pp. 153–164. Springer, London (2003). http://dl.acm.org/citation.cfm?id=648060.747263

66. Devlic, A., Reichle, R., Wagner, M., Pinheiro, M.K., Vanrompay, Y., Berbers, Y., Valla, M.: Context inference of users' social relationships and distributed policy management. In: Proceedings of the 2009 IEEE International Conference on Pervasive Computing and Communications Workshops (PERCOM Workshops), PERCOM '09, pp. 1–8. IEEE Computer Society, Washington, DC (2009). doi:10.1109/PERCOM.2009.4912890. http://dx.doi.org/10.1109/PERCOM.2009.4912890

67. Dey, A.K.: Understanding and using context. Pers. Ubiqut. Comput. **5**(1), 4–7 (2001). doi:10.1007/s007790170019

68. Dey, A.K., Abowd, G.D., Salber, D.: A conceptual framework and a toolkit for supporting the rapid prototyping of context-aware applications. Hum. Comput. Interact. **16**(2), 97–166 (2001). doi:10.1207/S15327051HCI16234_02. http://dx.doi.org/10.1207/S15327051HCI16234_02

69. Doerr, M.: The cidoc conceptual reference module: an ontological approach to semantic interoperability of metadata. AI Mag. **24**(3), 75–92 (2003)

70. Dourish, P.: What we talk about when we talk about context. Pers. Ubiquit. Comput. **8**(1), 19–30 (2004). doi:10.1007/s00779-003-0253-8. http://dx.doi.org/10.1007/s00779-003-0253-8

71. Ejigu, D., Scuturici, M., Brunie, L.: Coca: a collaborative context-aware service platform for pervasive computing. In: Fourth International Conference on Information Technology, 2007, ITNG'07, pp. 297–302. IEEE, New York (2007)

72. Endler, M., Skyrme, A., Schuster, D., Springer, T.: Defining situated social context for pervasive social computing. In: 2011 IEEE International Conference on Pervasive Computing and Communications Workshops (PERCOM Workshops), pp. 519–524 (2011). doi:10.1109/PERCOMW.2011.5766945

73. Etzion, O., Niblett, P.: Event Processing in Action, 1st edn. Manning, Greenwich, CT (2010)

74. Eugster, P.T., Garbinato, B., Holzer, A.: Middleware support for context-aware applications. In: Middleware for Network Eccentric and Mobile Applications, pp. 305–322. Springer, Berlin (2009)

75. Fensel, D.: Ontologies: A Silver Bullet for Knowledge Management and Electronic-Commerce. Springer, Berlin (2000)

76. Ferscha, A.: 20 years past weiser: what's next? IEEE Pervasive Comput. **11**(1), 52 –61 (2012). doi:10.1109/MPRV.2011.78

77. Fielding, R.T.: Architectural styles and the design of network-based software architectures. Ph.D. thesis, University of California (2000)

78. Filho, J., Miron, A., Satoh, I., Gensel, J., Martin, H.: Modeling and measuring quality of context information in pervasive environments. In: 2010 24th IEEE International Conference on Advanced Information Networking and Applications (AINA), pp. 690–697 (2010). doi:10.1109/AINA.2010.164

79. Finin, T., Joshi, A., Kagal, L., Niu, J., Sandhu, R., Winsborough, W., Thuraisingham, B.: Rowlbac: representing role based access control in owl. In: Proceedings of the 13th ACM Symposium on Access Control Models and Technologies, SACMAT '08, pp. 73–82. ACM, New York (2008). doi:10.1145/1377836.1377849. http://doi.acm.org/10.1145/1377836.1377849

80. Fong, P.W., Siahaan, I.: Relationship-based access control policies and their policy languages. In: Proceedings of the 16th ACM Symposium on Access Control Models and Technologies, SACMAT '11, pp. 51–60. ACM, New York (2011). doi:10.1145/1998441.1998450. http://doi.acm.org/10.1145/1998441.1998450

81. Forgy, C.L.: Rete: a fast algorithm for the many pattern/many object pattern match problem. In: Expert Systems, pp. 324–341. IEEE Computer Society Press, Los Alamitos, CA (1990)

82. France, R., Rumpe, B.: Model-driven development of complex software: a research roadmap. In: 2007 Future of Software Engineering, FOSE '07, pp. 37–54. IEEE Computer Society, Washington, DC (2007). doi:10.1109/FOSE.2007.14. http://dx.doi.org/10.1109/FOSE.2007.14

83. Gangemi, A., Mika, P.: Understanding the semantic web through descriptions and situations. In: Proceedings of the International Conference on ODBASE, pp. 689–706 (2003)

84. Geihs, K., Barone, P., Eliassen, F., Floch, J., Fricke, R., Gjorven, E., Hallsteinsen, S., Horn, G., Khan, M.U., Mamelli, A., Papadopoulos, G.A., Paspallis, N., Reichle, R., Stav, E.: A comprehensive solution for application-level adaptation. Softw. Pract. Exp. **39**(4), 385–422 (2009). doi:10.1002/spe.v39:4. http://dx.doi.org/10.1002/spe.v39:4

85. Golbeck, J., Hendler, J.: Inferring binary trust relationships in web-based social networks. ACM Trans. Internet Technol. **6**(4), 497–529 (2006). doi:10.1145/1183463.1183470. http://doi.acm.org/10.1145/1183463.1183470

86. Grandhi, S.A., Schuler, R.P., Jones, Q.: To answer or not to answer: that is the question for cell phone users. In: CHI '09 Extended Abstracts on Human Factors in Computing Systems, CHI EA '09, pp. 4621–4626. ACM, New York (2009). doi:10.1145/1520340.1520710. http://doi.acm.org/10.1145/1520340.1520710

87. Group, W.O.W.: Owl 2 Web Ontology Language Document Overview, 2nd edn. w3c recommendation 11 December 2012. http://www.w3.org/TR/owl2-overview

88. Gruber, T.R.: A translation approach to portable ontology specifications. Knowl. Acquis. 5(2), 199–220 (1993). doi:10.1006/knac.1993.1008. http://dx.doi.org/10.1006/knac.1993.1008

89. Gruber, T.: Ontology. In: Liu, L., Zsu, M.T. (eds.) Encyclopedia of Database Systems, pp. 1963–1965. Springer US, New York (2009). http://dx.doi.org/10.1007/978-0-387-39940-9_1318. doi:10.1007/978-0-387-39940-9_1318

90. Gu, T., Wang, X.H., Pung, H.K., Zhang, D.Q.: An ontology-based context model in intelligent environments. In: Proceedings of Communication Networks and Distributed Systems Modeling and Simulation Conference, vol. 2004, pp. 270–275 (2004)

91. Guarino, N.: Formal Ontology in Information Systems, vol. 46. Ios Press, Amsterdam (1998)

92. Guarino, N., Carrara, M., Giaretta, P.: Formalizing ontological commitments. In: Proceedings of the Twelfth National Conference on Artificial Intelligence, AAAI '94, vol. 1, pp. 560–567. American Association for Artificial Intelligence, Menlo Park, CA (1994). http://dl.acm.org/citation.cfm?id=199288.199324

93. Gummadi, K.P., Mislove, A., Druschel, P.: Exploiting social networks for internet search. In: Proceedings of 5th Workshop on Hot Topics in Networks, Irvine, CA, pp. 79–84 (2006)

94. Han, L., Jyri, S., Ma, J., Yu, K.: Research on context-aware mobile computing. In: 22nd International Conference on Advanced Information Networking and Applications - Workshops, 2008, AINAW 2008, pp. 24–30 (2008). doi:10.1109/WAINA.2008.115

95. Handte, M., Schiele, G., Matjuntke, V., Becker, C., Marrón, P.J.: 3pc: system support for adaptive peer-to-peer pervasive computing. ACM Trans. Auton. Adapt. Syst. 7(1), 10:1–10:19 (2012). doi:10.1145/2168260.2168270. http://doi.acm.org/10.1145/2168260.2168270

96. Held, A., Buchholz, S., Schill, A.: Modeling of context information for pervasive computing applications. In: Proceedings of SCI 2002/ISAS 2002 (2002)

97. Henricksen, K.: A framework for context-aware pervasive computing applications. Ph.D. thesis, The School of Information Technology and Electrical Engineering, The University of Queensland (2003)

98. Henricksen, K., Indulska, J.: Modelling and using imperfect context information. In: Proceedings of the PerCom Workshops, pp. 33–38 (2004)

99. Henricksen, K., Indulska, J.: Developing context-aware pervasive computing applications: models and approach. Pervasive Mob Comput 2(1), 37–64 (2006). doi:10.1016/j.pmcj.2005.07.003. http://www.sciencedirect.com/science/article/pii/S1574119205000441

100. Henricksen, K., Indulska, J., Rakotonirainy, A.: Modeling context information in pervasive computing systems. In: Proceedings of the First International Conference on Pervasive Computing, Pervasive '02, pp. 167–180. Springer, London (2002). http://dl.acm.org/citation.cfm?id=646867.706693

101. Henry, M.: Structure in Fives: Designing Effective Organizations. Prentice-Hall, Englewood Cliffs (1993)

102. Hoareau, C., Satoh, I.: Modeling and processing information for context-aware computing: a survey. N. Gener. Comput. 27(3), 177–196 (2009). doi:10.1007/s00354-009-0060-5

103. Hobbs, J.R., Pan, F.: An ontology of time for the semantic web. ACM Trans. Asian Lang. Inform. Process. 3(1), 66–85 (2004)

104. Hobbs, J.R., Pan, F.: Time ontology in owl. w3c working draft 27 September 2006. http://www.w3.org/TR/owl-time/

105. Hofer, T., Schwinger, W., Pichler, M., Leonhartsberger, G., Altmann, J., Retschitzeg-
     ger, W.: Context-awareness on mobile devices - the hydrogen approach. In: Pro-
     ceedings of the 36th Annual Hawaii International Conference on System Sciences
     (HICSS'03) - Track 9, HICSS '03, vol. 9, p. 292.1. IEEE Computer Society, Washing-
     ton, DC (2003). http://dl.acm.org/citation.cfm?id=820756.821849
106. Hong, J.I., Landay, J.A.: An infrastructure approach to context-aware computing.
     Hum. Comput. Interact. **16**(2), 287–303 (2001). doi:10.1207/S15327051HCI16234_11.
     http://dx.doi.org/10.1207/S15327051HCI16234_11
107. Horrocks, I., Patel-Schneider, P.F., van Harmelen, F.: From {SHIQ} and {RDF} to
     owl: the making of a web ontology language. Web Semant. Sci. Serv. Agents World
     Wide Web **1**(1), 7–26 (2003). doi:http://dx.doi.org/10.1016/j.websem.2003.07.001.
     http://www.sciencedirect.com/science/article/pii/
     S1570826803000027
108. Huhns, M.N., Singh, M.P.: Ontologies for agents. IEEE Int. Comput. **1**(6), 81–83
     (1997). doi:10.1109/4236.643942. http://dx.doi.org/10.1109/4236.643942
109. Jagtap, P., Joshi, A., Finin, T., Zavala, L.: Preserving privacy in context-aware sys-
     tems. In: Fifth IEEE International Conference on Semantic Computing (ICSC), pp.
     149–153 (2011). doi:10.1109/ICSC.2011.87
110. Jakkula, V., Cook, D.: Using temporal relations in smart environment data for activ-
     ity prediction. In: Proceedings of International Conference on Machine Learning,
     pp. 1–4 (2007)
111. Jayasinghe, D.: Quickstart Apache Axis2: A Practical Guide to Creating Quality Web
     Services. Packt, Birmingham (2008)
112. Jin, Y., Han, J.: Consistency and interoperability checking for component interac-
     tion rules. In: Proceedings of the 12th Asia-Pacific Software Engineering Con-
     ference, APSEC '05, pp. 595–602. IEEE Computer Society, Washington, DC (2005).
     doi:10.1109/APSEC.2005.55. http://dx.doi.org/10.1109/APSEC.2005.55
113. Juan, T., Pearce, A., Sterling, L.: Roadmap: extending the gaia methodology for com-
     plex open systems. In: Proceedings of the First International Joint Conference on
     Autonomous Agents and Multiagent Systems: Part 1, AAMAS '02, pp. 3–10. ACM,
     New York (2002). doi:10.1145/544741.544744. http://doi.acm.org/10.1145/
     544741.544744
114. Kabir, M.A., Han, J., Yu, J., Colman, A.: Scims: a social context information manage-
     ment system for socially-aware applications. In: Proceedings of the 24th Interna-
     tional Conference on Advanced Information Systems and Engineering, CAiSE'12,
     pp. 301–317 (2012)
115. Kabir, M.A., Han, J., Colman, A., Yu, J.: Sociotelematics: leveraging interaction-
     relationships in developing telematics systems to support cooperative convoys.
     In: Proceedings of the 2012 9th International Conference on Ubiquitous Intel-
     ligence and Computing and 9th International Conference on Autonomic and
     Trusted Computing, UIC-ATC '12, pp. 40–47. IEEE Computer Society, Washing-
     ton, DC (2012). doi:10.1109/UIC-ATC.2012.70. http://dx.doi.org/10.1109/
     UIC-ATC.2012.70
116. Kakousis, K., Paspallis, N., Papadopoulos, G.A.: A survey of software adapta-
     tion in mobile and ubiquitous computing. Enterp. Inf. Syst. **4**(4), 355–389 (2010).
     doi:10.1080/17517575.2010.509814. http://dx.doi.org/10.1080/17517575.
     2010.509814
117. Kalenka, S., Jennings, N.: Distinguishing social agent behaviour: a formal frame-
     work. In: 2002 Proceedings of the 5th Biannual World Automation Congress, vol. 14,
     pp. 13–20 (2002). doi:10.1109/WAC.2002.1049414
118. Kapuruge, M., Colman, A., King, J.: Road4ws – extending apache axis2 for adap-
     tive service compositions. In: Proceedings of the 2011 IEEE 15th International En-
     terprise Distributed Object Computing Conference, EDOC '11, pp. 183–192. IEEE
     Computer Society, Washington, DC (2011). doi:10.1109/EDOC.2011.15. http://
     dx.doi.org/10.1109/EDOC.2011.15

119. Katsiri, E., Mycroft, A.: Applying bayesian networks to sensor-driven systems. In: 2006 10th IEEE International Symposium on Wearable Computers, pp. 149–150 (2006)

120. Khalil, A., Connelly, K.: Context-aware telephony: privacy preferences and sharing patterns. In: Proceedings of the 20th Anniversary Conference on Computer Supported Cooperative Work, CSCW '06, pp. 469–478. ACM, New York (2006). doi:10.1145/1180875.1180947. http://doi.acm.org/10.1145/1180875.1180947

121. Kourtellis, N., Finnis, J., Anderson, P., Blackburn, J., Borcea, C., Iamnitchi, A.: Prometheus: user-controlled p2p social data management for socially-aware applications. In: Gupta, I., Mascolo, C. (eds.) Middleware 2010. Lecture Notes in Computer Science, vol. 6452, pp. 212–231. Springer, Berlin, Heidelberg (2010)

122. Lagoze, C., Hunter, J.: The abc ontology and model. In: Proceedings of the International Conference on Dublin Core and Metadata Applications, pp. 160–176 (2001)

123. Li, J., Dabek, F.: F2f: reliable storage in open networks. In: Proceedings of the 4th International Workshop on Peer-to-Peer Systems (IPTPS) (2006)

124. Li, D., Muntz, R.: Coca: collaborative objects coordination architecture. In: Proceedings of the 1998 ACM Conference on Computer Supported Cooperative Work, CSCW '98, pp. 179–188. ACM, New York (1998). doi:10.1145/289444.289492. http://doi.acm.org/10.1145/289444.289492

125. Loke, S.W.: Representing and reasoning with situations for context-aware pervasive computing: a logic programming perspective. Knowl. Eng. Rev. 19(3), 213–233 (2004)

126. Lovett, T., O'Neill, E., Irwin, J., Pollington, D.: The calendar as a sensor: analysis and improvement using data fusion with social networks and location. In: Proceedings of the 12th ACM International Conference on Ubiquitous Computing, Ubicomp '10, pp. 3–12. ACM, New York (2010). doi:10.1145/1864349.1864352. http://doi.acm.org/10.1145/1864349.1864352

127. Lu, Y., Tsaparas, P., Ntoulas, A., Polanyi, L.: Exploiting social context for review quality prediction. In: Proceedings of the 19th International Conference on World Wide Web, WWW '10, pp. 691–700. ACM, New York (2010). doi:10.1145/1772690.1772761. http://doi.acm.org/10.1145/1772690.1772761

128. Lukowicz, P., Pentland, S., Ferscha, A.: From context awareness to socially aware computing. IEEE Pervasive Comput. 11(1), 32 –41 (2012). doi:10.1109/MPRV.2011.82

129. Lupu, E.C., Sloman, M.: Towards a role-based framework for distributed systems management. J. Netw. Syst. Manag. 5(1), 5–30 (1997). doi:10.1023/A:1018742004992. http://dx.doi.org/10.1023/A:1018742004992

130. Maassen, J., van Nieuwpoort, R., Veldema, R., Bal, H.E., Plaat, A.: An efficient implementation of java's remote method invocation. SIGPLAN Not. 34(8), 173–182 (1999). doi:10.1145/329366.301120. http://doi.acm.org/10.1145/329366.301120

131. Manzoor, A., Truong, H.L., Dustdar, S.: On the evaluation of quality of context. In: Roggen, D., Lombriser, C., Tröster, G., Kortuem, G., Havinga, P. (eds.) Smart Sensing and Context. Lecture Notes in Computer Science, vol. 5279, pp. 140–153. Springer, Berlin, Heidelberg (2008). doi:10.1007/978-3-540-88793-5_11. http://dx.doi.org/10.1007/978-3-540-88793-5_11

132. Matheus, C., Kokar, M., Baclawski, K.: A core ontology for situation awareness. In: Proceedings of the 6th International Conference of Information Fusion, pp. 545–552 (2003). doi:10.1109/ICIF.2003.177494

133. McCarthy, J.: Notes on formalizing context. In: Proceedings of the 13th International Joint Conference on Artifical Intelligence, IJCAI'93, vol. 1, pp. 555–560. Morgan Kaufmann, San Francisco, CA (1993). http://dl.acm.org/citation.cfm?id=1624025.1624103

134. McGuinness, D.L., van Harmelen, F.: Owl web ontology language overview. w3c recommendation 10 February 2004. http://www.w3.org/TR/owl-features/

135. McKinley, P.K., Sadjadi, S.M., Kasten, E.P., Cheng, B.H.C.: Composing adaptive software. Computer **37**(7), 56–64 (2004). doi:10.1109/MC.2004.48. http://dx.doi.org/10.1109/MC.2004.48

136. McLaughlin, B.: Java & XML Data Binding. O'Reilly Media, Sebastopol, CA (2002)

137. Moran, T.P., Dourish, P.: Introduction to this special issue on context-aware computing. Hum. Comput. Interact. **16**(2), 87–95 (2001). doi:10.1207/S15327051HCI16234_01. http://dx.doi.org/10.1207/S15327051HCI16234_01

138. Obitko, M.: Web ontology language owl. http://www.obitko.com/tutorials/ontologies-semantic-web/web-ontology-language-owl.html

139. Parsons, D.: Dynamic Web Application Development Using XML and Java. Cengage Learning EMEA, Andover, MA (2008)

140. Patel-Schneider, P.F., Hayes, P., Horrocks, I.: Owl web ontology language: semantics and abstract syntax. w3c recommendation 10 February 2004. http://www.w3.org/TR/owl-semantics/

141. Pautasso, C., Wilde, E.: Restful web services: principles, patterns, emerging technologies. In: Proceedings of the 19th International Conference on World Wide Web, WWW '10, pp. 1359–1360. ACM, New York (2010). doi:10.1145/1772690.1772929. http://doi.acm.org/10.1145/1772690.1772929

142. Perera, S., Herath, C., Ekanayake, J., Chinthaka, E., Ranabahu, A., Jayasinghe, D., Weerawarana, S., Daniels, G.: Axis2, middleware for next generation web services. In: Proceedings of the IEEE International Conference on Web Services, ICWS '06, pp. 833–840. IEEE Computer Society, Washington, DC (2006). doi:10.1109/ICWS.2006.36. http://dx.doi.org/10.1109/ICWS.2006.36

143. Pitt, E., McNiff, K.: Java.rmi: The Remote Method Invocation Guide. Addison-Wesley Longman, Boston, MA (2001)

144. Raimond, Y., Abdallah, S., Sandler, M., Giasson, F.: The music ontology. In: Proceedings of the International Conference on Music Information Retrieval, pp. 417–422 (2007)

145. Ranganathan, A., Campbell, R.H.: An infrastructure for context-awareness based on first order logic. Pers. Ubiquit. Comput. **7**(6), 353–364 (2003). doi:10.1007/s00779-003-0251-x. http://dx.doi.org/10.1007/s00779-003-0251-x

146. Ranganathan, A., McGrath, R.E., Campbell, R.H., Mickunas, M.D.: Use of ontologies in a pervasive computing environment. Knowl. Eng. Rev. **18**(3), 209–220 (2003). doi:10.1017/S0269888904000037. http://dx.doi.org/DOI:10.1017/S0269888904000037

147. Ranganathan, A., Al-Muhtadi, J., Campbell, R.: Reasoning about uncertain contexts in pervasive computing environments. IEEE Pervasive Comput. **3**(2) (2004). doi:10.1109/MPRV.2004.1316821

148. Raychoudhury, V., Cao, J., Kumar, M., Zhang, D.: Middleware for pervasive computing: a survey. Pervasive Mob. Comput. **9**(2), 177–200 (2013). doi:10.1016/j.pmcj.2012.08.006. http://www.sciencedirect.com/science/article/pii/S1574119212001113

149. Reenskaug, T., Wold, P., Lehne, O.A., et al.: Working with Objects: The OOram Software Engineering Method. Manning, Greenwich (1996)

150. Riboni, D., Bettini, C.: Owl 2 modeling and reasoning with complex human activities. Pervasive Mob. Comput. **7**(3), 379–395 (2011). doi:10.1016/j.pmcj.2011.02.001

151. Riva, O.: Contory: a middleware for the provisioning of context information on smart phones. In: Proceedings of the ACM/IFIP/USENIX 2006 International Conference on Middleware, Middleware '06, pp. 219–239. Springer, New York (2006). http://dl.acm.org/citation.cfm?id=1515984.1516002

152. Rollinson, D.: Organisational Behaviour and Analysis: An Integrated Approach. Pearson Education, Harlow (2008)

153. Roman, M., Hess, C., Cerqueira, R., Ranganathan, A., Campbell, R., Nahrstedt, K.:
     A middleware infrastructure for active spaces. IEEE Pervasive Comput. 1(4), 74–83
     (2002). doi:10.1109/MPRV.2002.1158281
154. Rosi, A., et al.: Social sensors and pervasive services: approaches and perspec-
     tives. In: Proceedings of the IEEE PerCom Workshops, pp. 525–530 (2011).
     doi:10.1109/PERCOMW.2011.5766946
155. Rouvoy, R., Barone, P., Ding, Y., Eliassen, F., Hallsteinsen, S., Lorenzo, J., Mamelli,
     A., Scholz, U.: MUSIC: Middleware support for self-adaptation in ubiquitous and
     service-oriented environments. In: Software Engineering for Self-adaptive Systems,
     pp. 164–182. Springer, Berlin, Heidelberg (2009). doi:10.1007/978-3-642-02161-9_9.
     http://dx.doi.org/10.1007/978-3-642-02161-9_9
156. Sacramento, V., Endler, M., Rubinsztejn, H.K., Lima, L.S., Goncalves, K., Nasci-
     mento, F.N., Bueno, G.A.: Moca: a middleware for developing collaborative ap-
     plications for mobile users. IEEE Distrib. Syst. Online 5(10), 2 (2004). doi:
     10.1109/MDSO.2004.26. http://dx.doi.org/10.1109/MDSO.2004.26
157. Sancho, G., Bouassida Rodriguez, I., Villemur, T., Tazi, S.: What about collaboration
     in ubiquitous environments? In: 2010 10th Annual International Conference on New
     Technologies of Distributed Systems (NOTERE), pp. 143–150. IEEE, New York (2010)
158. Sandhu, R., Coyne, E., Feinstein, H., Youman, C.: Role-based access control models.
     Computer 29(2), 38–47 (1996). doi:10.1109/2.485845
159. Satyanarayanan, M.: Pervasive computing: vision and challenges. IEEE Pers. Com-
     mun. 8(4), 10 –17 (2001). doi:10.1109/98.943998
160. Scherp, A., et al.: F–a model of events based on the foundational ontology dolce+dns
     ultralight. In: International Conference on Knowledge Capture, pp. 137–144 (2009).
     doi:10.1145/1597735.1597760
161. Schilit, B.N., Theimer, M.M.: Disseminating active map information to mobile hosts.
     Netw. Mag. Global Int. Work. 8(5), 22–32 (1994). doi:10.1109/65.313011. http://
     dx.doi.org/10.1109/65.313011
162. Schilit, B., Adams, N., Want, R.: Context-aware computing applications. In: Pro-
     ceedings of the 1994 First Workshop on Mobile Computing Systems and Appli-
     cations, WMCSA '94, pp. 85–90. IEEE Computer Society, Washington, DC (1994).
     doi:10.1109/WMCSA.1994.16. http://dx.doi.org/10.1109/WMCSA.1994.
     16
163. Schmidt, A., Beigl, M., Gellersen, H.W.: There is more to context than location. Com-
     put. Graph. 23(6), 893–901 (1999). doi:10.1016/S0097-8493(99)00120-X. http://
     www.sciencedirect.com/science/article/pii/S009784939900120X
164. Schuster, D., Rosi, A., Mamei, M., Springer, T., Endler, M., Zambonelli, F.: Pervasive
     social context-taxonomy and survey. ACM Trans. Intell. Syst. Technol. 4(3), Article
     No. 46, 22 pp. (2013)
165. Searle, J.R.: Speech Acts: An Essay in the Philosophy of Language, vol. 626. Cam-
     bridge University Press, Cambridge (1969)
166. Shaw, R., Troncy, R., Hardman, L.: Lode: linking open descriptions of events. In:
     Proceedings of the 4th Asian Conference on The Semantic Web, pp. 153–167 (2009)
167. Sheng, Q.Z., Benatallah, B.: Contextuml: a uml-based modeling language for model-
     driven development of context-aware web services development. In: Proceedings
     of the International Conference on Mobile Business, ICMB '05, pp. 206–212. IEEE
     Computer Society, Washington, DC (2005). doi:10.1109/ICMB.2005.33. http://
     dx.doi.org/10.1109/ICMB.2005.33
168. Sirin, E., Parsia, B.: Sparql-dl: sparql query for owl-dl. In: OWL: Experiences and
     Directions Workshop (OWLED) (2007)
169. Smith, M.K., Welty, C., McGuinness, D.L.: Owl web ontology language guide. w3c
     recommendation 10 February 2004. http://www.w3.org/TR/owl-guide/

170. Srirama, S.N., Jarke, M., Prinz, W.: Mobile web services mediation framework. In: Proceedings of the 2nd Workshop on Middleware for Service Oriented Computing: Held at the ACM/IFIP/USENIX International Middleware Conference, MW4SOC '07, pp. 6–11. ACM, New York (2007). doi:10.1145/1388336.1388337. http://doi.acm.org/10.1145/1388336.1388337

171. Steimann, F.: The role data model revisited. Appl. Ontol. **2**(2), 89–103 (2007). http://dl.acm.org/citation.cfm?id=1412401.1412402

172. Strang, T., Linnhoff-Popien, C.: A context modeling survey. In: Proceedings of the First International Workshop on Advanced Context Modelling, Reasoning and Management, in Conjunction with UbiComp 2004 (2004)

173. Strang, T., Linnhoff-Popien, C., Frank, K.: Applications of a context ontology language. In: Proceedings of International Conference on Software, Telecommunications and Computer Networks (SoftCom2003), pp. 14–18 (2003)

174. Strang, T., Linnhoff-Popien, C., Frank, K.: Cool: a context ontology language to enable contextual interoperability. In: Stefani, J.B., Demeure, I., Hagimont, D. (eds.) Proceedings of the Distributed Applications and Interoperable Systems (DAIS). Lecture Notes in Computer Science, vol. 2893, pp. 236–247. Springer, Berlin, Heidelberg (2003). doi:10.1007/978-3-540-40010-3_21. http://dx.doi.org/10.1007/978-3-540-40010-3_21

175. Taconet, C., Kazi-Aoul, Z., Zaier, M., Conan, D.: Ca3m: a runtime model and a middleware for dynamic context management. In: Proceedings of the Confederated International Conferences, CoopIS, DOA, IS, and ODBASE 2009 on On the Move to Meaningful Internet Systems: Part I, OTM '09, pp. 513–530. Springer, Berlin, Heidelberg (2009). doi:10.1007/978-3-642-05148-7_39. http://dx.doi.org/10.1007/978-3-642-05148-7_39

176. Toninelli, A., Khushraj, D., Lassila, O., Montanari, R.: Towards socially aware mobile phones. In: First Workshop on Social Data on the Web (SDoW) (2008)

177. Toninelli, A., Montanari, R., Lassila, O., Khushraj, D.: What's on users' minds? Toward a usable smart phone security model. IEEE Pervasive Comput. **8**(2), 32–39 (2009). doi:10.1109/MPRV.2009.39. http://dx.doi.org/10.1109/MPRV.2009.39

178. Toninelli, A., Pathak, A., Issarny, V.: Yarta: A middleware for managing mobile social ecosystems. In: Riekki, J., Ylianttila, M., Guo, M.: (eds.) Advances in Grid and Pervasive Computing. Lecture Notes in Computer Science, vol. 6646, pp. 209–220. Springer, Berlin, Heidelberg (2011). http://dx.doi.org/10.1007/978-3-642-20754-9_22. 10.1007/978-3-642-20754-9_22

179. Vinciarelli, A., Pantic, M., Bourlard, H., Pentland, A.: Social signal processing: state-of-the-art and future perspectives of an emerging domain. In: Proceedings of the 16th ACM International Conference on Multimedia, MM '08, pp. 1061–1070. ACM, New York (2008). doi:10.1145/1459359.1459573. http://doi.acm.org/10.1145/1459359.1459573

180. Wang, X., Zhang, D., Gu, T., Pung, H.: Ontology based context modeling and reasoning using owl. In: Proceedings of the IEEE PerCom Workshops, pp. 18–22 (2004). doi:10.1109/PERCOMW.2004.1276898

181. Wang, G., Gallagher, A., Luo, J., Forsyth, D.: Seeing people in social context: recognizing people and social relationships. In: Proceedings of the 11th European conference on Computer vision: Part V, ECCV'10, pp. 169–182. Springer, Berlin, Heidelberg (2010). http://dl.acm.org/citation.cfm?id=1888150.1888164

182. Weber, M., Runciman, W.G.: Max Weber: Selections in Translation. Cambridge University Press, Cambridge, New York (1978)

183. Weiser, M.: The computer for the 21st century. Sci. Am. **3**(3), 94–104 (1991)

184. Wilson, C., Boe, B., Sala, A., Puttaswamy, K.P., Zhao, B.Y.: User interactions in social networks and their implications. In: Proceedings of the 4th ACM European Conference on Computer Systems, pp. 205–218 (2009)

185. Wishart, R., Henricksen, K., Indulska, J.: Context privacy and obfuscation supported by dynamic context source discovery and processing in a context management system. In: Indulska, J., Ma, J., Yang, L., Ungerer, T., Cao, J. (eds.) 4th International Conference of Ubiquitous Intelligence and Computing (UIC). Lecture Notes in Computer Science, vol. 4611, pp. 929–940. Springer, Berlin, Heidelberg (2007). http://dx.doi.org/10.1007/978-3-540-73549-6_91. doi:10.1007/978-3-540-73549-6_91

186. Xiang, R., Neville, J., Rogati, M.: Modeling relationship strength in online social networks. In: Proceedings of the 19th International Conference on World Wide Web, WWW '10, pp. 981–990. ACM, New York (2010). doi:10.1145/1772690.1772790. http://doi.acm.org/10.1145/1772690.1772790

187. Xing, B., Gronowski, K., Radia, N., Svensson, M., Ton, A.: Pocketsocial: your distributed social context now in your pocket. In: IEEE International Conference on Pervasive Computing and Communications Workshops (PERCOM Workshops), pp. 322–324 (2011). doi:10.1109/PERCOMW.2011.5766895

188. Ye, J., Coyle, L., Dobson, S., Nixon, P.: Ontology-based models in pervasive computing systems. Knowl. Eng. Rev. 22(4), 315–347 (2007). doi:10.1017/S0269888907001208. http://dx.doi.org/10.1017/S0269888907001208

189. Ye, J., Dobson, S., McKeever, S.: Situation identification techniques in pervasive computing: a review. Pervasive Mob. Comput. 8(1), 36–66 (2012). doi:10.1016/j.pmcj.2011.01.004

190. Zambonelli, F., Jennings, N.R., Wooldridge, M.: Developing multiagent systems: the gaia methodology. ACM Trans. Softw. Eng. Methodol. 12(3), 317–370 (2003). doi:10.1145/958961.958963. http://doi.acm.org/10.1145/958961.958963

191. Zheng, Y., Li, L., Ogata, H., Yano, Y.: Support online social interaction with context-awareness. Int. J. Contin. Eng. Educ. Life Long Learn. 17(2), 160–177 (2007)

192. Zhou, J., Sun, J., Athukorala, K., Wijekoon, D., Ylianttila, M.: Pervasive social computing: augmenting five facets of human intelligence. J. Ambient. Intell. Humaniz. Comput. 3, 153–166 (2012). doi:10.1007/s12652-011-0081-z. http://dx.doi.org/10.1007/s12652-011-0081-z

193. Zhu, H., Zhou, M.: Roles in information systems: a survey. IEEE Trans. Syst. Man Cybern. Part C Appl. Rev. 38(3), 377–396 (2008). doi:10.1109/TSMCC.2008.919168